Commercial
PHOTOGRAPHY

Commercial
PHOTOGRAPHY

A SURVIVAL GUIDE

John Tinsley

 BFP BOOKS London

© 1992 BFP Books

A catalogue record for this book is available from the British Library

ISBN 0-907297-27-7

Published by BFP Books, Focus House, 497 Green Lanes, London N13 4BP.
Printed in England by Redwood Press Ltd.

ACKNOWLEDGEMENTS

A book like this cannot be put together without the help of a number of people. I have been extremely fortunate in being able to call on the expertise of many friends and business associates, who have freely given up their time in providing information, checking manuscripts and advising me generally in their particular field of expertise. They are:

Nino Barresi of British Gas
Berry's Commercial Estate Agents
John Dinenage of Eastern Electricity
Michelle from Dun and Bradstreet
Terry from George Elliott
Peter Fitzgerald of KJP
Rebecca Grant of Crosfield Electronics
Tony Gray of Graytones Printers
David Parr from CNT
Morgan Reed of Studio Professional Sales
Melanie Smith of Johnson's Photopia
Steve Smith of Jessops, Leicester
Neil Suckling of Introphoto

Also, my particular thanks go to Harry Nash of Barclays Bank, Egham, for his considerable help on the banking sections, and to "M", a senior partner with a prestigious firm of chartered accountants, who checked the entire manuscript for accuracy from an accounting point of view.

With the exception of the manufacturers' product photographs, all the pictures in this book were taken by myself, and my thanks go to the following clients for their kind permission to reproduce them here:

Beckett Mitchell Associates, Stamford
General Medium Ltd, Whittlesey
HMD, Kings Lynn
The Design Factory, Oundle
S & M Design, Peterborough
SSL Ltd, Peterborough
T.W. Associates Ltd, Peterborough

Finally, I hope that my good-natured allusions have caused no distress to my Russian friends in particular and to the Russian people in general. If they have, then I apologise. I would hate to be barred from the finest parties in the world.

John Tinsley

CONTENTS

INTRODUCTION

This book is directed at anyone contemplating setting up a small commercial photographic studio to serve the needs of local commerce and industry.

Perhaps a businessman with some photographic knowledge who feels that a venture like this could be a good second career after redundancy; an amateur photographer or "semi-pro" who now wants to take the plunge and go full time; an established "high street" social photographer who wants to change direction, perhaps into the commercial field; even someone running a commercial business already who needs a helping hand in some areas.

All you need is a little capital, some basic photographic knowledge, and a real desire to succeed.

Up and down the country, outside the major city centres, there is a wealth of small, two or three person studios providing a complete photographic service for local ad agencies, design studios and business. The services range from standard brochure and PR photography through to advertising work, often with a good range of back-up services such as mounting and laminating for display prints, medium quantity runs of black and white prints for mail shots, duplicate transparencies, and copy negs. In many cases the people who run these operations have little or no formal photographic training, and for a number it is a second or third career.

However, any equipment supplier will confirm the almost horrific failure rate of these businesses, many not surviving the first year.

Yet these studios generally don't fail for lack of necessary photographic skills, or for lack of work, and less flounder these days because of poor business management. They go bust because their owners just do not understand the business – the money runs out before the end of the learning curve.

The situation is not helped by large, glossy books on advertising photography which teach techniques seldom needed at this level, and which demand an equipment armoury which few small studios can afford. Some of the amateur photographic press also confuses, emphasising the need for "art" and "creativity" in what is essentially a very pragmatic business.

Graduates of photographic colleges can join major studios as assistants and learn the business there, but others can make an excellent start with this book.

The business

I started in commercial photography after a first career in international marketing. At that time I had probably as much photographic knowledge as the average amateur; certainly no more.

My problem was that I could not obtain the kind of illustrations I required from the professional photographers in my area. I was marketing complex electronics equipment and I needed photographs for brochures and press releases that showed certain key features of the equipment, as well as comparative shots that showed features of one product against another. As hard as I tried, I could not obtain "straight" pics which showed that the connectors were gold-plated, or that fibreglass circuit boards were used, no matter how well I thought I had briefed the photographer.

I did get some very creative perspective effects and superimposed digital displays on the product; I even had palm trees waving gently over a humidity meter. Great though some of these shots were from a creative point of view – and maybe advertising campaigns could have been written around some of the themes – they were totally useless from a brochure or press release point of view. They simply did not show potential purchasers of my product what I wanted them to see. The fees, however, were substantial!

On this subject, I am always tempted to tell a story (probably apocryphal) told to me by a fairly senior executive in the military communications industry.

Many years ago, at the height of the "Cold War", his company had developed a short range radio set that worked well in helicopters. With determination he managed to bypass all the normal channels and eventually found himself face to face with a top army general in a hospitality tent at the Farnborough air show.

Clearing his throat, he started on his patter, and the general let him get well started before he interrupted, saying: "Tell me, young man, how many Russians does this thing kill?"

Totally thrown off balance, our hero babbled that this was a radio and not a guided missile, but was interrupted again: "Son, I get paid for killing Russians. That's all that interests me. Now, go away and when you can show me a gadget that kills Russians, come and see me again". And with that our hapless salesman was firmly ushered out of the tent.

Commercial photographs are used to sell products, not to admire for their beauty. Photographs which don't sell products are useless.

So finally I decided that I would take my own brochure shots and went out and bought a roll film camera and some studio flash equipment. A few years later I was running my own commercial studio.

This book is based on my own experience in commercial photography – not only in starting up and running my own studios, but also in helping others get their businesses off the ground. The principles have worked for me, and have given me a very satisfying and profitable second career. There is no reason why they should not do the same for you.

The book

We will start by looking at your own situation before you make the decision to go ahead – questions of motivation, things you should be warned about. You need to take into account family considerations, and how your partner feels about the whole thing.

We'll take stock of what you need in terms of knowledge and money, enough for you to know what to expect when you do go ahead. Then we'll move on to actually starting up, and making the all-important location decision.

Business plans and forecasts for the bank come next, assuming you are like most mortals and require bank financing of some kind or another. You will need to know how to put together a proposal that a bank manager will accept. We'll take a look at VAT and income tax, and talk about that other breed – the chartered accountant.

Premises are next, and we'll look at what you really require, the kinds of leases you may find, and, ultimately, how to convert it from a bare shell into a working studio.

Perhaps the biggest pitfall for many starting photographers is the amount of equipment they think they need. "Equipment poverty" is a common ailment in many new photographic businesses; cupboards overflow with gleaming, expensive gadgets that will hardly ever be used. I'll go into some detail discussing what you really have to have, and what is gilding the lily. Whether to have on-site processing facilities is another hotly debated point and we'll spend some time on that.

It is quite difficult to get business if no-one knows you are there, so you will need to know how to market yourself and your facilities. And we'll look at pricing.

Every business needs a certain amount of administration. Keeping tabs on what is going on is essential to the on-going health of your company. A firm collection policy will protect you against one of the most common causes of bankruptcy. We'll look at how you should look after your business, keeping sales and purchase ledgers, VAT returns, and how to prepare the annual accounts. We finish that section by looking at the personal computer – is it a help or a hindrance?

Up to now we have barely talked about the photography, but you are going to need to know what will be expected of you. We'll deal with the types of shot needed for different types of use, in some detail, especially the difference between photography for advertising and that for brochure and PR use. The role of the art director is discussed and we look at the terminology used, so that you will know what to do when asked for a "squared up" shot, or told that your work will be "cut-out". We will also examine some of the more advanced techniques you may eventually use, like special effects and front projection.

We will look in the darkroom to see what is needed there, and at other services you can offer your clients, such as processing, transparency duplication, internegative production, printing and mounting.

An understanding of what happens to your photographs when they leave you is important, so we take a look at design, production and reproduction techniques, finishing off with the final printing stage.

To round off, I've selected a number of standard commercial shots taken over the last few years. These are analysed as to what the objective of each shot was, how it was put together, the techniques and equipment used, and how successful in "killing Russians" the results were.

Now, if you are sitting comfortably, we'll begin...

FIRST CONSIDERATIONS

Most books on starting up a business include a section on "the correct personality profile". Some include chapters on psychological traits with enormous questionnaires on how you cope with decisions, adversity, likes/dislikes, etc. I was scared out of my wits by reading one of these many years ago, and had I taken the thing seriously, would never have moved out of my safe, secure, pensioned employment. However, I looked at a few friends who appeared to be doing quite well running successful small businesses, and decided that they would never qualify on those terms either, so I took the whole thing a little less seriously.

It is true that you do have to be a particular kind of person to run your own business, but I believe that anyone who has got beyond the dreaming stage generally has what it takes to make a go of it.

Far more important to success, in my opinion, is a down to earth realism in forecasting what life is going to be like. Advance warning of the problems that you will certainly have to deal with as you move from concept to start-up, and then into regular trading, will help you make the right decisions.

This chapter is about all of that. We are going to look at motivation, the problems you will encounter up front, and along the way, and how your lifestyle will change – not necessarily for the better or worse, but things will certainly be different. We also need to take stock of your current situation, not only financially but also with regard to your partner in life. And we need to look at your level of photographic knowledge, and identify any weak areas.

Motivation

A little self-examination will not go amiss, especially if your decision to "go it alone" is being made at a particularly difficult time. Judgment is clouded by emotion when employment changes or redundancies are in the air, and you must make sure that you are making decisions for the right reasons. I have seen people leap off into wild business ventures out of pique after an adverse pay review or having been passed over for promotion. But the grass in the self-employment field is not necessarily greener, and often the energy spent in trying to make a half-baked idea work would be much better spent in reconciling your own particular problems in your employment.

If you are in regular employment, and you are considering starting up your own business, then you must do so because you want to benefit from the many advantages of working for yourself, and are prepared for the solid hard work you will have to do. Rows with your boss, redundancy, or getting fired are not reasons, although these situations may present opportunities to bring already formed plans forward.

The first problem you will come up against is particular to the UK. In many continental European countries and especially in the United States, the man who creates business is viewed as making a definite contribution to the wealth of the country, and generally receives much more help and encouragement than his counterpart here in the UK. Whilst recent political emphasis has changed in favour of the small business, unfortunately, at the grass roots level, the starting small businessman is often viewed as someone not to be trusted, and in certain company is thought of as a failure before he even starts. It is a disgusting situation, and many would argue that some of Britain's ills stem from this attitude.

I remember visiting my bank manager when I was starting my first commercial photo studio. I had just left a senior position in sales and marketing. I had a little capital, a promise of a little work from my former employer, and a sound business plan. I had been careful to produce a realistic cash flow forecast showing fairly modest borrowings. I expected a very easy, congenial meeting.

I could not have been more wrong. A bank that was prepared to lend me thousands whilst I worked in a most insecure job gave me the third degree over a fifteen hundred pound overdraft. I considered the project to be as safe as houses – there was no local competition, I had a client up front and an expanding industrial estate on my doorstep. However the bank took a different view. How much experience did I have in the business? What security could I offer the bank? What were my contingency plans for repayment if the business failed? Would my wife work in the business or would she have a "real" job to help with the domestic budget? Surely the reason for there being no local competition was because there was no market. And so on.

I left the meeting feeling about six inches tall. I didn't even get my usual cup of coffee. It was for me, however, the best thing that could have happened. I realised right away that I was on my own and would have to fight for everything I gained. It was much easier after I accepted that.

You do have to get used to this change in attitude towards you, and it can be a little unnerving at first. Happily, bank managers' attitudes have changed a little over the years, and we'll be looking in detail at relationships with banks in a later chapter. However I still do get the feeling that bankers are happier with executives in high-risk city jobs than with the small businessman totally in charge of his own destiny, who is, in my book, a much safer and more secure proposition.

A new life

It is this control over one's future that makes all the problems of starting up a business worthwhile. However a business is a hard taskmaster, and if you are married and have children, you do need to consider the changes in family life that your new venture will bring.

Right from the beginning your family will have to accept that life will not be as organised as it was. You will not be able to rely on always going shopping on a Thursday evening. Mealtimes may become variable feasts, often taken on the hoof. Regular dinner parties will have to be replaced by the unplanned getting together of friends when everyone has an evening to spare at the same time. You must make sure that your family can cope with a totally disorganised existence, at least for the first couple of years, and that the needs of the business take priority.

Self-discipline is also needed. When you work for yourself, you are free to do what you want, and work on what you want. You are also free to lounge around all day and do nothing – there are no memos to force you into action. Retribution is swift, however. No work equals no money, and no money means no food on the table.

Thinking more positively, you will find that you make many new friends, most of them in the same self-employed situation as yourself. People who work hard tend to play hard, and we have found that our ad agency and designer friends are quite stimulating to be with. We found the first party we had where office politics and the boss's latest blunder were not on the agenda tremendously agreeable and refreshing. Another bonus is that because spare time is at a premium, you use it wisely, and find yourself doing things that you otherwise would not do. We have been to more concerts and visited more interesting places than ever before. A few hours off is much too valuable to spend in front of the TV screen. If this sounds as if it is the life for you, and your family can cope, then you have already overcome what many people find is the biggest hurdle in going self-employed.

Taking stock

The next thing you must do is to take stock of your current situation, not only financially. Is your partner/wife/husband totally committed to your venture? Whilst it is helpful, though certainly not essential, that he/she can contribute to the business in some way, it is an absolute prerequisite that they are with you every inch of the way, thick or thin, richer or poorer, in sickness and in health. If this is not the case, then you have no choice – you must alter your plans to suit your partner.

If you are used to sharing your life with someone, you cannot cope with the problems of the business as well as indifference or even disapproval from your better half. I know of more than one situation where a potentially viable business was starved of necessary cash because of a partner's reluctance to go the whole way and put in the family silver. Energy that should be spent in developing the business is spent in continual discussions and disputes about investment and financing the larger jobs. It really is tragic and disheartening to sit on the outside and watch businesses go to the wall because of lack of commitment somewhere.

Happily, I also know of several situations where a business has been saved by continual pressure from a partner not to give up, to stay on and fight, even when the situation looked hopeless. Never underestimate the positive effect of a totally motivated partner, and similarly, do not underestimate the chaos and disaster that a uninterested mate can wreak. Commitment is king. Remember the old saying that if you risk a little, you may lose a little or gain a little. If you risk a lot, you may lose a lot or you may gain a lot. It is impossible to risk a little and gain a lot.

There is one other area that needs consideration at this stage. Commercial photography is all about producing photographs for industry and commerce to use in brochures, advertisements and for PR in magazines and newspapers. You need to be located in an area where there is a good supply of commercial clients. More often than not you will find customers on your doorstep. On the other hand, you may need to move to another area of the country. The whole question of location is dealt with later on, but for now, don't ignore the fact that you may wish to move – some people find moving more traumatic than others.

The next thing you need to look at is your state of health. *Before* you launch your business is the time to have a full check-up; when you start up you will simply not have time to fix your teeth, or get your eyes retested, or get a spare pair of glasses. The first two years of a new business are exhausting, and you need to be fit to work an 80 hour week most weeks during that time.

Photographic skills

Up to now, I have not touched upon photographic skills. In commercial photography, the skills you need are principally technical; the creative or artistic input usually comes from your client in one form or another. For this reason, your level of skill at this stage is not too important providing you do know what your current level is compared to what eventually will be required of you. You can then spend time now in filling the gaps and getting up to speed, so to speak.

It is in this area of necessary skills that I find most confusion in budding commercial photographers, and frankly the situation is not helped much by the profusion of advice offered by some amateur photographic magazines, which have about as much idea of what really goes on in the average small commercial studio as Renoir would have in an industrial design house.

In later chapters we will look at the photographic side of the business, but for now, before you open your studio, you need to be proficient in certain areas. I cannot overemphasise the need for a firm grounding in basic photographic theory (Appendix C will help you fill in any gaps). It's boring and dull and all that, but when the latest piece of high-tech equipment breaks down on you in the middle of a shoot, you will always get through if you really know what is going on, and it is not that difficult to learn. This is what you need to know:

Basic optics: In basic optics you should know how a camera lens focuses an image on the film, and how the shutter works. Also the effect of lens extension on reduction and magnification of the image, and the simple formulae which allow you to calculate one from the other. You should know what "hyperfocal distance" is, and how to calculate it. Familiarity with depth of field is important, and, if you are likely to take on banquet and reception photography, you should be able to calculate it from first principles. Absolute sharpness in the image is one of the chief differences between a good professional photograph and most amateur pics, and it usually comes from a good knowledge of depth of field. You should be familiar with perspective, and how to modify it by changing camera position and by changing lenses.

Exposure theory: Basically, you need to know how illumination is measured, and have an idea of the relative intensity of different sources of light. You need to know about the inverse square law when using artificial light sources, and the way exposure and f numbers are linked. A good knowledge of how exposure meters work is necessary, as is familiarity with both reflected light and incident light measurement techniques, and little knowledge of the zone system won't hurt.

Camera knowledge: You will be mostly using two different cameras, the roll film reflex and the 5x4in monorail. You need to be familiar with their use, in particular the use of Polaroid backs and materials, wide and long lenses, double exposure devices, and the rapid loading of film backs. Whilst I would not go so far as to encourage competitions in loading backs blindfold (as does one prestigious camera manufacturer), it does need to be second nature. As far as the 5x4 is concerned, don't worry about that for the time being. As you build your studio and get your lighting right, you will have ample time to become familiar with this camera and its accessories.

Studio flash knowledge: Again, most of what you need to know in this area you can gain as your studio takes shape. However, look at flash equipment, see the difference between monobloc and separate pack/head equipment, and also the different types of softboxes, brollies, reflectors and snoots available. Flashmeters are important, you should know how they work.

Processing: To start with, all you need to know is how to develop black and white film, produce contact prints and enlargements. The use of variable contrast paper like Multigrade or Polycontrast saves time and money, and you should also be able to manipulate negative contrast by under/over exposure with development compensation. You will be asked to produce black and white internegs from colour transparencies, and to produce negs from flat copy. The ability to keep contrast under control is essential.

Location flash: If your work is likely to contain much location work, then a good knowledge of fill flash using portable battery flash units in daylight is essential.

Don't be put off by this list – most of it is common sense, and all the subjects are dealt with at length in Appendix C. Don't worry if there are areas which are completely new to you; when you are putting your studio together, you will have ample time to experiment with new techniques and to fine-tune the skills you already have. Meanwhile, read up on basic photographic technique avidly. If you know what is actually going on in a camera when a shot is taken, then you will not have a problem.

Commercial photography for brochures and advertising is not just popping a Metz flash on a Bronnie and setting everything to auto!

Financial considerations

Finally, we need to know whether you have enough money to start with. Firstly, you will need some basic camera outfits, 35mm, roll film and sheet film. At this stage, we are only interested in broad estimates as the whole question of acquisition of equipment is dealt with in detail in Chapter 4. Also, as there is the choice between budget, standard and deluxe equipment, for the purposes of these estimates I have assumed that you will generally purchase new, standard "base model" equipment. Because I have assumed you will make a voluntary registration with the Customs and Excise, these prices do not include VAT. This is what you need to budget for:

A basic manual 35mm camera, complete with standard, wide, and tele zoom lenses, a few filters and a small flash unit. Allow £750.

A roll film reflex camera, complete with standard and long lenses, two film backs, a Polaroid back and a "compendium" lens hood. Allow £2,250.

A 5x4in monorail camera complete with two lenses, a Polaroid back and a few dark slides. Allow £1,500.

Studio flash equipment, power packs, heads, softboxes, accessories, flashmeter. Allow £2,750.

General accessories such as a good camera stand, a background roll support system, filters, and odd "bits and bobs". This is one area where you should be able to buy good stuff second-hand. Allow £600.

If you intend to do location work, then you should add a wide lens, a tripod and a bigger battery flash unit – this would add another £1,000 to the overall figure above.

These prices will enable you to acquire good, basic equipment which you can build on in the future.

You should then budget for equipping a darkroom and processing area. £3,500 will set you up with an enlarger, lenses, an E6 processor, driers and accessories. If you want more automation, and a fancier enlarger, then you can double that figure.

This little lot comes to between about £11,500 and £16,000 plus the dreaded VAT. However, most people who have aspirations about "going pro" will already own a certain amount of photographic equipment. Whilst the gear you own may not all be appropriate for commercial work, some of it will be, and the rest can be traded in against what you need.

You then need cash for fitting out the studio premises, and I have made the assumption that you will be dealing with a modern "starter" type industrial unit, of about 1,000 square feet. There are substantial savings to be made by doing the work yourself, so these estimates are for materials only, and include main studio, darkroom and office areas.

Timber, plasterboard, bench materials and a sink should cost no more than £1,500, plumbing cold water and drain should be done for about £150, and wiring and heating (professionally done) will cost about £1,000. Decorating the reception area, carpets, office furniture, and a computer/word processor will add about £1,650.

Much depends on individual requirements, but you are looking at between £16,000 and £20,000. On the credit side, you probably already own about £3,000 worth of gear, so this can be deducted from the total figure, bringing it to a more affordable £13-17k. On top of this you need to add enough to finance the first four months operations and living costs. You will need to start an inventory of film, chemicals and studio consumables, provide rent and rates (although you will probably be able to negotiate a two to three month rent free period), and still have enough money to live on for the first four months or so. My estimate of this is about £10,000. All in all, you are going to need about £25,000.

So, what are you worth? Firstly, if you own a house, take the difference between the mortgage outstanding and what sensibly you would be able to sell the house for. Then, after deducting selling costs and legal fees, add this sum to your current bank balance, and any building society deposits you may have. Then add the value of any non-essential assets you have for disposal – you are not going to have time to play golf anyway! Deduct the value of any hire-purchase agreements, bank loans and credit card debts. The result is your net worth, and will be made up of cash (bank and building society deposits) and equity (in your house). In the current case, if you have about £12,000 in cash and about £15,000 in equity, then you should have no problem in financing your business using conventional means. I have assumed that you have a car which will keep going for the next year without major problems.

This has probably been a very difficult chapter to take in; it certainly wasn't easy to write. I have tried not to pull any punches, and I have tried to tell it the way it is. If you have stayed with me this far, and the figures add up, then there is absolutely no reason why you should not be running a profitable commercial photographic business in a year from now. The next chapters are all positive – it's easier from now on.

GOING AHEAD

Right. The decision is made, you are going into business for yourself as a commercial photographer. Go and have a celebration – you are going to be busy from now on.

Location

The first decision you have to take, and arguably the most important, is where to locate your business.

In commercial photography, we are lucky in that we only need to consider a broad area. The high street GP photographer on the other hand, is more interested in a good address within an acceptable town. His business is in dealing mainly with members of the general public, and then for only a few commissions – a wedding and some portraits for instance. He needs a location that will "pull" people off the street into his studio, and impress them sufficiently to take an order there and then. It is almost what the Americans call a "specialty" business, one in which you only make a few repeat sales.

Your business, on the other hand, will have a limited number of clients who will use you regularly, month in, month out, and year in and year out. Whilst the GP photographer can just survive if he chooses a poor town but an excellent address, the commercial photographer will fail if he locates in an unsuitable area, irrespective of the address.

It is understandable for anyone considering a new business to only think about locating it in the area where they already live. There are certainly very good reasons for this. If you have lived in an area for a while, and have built up good contacts in the commercial world, you will be in a better position to evaluate your chances than someone in a new and strange area. If this is your situation, and your research among your contacts indicates that there is a market to build on, then you are already streets ahead. You may be fortunate also in that, if you are currently employed in the area, your current employer may be able to give you work when you start up – this helped me at first.

Starting your business where you live is certainly the easiest option. However, if you are unsure about the viability of your own area, then you must look elsewhere for possibly greener fields, if only for comparison.

So where do we look, and what do we look for? To start off with, the area should be growing and not in decline. It should be attracting new industry and commerce, and this growth should be visible. Try and put yourself in the position of a medium sized company relocating in the UK. Think of the factors they would consider important, such as availability of suitably qualified labour, availability of land or buildings, good rail and motorway connections, and pleasant surrounding countryside to attract executive staff. Make a list of towns that you would consider if you were going to move a computer assembly plant, for instance. You may find that your list contains many towns which are designated "new towns" by the Commission for New Towns (CNT), or they may have a Development Corporation. If so, so much the better, as there are positive advantages to starting a business in these particular areas.

Then get into your trusty car and visit each of the areas in turn. Visit all the industrial estates first. Look for new construction, and plenty of "Sold" and "Let" signs. Look for wealth-creating growth industries like computers, computer peripherals, instrumentation, leisure products, biochemical and pharmaceutical companies. Importers and distributors to the retail trade are vast consumers of photography. Look for evidence of healthy service businesses like accountants and solicitors. A firm of chartered accountants with a line of this year's Jaguars and BMWs in the car park says a lot for the commercial health of an area!

Then, do your weekly shopping in the local Sainsbury's or Waitrose. Look at the products on sale. If the area is not short of cash, then what is being offered will reflect it. The average purchase at the tills says a lot, as does the age of the cars on the road. You will, after a couple of towns, start to get a "gut" feel for an area. When you do have a positive feel for a town, look in the Yellow Pages under advertising agencies, graphic designers and PR consultancies. Drive round and see if they look as if they are doing well or not.

Finally, see if there are any serious commercial photographers around.

This is not as easy as it may seem. We have all seen ads in the Yellow Pages for "Specialists in Weddings, Portraits, Pets, Aerial, Industrial, Commercial and Advertising Photography". Unless the firm concerned is a major photographic studio with staff in double figures, ignore it. Your competition is more likely to be found under the "Photographers – commercial and industrial" section of the Yellow Pages. They will also be found in small factory units on the industrial estates themselves, or in converted chapels, schools or warehouses near by. For the time being, just note their presence.

Market research

After a while, one or two places will impress you more than others. You now have somewhere to compare with your home town, and you will have to refine your selection criteria in order to make the final choice.

At this stage most books on business will advise you to do a detailed market survey, calling on potential clients in the area to find out if they are users of photography and if so how much, and possibly to gauge the competitive activity. If I felt that the answers you would get at this stage would be accurate, I would suggest this as the next step. However, my own experience of this kind of thing is that it is probably not worthwhile. Before everyone recoils in horror at this marketing heresy, I have found, in creative services particularly, that what you get told in response to a general enquiry can be very different to what you may find once you have set up shop.

Some years ago I opened a studio in a new town where several ad agencies and designers were in business, apparently doing quite well. Yet for the first few months I could not get any business from

There is little point in opening a photographic studio in a poor or run-down area

them, other than the odd dupe tranny or copy print. Each time I asked for some studio work I was given the standard answer that "they didn't use photography that much". When I managed to persuade them to visit my studio, and got them talking a little, it transpired that they used to use photographs in their brochures and ads, but had so much trouble getting the local photographers to produce work that was usable that they finally gave up and started producing their own illustrations using airbrush and standard art techniques.

When I was shown some of the work produced, I began to see why. I saw work done on 6x4.5cm format that was intended for use as an A3 spread for food products; transparencies vastly under and overexposed; catalogue and product shots that had insufficient depth of field. One designer even kept a file which he called his "chamber of horrors" of photographic work, produced by a local "Specialist in Wedding, Portrait, Pet, Aerial, Industrial, Advertising and Commercial Photography"!

My experience is that until these clients have seen a professional studio set up with the right equipment, together with some examples of good professional photography, they will not take you seriously. As a consequence, they will not discuss their business and photographic requirements in any detail. The positive side of this is that once they see you have invested seriously in the business, and have seen a sharp, bright 5x4 on the light box, then gradually they will change their policies to include more photography – and it will be your photography that they choose.

Further research

In locating to a new area you are in a "Catch 22" situation. Unless you have a brilliant portfolio (and even that doesn't always work), you are not going to obtain any worthwhile commitment from your potential clients until you are up and running. It is a risk, therefore, but there is still a lot that you can do to help you to the right decision. Personally, I would rather evaluate a totally new area by looking intelligently at the town, its industry and people, than by undertaking a market research exercise that probably will not leave you any the wiser.

How do we go about this refined study? Firstly, make sure the town is really growing. Talk to the local Chamber of Commerce – they will have lists of companies in the area complete with their activities, and can give you much background information. Remember that at this stage you are in an information gathering mode; don't give away too many details about yourself. The local Council may well have lists of businesses in the town, and, if you are looking at a "new town", the local Development Corporation or CNT office will have a lot of of data which should be reasonably up-to-date on what is going on.

Go back and have a second look at the ad agencies and graphic designers. Three or four active agencies can provide a very good base business for a small studio if you can learn to satisfy their particular requirements.

Look again at the companies in the industrial estates. High-tech companies often produce "capabilities" brochures and there is usually a constant flow of press release product work. Companies which supply the retail trade produce enormous catalogues in which every product is photographed, and all new product ranges need press release shots taken, with appropriate print runs. Typical prospects in this category include companies which import DIY goods, furnishing accessories, sports goods, toys, etc. Pop into some of these and ask for a copy of their current catalogue.

Look for advertising and brochure-related service businesses. Every colour photograph printed requires separation negatives produced by reprographic companies. These companies work for agencies and magazine publishers. You should be able to tell from the display of work in the reception area whether their main work is in ads and brochures (good for you) or magazines (not good for you).

Next, look at the competition, ignoring the local cowboys of course. I believe that the presence of serious competitors is not necessarily a bad thing. First of all, if the area is growing, then each day that goes by means there is more and more business to share. Secondly, a competitor means that someone else in addition to yourself is promoting good photography, and improving the effective market size. It may be nice to be the first into a new industrial area, but bear in mind that you will then be alone in promoting professional services. Remember too, that many of your direct accounts may never have seen a good, bright, sharp professional transparency. A good competitor or two need not be a reason to reject an otherwise promising town, and it also confirms that there *is* a market.

Premises and accommodation

Finally, you need to look round to see if there are suitable premises for your business. If you are in a new town situation, then you have a tremendous advantage in that small industrial starter units are readily available on very flexible lease arrangements. If not, then you have to do the rounds of the estate agents, who will usually try to persuade you to take on too much for too long.

Try for a modern industrial unit of about 1,000 square feet, on a three year lease. Converting old chapels, pubs and the like is a great pastime for an established company that can afford to sub-contract the major work, but will involve a start-up company in far too much time and money.

If your chosen town is not near your existing home you also need to find suitable accommodation for yourself and your family. Don't be too fussy; you can have your mansion after a few years when you've made your pile. Again, new towns sometimes have rental accommodation available that can really ease the move, both financially and emotionally, but these days you have to be quick, as there are not too many left. If you do move in to a new town from a distance, the Development Corporation or CNT office will usually do their utmost to get you housed in order to attract you to the town.

A hi-tech business environment is a good place to locate

You now make your choice of location. Generally, new towns offer more growth prospects than established business areas, and their industrial and commercial scene is usually a very dynamic one, but on the other hand the latter do tend to be more stable and reliable. Also, don't forget that the chances are that your information about your own home town is more likely to be accurate than your estimates about a new and strange area, however inspired they may be. Take a weekend off and think about it, then make your decision.

Having got that one out of the way, the rest of this chapter will be devoted to looking at the different ways in which you can trade, what professional help you may need, who you should formally notify, how to make your business plan, and last but not least, how to raise the money you need.

Trading formats

The simplest form of running a small business is the sole trader format. Basically, you personally own the business, are liable for all its debts, and pocket all the profits. You are liable for tax as a self-employed person, which means that you pay tax on the profits at the normal rates in force at the time, after deduction of your personal allowance.

You do not have to register the business with any authority, and you can use almost any name you wish to trade under. The only problems you may have in that area are that if you use the same name as another company trading locally they can object, and obtain an injunction to prevent you trading under that name. Also, there are certain words that you may not use such as "Limited", "Trust", "Royal", "English" etc. But it's all common sense. If you are concerned about these, you can get a list of "taboo" names from Companies House.

The only absolute requirements are that you pay National Insurance contributions for yourself and staff (if any), submit annual accounts to H.M. Inspector of Taxes, and register for VAT with H.M. Customs and Excise if your business qualifies or is likely to do so. It is the simplest formula, and is the form that most small businesses use, including my own.

Next on the list is the partnership, when the firm has two or more proprietors. The rules are the same as for a sole trader but with a few major additions.

Firstly, the tax situation on partnerships is more complex, and secondly, the liability for debts is jointly held among the partners. The exact terms of the law are that all the partners are "jointly and severally responsible". What this means is that if all the partners except you do a moonlight, you, and you alone, are left holding the baby. It's up to you personally to recover their share, if you can.

I cannot say that I am much in favour of partnerships for small business start-ups. Two colleagues who are the best of friends may not remain so in a business situation, and like going on holiday with your best friend, you don't know how you are going to get on in a closed environment. And even a wonderful relationship with your wife/husband can sour very quickly. Also, I believe that one of the reasons many small businesses succeed is because of the autocratic rule of the entrepreneur; management by committee just doesn't work in the small business environment. However if you must do it, draw up a partnership agreement with the help of your solicitor, who will know what to put in it to protect everybody's interests.

The third option is the Limited Company. A Limited Company is a legal creation which can buy and sell, and therefore can have debts and debtors. It is formed by two or more investors (shareholders) who contribute money to the business and thus are allocated "shares" in it. The value of these shares in the beginning is usually the value of the money each has committed. As the company trades, the value or net worth of the company is calculated on the balance sheet, which basically is a form showing all the assets and liabilities of a business (we'll go into that later). The value of the shares then is the net worth of the company divided between the shareholders in the ratio of their initial contribution.

The Limited Company must have at least one Director, and a Company Secretary. These two people are often the shareholders in a small company. The apparent attraction of the Limited Company to many people is that the directors' liability to pay debts is strictly limited, and in most cases is zero. This means that in high risk situations directors can take chances knowing that they do not face personal ruin if it all goes wrong – in theory. In fact, to run up debts you need to either borrow money or establish credit. Most banks and suppliers will require a personal guarantee of repayment from a director before doing this in a start-up situation. This means that if your company goes belly-up while still owing the banks, they will be round knocking on your door.

The Companies Act also regulates what directors can and cannot do, and stipulates that the annual accounts must be audited by a qualified chartered or certified accountant, which, at the end of the day, also means that an accountant is going to have to prepare those accounts. Your accountancy bill is likely to be in the order of £2000–£3000.

Finally, the tax situation is a little more complex than for a sole trader business. As directors are paid a salary, they will pay tax on a PAYE basis. In addition, the "company" pays tax on the profits.

There are many advantages to the Limited Company formula for larger or more complex companies. For the sort of small business we are talking about I frankly don't think it makes much sense, certainly in the early years. My recommendation is that you trade as a sole trader, and I have written this book on that assumption.

Professional help

Many people assume that if you run your own business you must appoint a firm of accountants to "look after you". Whilst this may be true in many cases, there are equally many where it is not.

Accountants do have the reputation of having voracious appetites for money, but one should look at the services they provide, and how they provide them. Accountants are usually appointed to take away the chore of preparing ledgers, VAT returns and the annual set of accounts. They will also deal with the taxman for you, and sometimes find you risk or venture capital.

If, as many retail businesses do, you have a large cardboard box in the corner into which you tip the day's mail, and expect an accountant to take over from there, then this service is going to cost. They will employ junior staff at anything up to £20 an hour cost to you to sort out all the invoices, prepare the VAT returns, post them, pay your creditors and so on. It is not difficult to run up a substantial bill this way, and it is hard to criticise accountants for charging under these circumstances.

Where you can get into trouble is in trying to limit the damage by doing a percentage of the work yourself. Some accountants will argue that in order to put their name on the accounts they need to check all the work done. This can cost almost as much as the "cardboard box" exercise. You don't need to enter this debate if you do the whole thing yourself, and certainly, whilst your business is small, this is not difficult and won't take up much of your time. Similarly, VAT returns only take half an hour to prepare from good records.

In addition to the preparation of accounts, accountants provide other, perhaps more useful facilities. The first is in the area of tax counselling, and we'll deal with this crucial area later. The second facility is in assisting you in finding capital if you do not want to place yourself totally in the hands of the bank. Most accountants know of local sources of money and, if they are convinced you are on to a winner, will recommend you to a potential investor. Finally, an accountant will give you day-to-day advice on the running of your business.

Leaving aside the tax considerations for the moment, you should look at hiring an accountant in the same way as you would look at a new camera or accessory. Do you need the paperwork assistance? Do you need the day-to-day advice? Do you need the access to sources of capital? If you do, then you should appoint an accountant and expect a bill of £1,000 upwards every year. Certainly, having a firm of accountants on the end of the phone can be very reassuring at times, but do not forget you are paying for every minute. On the other hand, if you think you can manage on your own, then don't enter into an arrangement with a firm of accountants, and do your own accounts. I'll show you how later on.

Where you must have professional advice is in the area of tax. It is impossible for anyone who is not involved on a daily basis to know the ins and outs of the latest tax legislation. Many accountants have been tax inspectors, or are members of the Institute of Tax, and can save you thousands of pounds by merely showing you how to avoid (not evade) situations which make you exposed, and by making sure you avail yourself of all the allowances which you are legally entitled to claim. Good tax advice is invariably worth the cost, especially when you go from a salaried position to a self-employed situation. If you have elected to appoint a firm of chartered accountants, then this service will be available to you as part of the deal.

On the other hand, if you have decided to "go it alone" then my advice is to find someone properly qualified in this field, preferably a member of the Institute of Tax, and deal on a freelance basis. This expert will look over your annual accounts, suggest modifications, and help with your tax computation, and all for a fee less than you would face if you gave your business lock stock and barrel to the local firm of chartered accountants. Also, you will probably find that with the local firm a junior member of staff will be dealing with your account, whereas with your own tax consultant you will benefit from a much higher level of skill and expertise.

Getting started

Your first step is to talk to your tax advisor, either your accountants if that is your choice, or your own expert. Do not delay this meeting, especially if you are moving into self-employment for the first time.

At the time of writing, under certain circumstances the Inland Revenue will allow the losses of new businesses to be set against tax paid in previous years. This means that if you make a loss in your first year, you can claim for repayment of tax, at the rate the tax was paid, equal to the loss. This is an exercise that is certainly best left to your advisor to arrange, and is a very welcome source of cash when you first start up. The arrangement can go on for a year or two until your business turns the corner.

Another decision that can affect your tax liability is the date you decide for the end of your financial year. Again, take proper professional advice before plumping for your wife's birthday! Then, you need to write formally to your local tax office. You must inform them that you are leaving salaried employment, and that you are going to be self-employed in the field of commercial photography. Don't forget to tell them your trading name and address if you know it, and advise them of your decision regarding the start and finish of your financial accounting period. Let your advisor have a peep at the letter first, then get it on its way.

Then you must also write to your local office of the DSS informing them that you will now be paying contributions as a self-employed person. These, initially at any rate, will be weekly flat rate Class 2 contributions.

Your next step is to apply for voluntary registration for VAT. There are several important reasons for doing this, the first being that VAT registration will improve your image in the eyes of your customers. They will all be registered for VAT anyway, so it is not going to cost them any more to deal with you. The second reason is that you will be acquiring substantial amounts of capital equipment, and the ability to recover the VAT will help your cash flow substantially. Thirdly, in the case of purchases of capital equipment used in your business, the VAT office will, in most cases, allow you to reclaim VAT paid on purchases made prior to your registration, and this can be as much as three years before registration. Again this means a nice cheque at the start when you need it most.

The business plan

One complaint I hear frequently, usually from bank managers, is that small business proprietors know little about how their businesses are really doing, and don't plan ahead. Most "seat of the pants" entrepreneurs argue that they are too busy making money to worry about such trifles. This attitude is fine whilst they really are making money, but then how do they know? Nobody is more surprised than the "up and at 'em" businessman when all of a sudden he is facing disaster because there isn't enough money in the bank to pay the rent or the bank interest. You need a plan, and you need to know how you are doing against this plan to run any kind of business, especially these days.

The first element of the plan is your sales forecast, which is simply your best guess at the amount of business you are going to do in the next twelve months. To do this, you have to make some basic assumptions. If you are setting up shop in your own home town then your assumptions will probably be more accurate than in a new environment, but don't let that bother you at this stage. What is important is that you know what your assumptions are, so that in days to come you can see which assumptions were right and which were wrong.

In commercial photography it is safe to assume that most direct accounts will give you a small job to do "to try you out". Direct accounts are those in which you are dealing direct with the end user, with no agency in between. For the sake of argument, assume that a third of the clients you visit will commission you to do work on an increasing basis, and that you will begin to deliver work two months after your first sales visit. Ad agencies and designers will be a little more reticent, allow a three months lead time, but also include a little lab work like black and white print runs or the odd dupe tranny. Name each client that you intend to prospect and allow an invoice value of between £400 and £500 per day for each job.

Write down your assumptions so that you can refer to them later when you are a few months in. You are going to need this sales forecast to prepare the first planning document, your "Profit and Loss Forecast".

The profit and loss forecast

The Profit and Loss Forecast, Table 1, illustrated here, was prepared using a PC and spreadsheet program. If you look at line 7,
you will see a typical sales forecast for a start-up situation. These
figures are, in fact, very close to the first months of trading for a
studio I started up in Peterborough a few years ago, with only a
very small increase for inflation. You should do at least as well as
this, possibly better.

Note that at this stage, "Sales" is the value of your invoice to
the client, less VAT. As VAT is recoverable, it does not form part of
your accounts, and all the figures we will discuss here do not
include it. We will need to consider VAT when we talk about "Cash
Flow", but we are not there yet.

The next thing we need to estimate is the "Gross Profit" on our
sales. Gross profit is the profit we earn when we buy materials and
services, and sell them on at a profit without taking overheads into
account. Overheads are items such as wages to staff, rent, electricity and other expenses. In our case, gross profit is the difference
between the selling price and the cost of materials such as film and
processing. Also included in these "direct" costs are any bought-in
items or services specifically needed for the job, such as background rolls and modelling fees.

As you, the photographer, get paid out of overall (net) profits,

Blankfrawe Photography, Profit/Loss Forecast, Jan 1992/Dec1992

		Jan	Feb	Mar	Apr	May	Jun	Jul	Aug	Sep	Oct	Nov	Dec
7	Sales:			250	850	1350	1600	1850	1600	2400	2900	3000	3250
9	Gross Profit:	0	0	175	595	945	1120	1295	1120	1680	2175	2250	2438
10	(%age)			70%	70%	70%	70%	70%	70%	70%	75%	75%	75%
12	Expenses:												
14	Rent				500	500	500	500	500	500	500	500	500
15	Rates	100	100	100	100	100	100	100	100	100	100	100	100
16	Insurance	60	60	60	60	60	60	60	60	60	60	60	60
17	Repairs & Renewals	0											
18	Gas & Electricity			400			175			125			300
19	Stationery	400					200						
20	Telephone	200		200			200			200			200
21	Car Lease												
22	Car Fuel & Service	35	35	35	135	35	35	35	35	35	35	35	35
23	Car Tax & Insurance				350								
24	Bank Loan Interest				150	150	150	150	150	150	150	150	150
25	Bank Charges	25	25	25	25	25	25	25	25	25	25	25	25
26	Overdraft Interest		16	11	0	0	18	47	56	62	75	82	78
27	Entertainment			50				50					
28	Adv & Publicity		250		150								
29	Depreciation	250	250	250	250	250	250	250	250	250	250	250	250
30	Prof. Fees						1000						
31	Sundries	50	50	50	50	50	50	50	50	50	50	50	50
33	Total Expense:	1120	786	1181	1770	1170	2813	1217	1226	1557	1245	1252	1748
35	For Month:												
37	Net Profit/(Loss):	-1120	-786	-1006	-1175	-225	-1693	78	-106	123	930	998	690
39	Cumulative:	-1120	-1906	-2912	-4087	-4312	-6005	-5927	-6033	-5910	-4980	-3982	-3293

Table 1.
Profit & Loss
account

the gross profit in a photo business is very high, figures of 85% and higher not being uncommon. To calculate gross profit as a percentage you divide it by the selling price and multiply by 100. As you will be wasteful of materials to start off with, take a figure of about 70% for the first few months and increase it very gradually as you start to become more efficient. Line 9 shows the gross profit you have just calculated.

We now need to deduct our overheads from the gross profit, starting off with the general items such as rent and rates, Lines 14 and 15. I have assumed you have negotiated well and obtained a three month rent holiday. Rent has been calculated on a 1,000 sq ft unit at £6/sq ft/year. Rates are estimated at £1,200 p.a. You will need to carry insurance and this is costly. As rates are constantly going up, the £720 on line 16 may need to be revised upwards. You will note that I have assumed you will appoint an accountant, simply because I wanted to show expenses at a maximum in this particular exercise.

The rest of the expenses lines are self-explanatory except for the bank and depreciation entries. You will note there are three lines of bank expense, lines 24 to 26. These are to cover the bank loan interest, charges and overdraft interest. You cannot, on a profit and loss forecast like this, include the actual payments on a loan as these include capital which adds to the worth of the business. Similarly, you can't allow money spent to acquire capital goods like cameras, as they are also part of the wealth of your business and are accounted for elsewhere. Expenses here mean just that – they are expenses only and not sums of money invested to acquire cameras and lighting, or to improve the premises.

In this fictitious business I have assumed that you will borrow £10,000 from the bank as a loan, and line 24 is my estimate of the interest-only portion of your monthly payment. Next, you will be charged for transactions on your business account at the bank, and line 25 is my "guesstimate". Finally, part of your bank borrowing will be in the form of an authorised overdraft. This facility from the bank is to provide cash to cover short-term ups and downs, and is at a cheaper interest rate than a loan. We calculate the actual interest from the "cash flow forecast", but, for the time being, just take my figures in line 26 for granted.

When you buy capital equipment, it is assumed that it will wear out and need to be replaced. Accountants therefore allow for "depreciation" of these assets, and there are several ways of calculating this, some more complicated than others. How you calculate it is really not that important, because the Inland Revenue will not allow depreciation as a valid expense to be set against tax. You do need to include it here though, because you need to have some idea that your business can afford to replace expensive equipment as time goes by.

	P & L Summary		
3			
4	-------------		
5		1992	1993
6	===		
7	Sales:	19,050	45,000
8			
9	Gross Profit:	13,793	33,750
10	(%age)	72.5%	75.0%
11	---		
12	Expenses:		
13	---------		
14	Rent	4,500	6,000
15	Rates	1,200	1,320
16	Insurance	720	790
17	Repairs & Renewals	0	300
18	Gas & Electricity	1,000	1,100
19	Stationery	600	250
20	Telephone	1,000	800
21	Car Lease	0	3,000
22	Car Fuel & Service	520	700
23	Car Tax & Insurance	350	400
24	Bank Loan Interest	1,350	1,800
25	Bank Charges	300	500
26	Overdraft Interest	445	550
27	Entertainment	100	200
28	Adv & Publicity	400	500
29	Depreciation	3,000	3,000
30	Prof. Fees	1,000	1,250
31	Sundries	600	660
32			
33	Total Expense:	17,086	23,120
34	---		
35			
36	Net Prof./(Loss) for year:	(3,293)	10,630
37			
38	===		

Table 2.
P&L Summary

My depreciation calculation is as follows, with apologies to my many accountant friends.

The assets that are subject to the depreciation calculation are cameras and other capital equipment, your car, and the work you will do on the industrial unit, normally called "leasehold improvements". I normally calculate depreciation over five years, subject to a "residual value". This is what the asset is worth after five years and is unlikely to change. A Nikon F3 will always be worth about £100 for instance, or an old banger will always fetch £500 or so. We are talking about £12,000 worth of capital gear, so if we take a residual value of 20% we are left with a balance of £9,600 to depreciate over five years, which equals £160 per month to set aside from profit. I have assumed that your car is worth about £4,000, so on the same basis you will need to set aside £50. The leasehold improvements, in my opinion, will have nil residual value, but will last longer, so I have depreciated this over ten years, thus giving £40 per month. This little lot equals £250 per month to be allowed for, on line 29.

We now have a forecast of income and expenditure, our "P&L Forecast" to give it it's Sunday name. This forecast is the one that tells you when your business becomes profitable, and by how much. In this fictitious plan, our business starts to make a profit consistently in September, but cumulatively, for the year, loses £3,293. This is a typical result; don't forget that you are starting from zero and you need to build up the business. However you do need to show that you will make a profit one day, and to this end I have made a forecast for the following year, shown here as Table 2.

I have gently moved up the rate of doing business to £3,750 per month, averaged, and also improved the gross profit percentage to 75%. I have also included a leased car, and a full year's rent. You will see that I am forecasting a profit of some £10,000 out of which you have to pay yourself and the taxman. Your tax should be minimal if you have taken the correct advice, so you are now financing your own income of about £800 per month out of the profits of your business. Having established that your business is viable, we now go on to probably the most important plan you must make, the "Cash Flow Forecast".

The cash flow forecast

One of the biggest traps to fall into is that of confusing profit with cash. Businesses require cash to acquire cameras and lighting, to buy stocks of film and materials, and to finance the period between giving your client your invoice and getting paid. Proper cash forecasting will ensure the smooth progress of your business, and sloppy "back of fag packet" estimates will surely lead to your ruin. The profit calculation is a paper one to ensure that you are trading profitably – the cash forecast will make sure that your cheques won't bounce when you pay your suppliers' bills, and, more importantly perhaps, there will be enough money for you personally to draw on to pay the grocer.

The first thing to do is calculate the input of cash to the business from your sales forecast – line 7 of the P&L forecast, Table 1. Most businesses in the UK work on what is euphemistically called "net monthly" terms. What this means is that invoices issued in one month are paid at the end of the following month. As they tend to be paid at the end of the first week of the month after that, you are granting somewhere in the region of 40 to 70 days credit, free of charge. (Our American cousins think we're crazy, they think in terms of 14 to 21 days as a credit account.) Also, if you don't chase your money vigorously, that can very easily be extended into 70 to 100 days, or beyond. We'll look at this shameful situation later on, but, for the purposes of our plan, let's enter the cash line as the sales line, but two months further on, adding VAT at the current rate (17.5%). This now becomes line 12 in our "Cash Flow Forecast", Table 3, for our fictitious business. We'll go through it, line by line.

Line 13 is for any asset sales – unsuitable cameras, or lenses you don't like, for instance. The figures should include VAT at the current rate. Line 14 is for the introduction of cash into the business, such as a bank loan or a postal order from Uncle Harry. The total of these is line 16, "Total Receipts", which is the flow of cash into your business, its life-blood.

Each month you will have standing orders and cheques written

		Jan	Feb	Mar	Apr	May	Jun	Jul	Aug	Sep	Oct	Nov	Dec
1													
2	Blankframe Photography, Cash Flow Forecast, Jan 1992/Dec1992												
3	------												
4													
5		Jan	Feb	Mar	Apr	May	Jun	Jul	Aug	Sep	Oct	Nov	Dec
6	=====												
7	Invoiced Sales:												
8	(From P/L F'cast)		250	850	1350	1600	1850	1600	2400	2900	3000	3250	
9	=====												
10	Receipts:												
11	---------												
12	from Sales:					294	999	1586	1880	2174	1880	2820	3408
13	from Asset sales:												
14	Cash introduced:			10000	0								
15													
16	Total Receipts:	0	0	10000	0	294	999	1586	1880	2174	1880	2820	3408
17	------												
18	Payments:												
19	---------												
20	Drawings	750	750	750	750	750	750	750	750	750	750	750	750
21	Rent			500	500	500	500	500	500	500	500	500	500
22	Rates	100	100	100	100	100	100	100	100	100	100	100	100
23	Insurance	60	60	60	60	60	60	60	60	60	60	60	60
24	Materials	500		0	100	175	250	300	275	350	500	500	550
25	Lab services			50	75								
26	Gas & Electricity			460			200			145			345
27	Stationery	460					230						
28	Telephone	230		230			230			230			230
29	Car Fuel & Service	40	40	40	155	40	40	40	40	40	40	40	40
30	Car Tax & Insurance				350								
31	Capital items	6400	1800	1800									
32	Start up costs	2500	2500										
33	Bank Loan				325	325	325	325	325	325	325	325	325
34	Entertainment				50			50					
35	Adv. & Publicity			290		175							
36	Prof. Fees							1150					
37	Sundries	60	60	60	60	60	60	60	60	60	60	60	60
38													
39	Total Payments:	11100	5600	3600	2650	2010	3945	2135	2110	2560	2335	2335	2960
40	------												
41	VAT Calculation:												
42	----------------												
43	Input Tax:	1518	699	393	84	41	322	60	56	123	89	89	182
44	Output Tax:	0	0	44	149	236	280	324	280	420	508	525	569
45													
46	VAT payable(Refund):	-350			-2566			218			785		
47	------												
48	Net Cash Flow:	-10750	-5600	6400	-84	-1716	-2946	-767	-230	-386	-1240	485	448
49	------												
50	Opening Bank:	12500	1725	-3916	2448	2339	597	-2387	-3220	-3525	-3992	-5327	-4943
51	O/Draft interest:		-16	-11			-13	-42	-50	-56	-69	-76	-71
52	Bank Charges:	25	25	25	25	25	25	25	25	25	25	25	25
53	Closing Bank:	1725	-3916	2448	2339	597	-2387	-3220	-3525	-3992	-5327	-4943	-4592
54	=====												

Table 3. Cash flow forecast

on the business bank account. These come next. You may be a little puzzled over "Drawings". No, you are not employing an artist – in a sole trader business your income is the net profit, after tax, you make on your sales. However, you don't know what this profit is until the end of the year, and it may well be negative. You therefore decide on a sum of money you will "draw" each month, "on account", in anticipation of the profits you hope to make. This is not a salary or wages, and tax is not deducted. It is your advance on profits, and you set the level according to your needs and the profit you have anticipated in your P&L forecast (Tables 1 and 2). I've allowed £750 per month; you set what you want. Later on, when you get going, you can arrange a credit transfer into your personal account for this amount at the start of every month.

Next are the payments you make for each of the headings outlined in lines 21 to 37. Note that in the cash flow calculation we are dealing with every payment irrespective of purpose, so we can see here cash out for cameras, for doing up the industrial unit, and the full amount of a bank loan, all inclusive of VAT. For some items, you will probably obtain "monthly" credit terms from your suppliers, and in this case, the cash would go out about 60 days after the purchase. To make life simple here, I've ignored monthly accounts for purchases, but not for our sales.

Then, there is the VAT calculation of "Input Tax", the recovery of tax charged by your suppliers, and "Output Tax", the tax you charge your clients, and which must be rendered unto Caesar. This calculation is normally done every quarter, and you will note that the cheque is positive (the Excise gives you money) at the end of the first quarter. This is because of your profligate spending and low sales. Also, at the beginning there is another repayment of VAT. This is the expected recovery of VAT on items you bought before you registered. Regrettably, this flow of cash from the Customs and Excise is short lived, and later on in the year you will be paying them.

Line 48 is the one that interests your bank manager, your "Net Cash Flow", which states whether money is flowing in to your business on average, or flowing out of it, and by how much. It is the total receipts minus the total payments plus or minus any VAT adjustments. On this plan, you can see that our fictitious business only goes "cash positive" on a monthly basis in the last two months of the year, whereas if you look at Table 1 again, you will notice that we go into profit earlier. This is normal, and underlines the fact that a profitable business can be negative on cash flow quite easily, and worse, if you plan a very vigorous growth, you can be in cash flow trouble for a very long time. Indeed, more small businesses are limited in their ability to grow quickly because of cash constraints than for any other reason. Three-month credit terms don't help them either.

The last section on the plan is the bank situation. Here, I have assumed that you have invested £12,500 of your cash in the business, and you have succeeded in persuading a bank manager to lend you £10,000 in the form of a term loan, and to grant you overdraft facilities. As you trade you will notice that during the year, your balance changes from £12,500 at the start, to a maximum of £5,400 overdrawn in October. Your overdraft decreases from that point as your net cash flow (line 48) goes positive. This means that you need authorisation for a maximum overdraft of £5,400, and I would ask for £6,000.

The nice thing about overdrafts is that the bank calculates interest on a daily basis, on a negotiated rate over the bank rate. "3% over base" is a nice rate to get, and I have used this rate in my (inaccurate) estimate of overdraft interest in line 51. Now you know where I got my figures from for line 26 in the P&L Forecast, Table 1. The bank charges, line 52, complete the cash flow forecast.

You now know all you need to know about your business, what your sales must be, how much profit you will make and when, and what your cash requirements will be. If you already have a computer you can use a spreadsheet program to play with the figures and make sure you understand every one.

Spend some time on this stage, and make sure you are really happy with all the assumptions, especially the sales figures. When you are, you can go on to the next stage of raising the finance and starting up your business.

Raising the money

There are several ways of raising money to start up a business, but the general principle is to borrow as little as you need to. "Never a borrower nor a lender be" is perhaps going a little too far, but many bank managers will tell you that most small businesses borrow too much and so spend most of their time working for Barclays or Nat West.

You will need two kinds of money: term borrowing, which as the name suggests is a loan with monthly repayments over a fixed term, rather like HP, and a short term credit facility, an overdraft, which allows you to overdraw on your current account as and when you need the money. Looking at the term borrowing first, this is the money you need to purchase capital equipment and to fit out your studio. You can obtain this money from the bank in the form of a "business loan", from a private source located by your accountant if you have one, or you may be able to raise it yourself.

I'll deal with negotiations with a bank more fully in a moment, and if you are getting facilities with the help of your accountant then you will discuss the terms with them. Do not, however, dismiss raising the cash yourself – it will make your life so much easier if you can.

Firstly, can you borrow from a relative? Formal agreements can be cheaply set up through the family solicitor, and there is nothing wrong with it if you pay a commercial rate of interest. Have you any insurance policies with surrender values? What about a second mortgage on the house – a bank almost certainly would want to take it as security, and if the equity is good enough for the bank, it certainly will be good enough for another lender such as a building society.

I personally avoid the unpleasant business of a bank having my home as security for my business like the plague, and this is one way around it. There are others too, which we'll look at later. If you do remortgage your house or take a second mortgage, then you have the distinct advantage of not linking that debt with the performance of your business. The interest rate will be substantially lower than a bank loan, especially if you remortgage, and you may be able to claim full tax relief if you can convince the tax inspector that the loan was necessary for the start up of your business.

Whether you provide the initial money yourself or borrow it, you need to open a business account with a bank, and persuade the manager to do business with you. We'll spend a little time on this subject, because the high street bank can be a tremendous help if you understand the role it has to play in your business.

Leaving aside merchant banks who provide "risk" capital (at a suitable price), the high street bank is there to "oil the wheels" and help you achieve your objectives, but at little overall risk. You must take the risk; don't expect your local branch of Barclays to do it for you. Also, just because you have thousands of pounds worth of security, don't think it is your right to demand a loan because it will be adequately secured. A bank is not a pawn shop. A bank will lend on a business only if it thinks it is viable. There is little point, from the banker's point of view, in wasting time lending on a hare-brained scheme that will never get off the ground, even if the security is good. The bank will have lost good management time and effort that would have been better spent on a more worthy cause.

Security for borrowing is a subject that often causes a great deal of emotion. When a bank (or anyone else for that matter) lends money, it needs to know that it has a good chance of getting paid back. One way that it can judge this is from the degree of commitment to the venture that the borrower has. If a borrower needs say, £20,000, and has already £15,000 of their own money to invest, then the bank is pretty sure that his commitment to the venture is solid. If the venture itself looks viable, then a bank is unlikely to ask for security on the loan. The only minor disadvantage you will have in these circumstances is that the interest rate on unsecured borrowing is slightly higher. On the other hand, if in the case of our £20,000 requirement, the borrower only had £5,000 to invest, then the bank would certainly require security. In this case, it is doubtful that the bank would play anyway.

It is very difficult to lay down hard and fast rules, but if you are prepared to put in half of the money from your own resources, the bank will generally lend the other half, but will require some form of security. If you can manage to increase your contribution to two thirds, then you will probably be able to persuade the manager to lend without security.

In our fictitious example, I have assumed that you have £12,500 of your own, need a term loan of £10,000, and require an overdraft facility of about £5,000. Theoretically, you are a little short of the 50% rule at 45.5%, but you should be OK with security. If, however, you decided to raise an additional £10,000 yourself by remortgaging your house, for example, then you would only require a £5,000 overdraft facility for a total investment of £27,500. The bank would be unreasonable in asking for security under these circumstances.

The security that a bank will accept includes any asset that is reasonably easily converted into cash. Stocks and shares, insurance policies and guarantees from third parties are all acceptable, as is your house if your equity is sufficient. It really is your decision as to whether you want to put your house on the line; my views on the subject have already been stated.

Finally, you need to know what value the security should be. This obviously varies from manager to manager, but you should work on between 1.25 and 1.5 times the value of the debt. If you are going to ask a bank to finance £15,000, then they will need to see between £18,000 and £22,000 worth of security.

Another solution to obtaining a loan if you can't raise enough security is the Government's Loan Guarantee Scheme. The Government guarantees 70% of loans over two to seven years in return for a small premium on the guaranteed part of the loan. Your bank will have details. I find it all a very unpleasant and sordid business, and if you can avoid term borrowing from a bank, then you should do so.

You should now be in a position to approach a bank. Make the appointment with the branch manager; you may as well deal with the boss, as most business lending situations will end up with him/her eventually. You should take with you your sales forecast together with your assumptions, your profit & loss forecast and the cash flow forecast. If you are going for a term loan as well as an overdraft facility, decide how much you want as a term loan and how much on the overdraft. Bear in mind that although an overdraft is much more flexible, it is only meant for smoothing out ups and downs and not for "hard" borrowing. If you try to fiddle it that way, you will get your fingers rapped very quickly by the manager. Also, an overdraft facility is one which is temporarily granted by your manager, and can be withdrawn at little or no notice, unlike a loan, which, providing you make the payments on time, is cast in concrete, as, usually, is the interest rate. Remember, interest rates can go down as well as up.

Take your partner along as well; two committed people are better than one. Bank managers have the reputation of being tough, difficult people, but most of the examples I've met have been quite easy to get on with. One informed economist described them as "the most romantic and least realistic of men..."

When you meet the bank manager, remember all the time that he or she is trying to assess you as well as the venture. Your character is as important as the figures you will present. A bank needs to be comfortable with the people it deals with, and will look for signs that you are a trustworthy person and that you will honour your promises. The manager will also look for signs of over-optimism, but be careful here not to go to the other extreme and be overcautious. They will look for some evidence that you know what you are doing. If you can link your previous experience in some way to your venture, then they will know you are not going in cold.

Above all, they will be looking for commitment to the project – they do not want you to cut and run the moment the going gets tough. Also, if the bank you are visiting is not your own bank, be prepared for questions as to why you have come to them. It is only natural to assume that you have been turned down elsewhere. If you have, say so. The fact of the matter is that a bank wants you to succeed in your plans as much as you do. Little businesses become big businesses and banks like big businesses.

Managers of banks have a large amount of discretion, and rarely apply fixed rules in their dealings. If he/she takes a shine to you, and the figures add up, then you may be surprised at a bank's level of co-operation. But if a bank manager thinks you are trying to con them, then you will be shown the door gently but firmly.

Generally, you will get a decision on the spot. If it is negative, don't be too concerned at first. The "chemistry" may be wrong, or they may have had a bad day. Present your plan to another bank. Only if you get a number of refusals should you think about revising your plan.

THE STUDIO

Armed with our finances arranged, we can now, at last, start to think about photography, and turn our attention to designing, finding and fitting out our studio.

Space considerations

A commercial photographer has to design his studio around the largest product he is likely to have to shoot. The specialist is lucky – I know of a photographer who shoots jewellery on 10x8in in a converted living room, while at the other end of the scale there is a cavernous studio in the Midlands where they undertake photography of commercial vehicles. The specialist can "tailor" their studio exactly to their particular needs. We, on the other hand, have to make some compromises, knowing that there will be situations where our studio is too small, or too large. The trick is to make sure these occasions are rare.

Most localities tend towards one kind of business or another, and this is reinforced with time. As specialised service industries gather around their clients, they in turn attract more similar clients, and so on. This obviously does help in designing our studio, and in keeping costs to a minimum. There is no point in fitting out a 50x60ft studio in a town that specialises in semiconductor production, for instance.

These considerations, however, only affect the studio itself, and the access to it. The darkroom and office will be common to most applications, and the only other "client variable" feature will be a changing room for models, which you are likely to need at some time in most applications.

The other subject you need to address is that of in-house processing. Most agencies and many direct clients these days expect a photographic studio to provide a full range of services. If you live within a mile or so of a friendly professional processing lab, then you may be able to dispense with this expensive accessory. Having said that, you must be sufficiently friendly with them to have them waiting around half the night to process a dozen sheet films without rancour. This facility is present in many major towns, but in the small towns and "boonies" where you are likely to locate your business, you are going to have to have your own processing facilities. This is not too big a problem providing that you keep your feet on the ground and tailor your services to the needs of your clients.

The minimum that you must be able to offer is black and white negative processing for 35mm, roll film and sheet film, B&W printing from 5x7in to about 20x16in, and, from time to time, largish enlargements using 30in rolls. You must also be able to produce mono internegatives from transparencies, on 5x4in format.

In colour, you must be able to process E6 roll film and 5x4in sheet film, and be able to offer a dupe transparency service. Finally, you should be able to take a colour internegative from a transparency, even if you leave the printing to a lab (you may not have the time to let the lab have the tranny).

Bearing in mind the low volume of your work, you will be able to achieve this with a couple of darkrooms taking up a total of 150 –175 square feet or so, less if you combine all operations into one room.

Before leaving aside considerations of lab space, there are another couple of services which you can offer, which, whilst not essential, can be very profitable. The first is a copying facility, to copy artwork or photographs on to transparency film or mono negative film. Many clients need this service when including illustrations in ads or brochures.

The second is to offer a cold mounting or lamination service. This is usually used to mount large prints on to foam board for displays, and, despite the relatively high cost of the mounting rollers, can be extraordinarily profitable. Allow for a bench about 6ft by 3ft for the copying stand, and for a bench about 8ft by 3ft 6in for the mounting rollers.

Having put the cart before the horse so to speak, we'll now look at the main studio – where we are going to take the pics. There is a starting point: I like to think in terms of taking a full length figure on a landscape format, on either 6x7cm or 5x4in, using 127mm or 180mm lenses respectively. Allowing for a little top and bottom, the reduction on 6x7cm is about 1/35 (reduction = image size/object size), and on 5x4in is about 1/24. Add two focal lengths each (the formula is in the back of this book), and the subject/film distance is about 16ft in both cases. I like about four feet behind the subject to let the background roll go out of focus, and you need (especially on 5x4) three to four feet behind the camera. Voila! Your minimum studio length is about 24ft.

As far as width is concerned, I like to have about six feet either side of an eight foot shooting width in front of the background. This means that the starting point for the studio size is 20ft wide by 24ft long. These dimensions are not cast in concrete, and they can be increased or decreased depending on the kind of photography contemplated.

Let's look at two very different studio installations, both of which I have been associated with at some time or other over the last few years.

An economy studio

The first studio was located in small industrial unit in a multi-unit building of nine, located in a "high tech" new town. The local business was almost completely based on the electronics industry, with activities varying from advanced avionics manufacture through to miniature electronic components. There were a number of firms importing or manufacturing computer peripherals equipment such as disc drives, PC expansion cards and the like, together with a number of businesses providing intermediate products for local companies: printed circuit boards, steel cabinets, silk screen print-

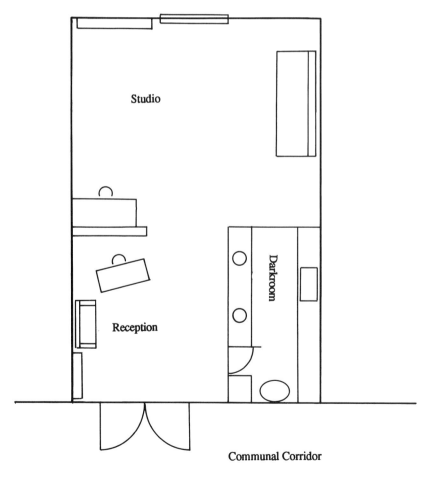

Figure 1.
Economy studio
floor plan

ing. Finally there were several one or two man sub-contract businesses, providing wiring and assembly services.

The scene was completed by one or two graphic designers locally, and one full blown ad agency in a nearby town. Professional processing facilities were available some thirty miles away with a twice weekly pick-up and delivery service.

I have found that this profile is fairly typical of many small new towns, and, of late, of areas around the newer industrial units in larger towns.

For this studio, obviously, a large area was not going to be needed, and the unit size in fact was only 700 square feet. The floor plan is shown in Figure 1. One of the advantages of taking a "starter" unit like this in a small multi-unit building is that your main doors give on to a corridor, and not the cold world outside. If the main building is heated, the advantages are obvious. Also, this particular building had a receptionist's office at the main entrance, which, on the rare occasions when it was staffed, was a great help to a one person business.

The cost of fitting out this unit was less than £1,000, including plumbing and a removable security grill on the window. Electric Economy 7 heating was installed by the landlord. The studio area measured only 17ft by 22ft, smaller than the "start point" studio, but totally capable of handling the kind of work demanded of the studio. Most of the work in the area consisted of small "product table" work, and this was done in the centre of the studio on a home made small product fixture. At one end of the studio there was a small bench supporting a Bowens Illumitran slide copier, and a microscope carrying a 35mm camera for photomicroscopy of integrated circuits.

At the far end of the studio was a Courtenay fixture carrying up to three 9ft Colorama rolls with chain drive. The window was fitted with a blackout panel which could be removed for ventilation purposes. The floor of the studio was left as sealed concrete flooring slabs.

The darkroom measured 7ft by 14ft, a little cosy, but contained two enlargers, one colour, one cold cathode black and white. Facilities were also provided for E6 film processing, and there was a 5ft sink for black and white print processing in dishes. There was also a hand-washing sink, together with film and print driers. The darkroom walls were made using 2x3in stud and plate construction, with plasterboard used inside the darkroom, and decorative veneered wood panels on the reception area side.

The floor had two thicknesses of thermoplastic tiles. Benches were converted kitchen cabinets from MFI, with the bases sealed to the floor tiles. Water heating was provided by a small electric six litre storage heater, mounted on the wall over the main sink. A light baffle was fitted on the dry bench, and entry to the darkroom provided by a standard door.

Finally, the reception area was carpeted with carpet tiles, and contained a desk, two comfortable chairs and a bookcase. The entry to the studio was via two doors opening to a width of 6ft, with easy access to the studio area from the entrance.

This studio was compact and easy to run. It showed itself quite capable of responding to the photographic needs of the area, and was easily run by one photographer and partner. It was so successful, in fact, that it became the subject of detailed attention from a competitor. Why not, it had all the pluses for a successful business – it provided the services the area needed, but no more, and carried minimum overhead expense.

A standard commercial studio

The next example is a more substantial studio located in a developing town in the East of England. The town itself is a designated "new town", the activities of an aggressive Development Corporation having come to an end. The local businesses combine old, traditional engineering with newer imports from the South East, plus new starting businesses in just about every field. If there was a trend developing, it was in wholesaling for the retail trade. However, no studio based in this area could afford to ignore the substantial engineering presence.

For this reason, a larger than usual studio was envisaged, with good access for large and heavy products. A standard independent industrial unit was chosen, on a reasonably central industrial estate. This location made it convenient to the several industrial estates around, as well as being only a couple of miles from the central town area, where lurked the major design and advertising agencies. The unit chosen was about 1,350 square feet in size, and the plan is shown here (Figure 2).

The main studio area was 29ft wide by 25ft long, but this area was eaten into at one end by a small model changing room and a mounting and lamination bench. Shooting was done along the 25ft dimension, leaving plenty of room at the side to stack products for photography. Access was through an 8ft square roller-shutter door leading into a small unloading area with swing doors giving on to the studio. Although this space was essentially wasted, it did give an extra set of doors between the studio proper and the outside world, and yet you could still get a fork-lift truck into the studio with no problems. The background roll system was attached to the far wall using Bowens triple hooks.

The changing room did get in the way, and had the decision not been made to include colour printing facilities, the main darkroom could have been made smaller and room found for the changing room on the left hand side.

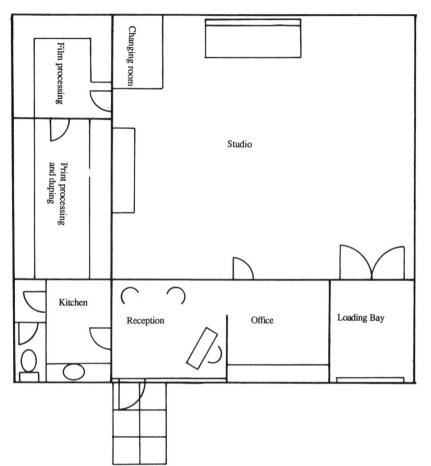

Figure 2.
Standard com-
mercial studio,
floor plan

Originally, this studio started life with only one darkroom, in which all processes were carried out. As the volume of copying increased, space had to be found for a Polaroid MP4 copying set up. This coincided with in an increase in 5x4in and 10x8in dupe tranny work as well, and if the area at the end of the darkroom was closed in, an extra E6 machine could be accommodated as well. When all the work was finished, the main darkroom just handled printing and dupe exposing, and the room tacked on to the end handled E6 and copying. It also served as a "light trap" for people going in and out of the main darkroom, although I was never sure about the legality of this arrangement. The construction of the darkrooms was again 2x4in stud and plate; the model changing room was of lighter construction using 1x2in timber.

At the front of the building there was a personnel door with two floor-to-ceiling windows. This arrangement, unusual for an industrial unit of this size, enabled a very pleasant reception area to be built. Many industrial units only have a small "people" door built in as part of the larger main entrance, but this separate entrance made an excellent impression on visitors and customers alike. In this particular studio, it meant that the "Girl Friday" (receptionist, switchboard operator, accounts clerk, typist, hirer of models, payer of bills and maker of coffee) had a desk near to a window so she could keep in touch with the outside world.

Again, the reception area and office construction was 2x4in stud and plate with a false suspended ceiling. Carpet tiles were used on the reception area floor, ordinary tiles on the office floor. On the other side of the reception area was a small kitchen for making sandwiches and coffee, and a toilet. Electric Economy 7 heating was installed; full heating in the office/reception area, background-only heating in the studio. The darkrooms were fitted with simple convector heaters which were only used at the start of very cold days and then turned off.

This studio was run by one photographer, his wife and a succession of trainees. The studio itself was booked for a minimum of three days every week, and also provided a range of services which included dupe and composite transparencies, mounting and lamination, copying, hand colour printing, and E6 processing for clients willing to pay the price. It is this studio that has been used as a model for this book.

Hopefully, having looked at these two examples, you should now be able to go out to look at units, and perhaps have a better idea of what you need. If you are looking at a new town then call the Development Corporation or the local office of the Commission for the New Towns, otherwise talk to the commercial divisions of the local estate agents.

Unit hunting

While you are trudging round industrial units, don't forget that generally overhead or fixed costs are directly proportional to floor area. Special deals for a bigger unit always cost you more money.

The whole subject of pricing is covered later, but today's commercial photographer is facing a customer who is much more cost-conscious than ever before. Most clients know that photography, especially good commercial photography, is expensive, but many feel that they have been overcharged in the past. You must therefore be very careful when you make decisions that affect your overhead costs. You cannot just automatically assume your client will pay for it, because he may not. You are then left with the unpleasant but not uncommon situation of a business that can't support its overheads – the end is just around the corner.

Generally, you will be limited by what is available on the industrial estates in the area, but don't be put off by premises in other locations. There are lots of buildings which have housed very different businesses that can be successfully converted into photographic studios. However, steer clear of old chapels, pubs, cinemas and the like unless you have piles of money and lots of time. Industrial units tend to have high roofs or ceilings, in the order of 12 to 14 feet, which give adequate clearance for large softboxes and makes it easy to construct mezzanine platforms for a high camera position. Make sure that that ex-undertaker's has sufficient height for you to work in!

Generally, my advice is to start off with a standard "starter" type industrial unit built in the last ten years or so. These buildings are easy to fit out, tend to be well insulated and thus don't cost a fortune to heat, have space for a few cars to park in front, and have large doors to allow easy access for cumbersome products. They also say "I'm a serious business", not here today and gone tomorrow.

Advertising agencies and graphic designers will be major clients for your business. Although these companies tend to gravitate towards the more expensive areas of town, the service companies they deal with will have less expensive tastes. Seek out the reprographic companies, the typesetters and colour printers – these companies are regularly visited by your potential clients. Put your business next door to a repro house and you will have curious visitors almost from day one.

You will probably not be as lucky as that though, so you should look carefully at the kind of businesses around any unit you plan on taking. A car repair shop next door is not going to help your image (see below). The problem is that the variety of businesses that can be operated from small starter units is large, and it is virtually impossible for planning or other regulations to stop what you may consider to be an undesirable activity starting up next door.

Vetting your landlord

We had a situation once in our studio when the unit directly behind us was let to a problem tenant. His declared business was distributing automotive parts to the garage and retail trade, but when trading started it was obvious that the real business was repairing cars for the general public. To make matters worse, the dividing wall between our unit and theirs was only concrete block up to a height of 10 feet or so, the remainder being four feet of plasterboard, and this unsealed. As a result, we were assailed by fumes from a trichlorethylene degreasing plant, petrol fumes, music at 50 watts and foul language.

Matters came to a head when we were photographing perfumery products for a local company, art directed by two quite genteel ladies. All was going well until, behind us, a piece of car appeared to have fallen on a delicate part of someone's anatomy.

The resultant oaths enlarged my already quite extensive vocabulary, and must have been quite a revelation for my client guests.

The following morning, a full petrol tank emptied itself on their concrete floor, and we had to shut down operations for two days until the vapours cleared.

Because the lease did not contain specific clauses about operations that resulted in a real nuisance to neighbours, there was very little we, or the landlord, could do about the situation. Unluckily for them, but happily for us, the business ran out of cash four weeks after the end of the rent free period, and the problem went away. But it could have been quite serious for us; closing down and moving had to be our only option.

I mention this because your only recourse in these matters is to the landlord, and his attitude is reflected in the terms of the lease. There are developers and landlords who are only interested in the real estate equivalent of "bums on seats" – a rented unit is better than an unrented unit, and the quality of the tenant is unimportant providing he pays his rent.

There are other more enlightened landlords who believe that if they can create an "upmarket" estate with mainly professional tenants, then they can charge higher rents and make more money. Every town has a few areas like this, and you should seek them out.

If your landlord wants to maintain a high standard of amenities on his estate, then that will be reflected in the lease, and in his attitude to tenants who annoy. Ask to see a draft lease fairly early on in your talks with your prospective landlord. You are on the right track if it contains clauses which give the landlord discretion in deciding what is an acceptable activity and what is not.

Do not object to close questioning about your own activities; it is in your own interests.

The lease

The kind of lease that you will be offered will depend upon whether you are dealing with an estate agent or, in the case of a new town, the CNT or Development Corporation. Starter units let by the CNT or a DC usually have leases that run for three years. This short term is based on the premise that after three years an expanding business will want something bigger, or an unsuccessful business will want out. These leases are extremely flexible, and rightly so.

Every lease contains a renewal clause at the end of each three year period, so it can be seen as a three year rent review for those that are happy with their unit and wish to stay more or less permanently. The concept of new towns is to create an environment which allows business to flourish, and not simply to rent buildings. Development Corporations and people from the CNT are generally nice people to deal with, and usually you will be able to negotiate a rent free period up front. The purpose of this is to help your cash flow whilst you get your business up and running. However, four months is the most you are likely to get.

If, on the other hand, you are dealing with an estate agent, the situation is very different. Estate agents are charged with the job of renting units to the most stable tenants for the maximum rent and the longest period. They are imposing conditions upon you which are essentially the same conditions imposed upon them by the landlord.

Occasionally both they, and you, will come across a property developer who feels he can rent his 1,500 square foot starter unit to the same tenant for 25 years with a rent review every year and an initial premium of £10,000. When you mention a break clause they have a fit of apoplexy. Don't always blame the agent – he may have been telling the developer for months he'll never get it.

Generally, with a private developer, you will have to sign a lease for a longish duration. I am told that this has something to do with valuing the lease from a financing point of view, and I suppose it sounds plausible. Where you can protect yourself is to insist on a break clause being inserted in the lease. This means that you can break the lease without penalties at specific times should the building, or environment, prove unsatisfactory. If you can also agree that the rent reviews coincide with the break points, then the situation is totally under your control.

For the type of building we are talking about, you should be able to negotiate a twelve year lease, with break points at three or five year intervals, and with rent reviews at the same time. Whether you have rent reviews at three years and the break at five, or vice versa, depends on how good a negotiator you are. Believe me, it is possible, but there still are a lot of dreamers out there, especially in the property development business. And don't ever, ever accept a sublet clause as a replacement for a clean break.

Another sore point when renting in the private sector is the "premium". A premium is a sum of money you pay when you sign a lease, which is designed to compensate for improvements made to the property. If the previous tenant, or the landlord at the previous tenant's wishes, has built an office area, or has installed a burglar alarm, or has made any addition to the bare walls of the unit that makes it more attractive or useful, then it is normal to charge a premium for this work. You, in turn, will negotiate a payment at the end of your lease, so it is important that the premium is for some real improvement, and not just a further payment to negotiate at the start of your tenure. You don't get "owt for nowt", but make sure you are not paying out for nowt.

You will be expected to pay the legal costs of drawing up the lease, together with stamp duty, and maybe there will be a charge for putting up a sign with your name on it.

There really is no benefit in having a solicitor read through your lease, except to the solicitor. If you are dealing with a reputable company you should have no problem.

Finally, don't forget that the council dustmen don't collect from industrial premises, so you will have to make some arrangement for refuse collection. Most estates have a service with one contractor, and it is best to sign up with them, but, think about the amount of waste you will have. You will probably never fill their smallest container, so buy the minimum service.

You then get your keys.

Fitting out the unit

The first decision you should make is how to heat your unit. You usually have the choice between gas and electricity, and this choice rests on whether you wish to pay more for installation in return for lower running costs, or vice versa. Electric storage heating is excellent for a photographic studio, has a low installation cost, but can be expensive to run, especially if you need to top up the heat during the day with peak rate energy.

Gas, on the other hand, costs between two and three times the amount to install, but has a lower running cost, especially when you take into account the fact that you use gas as you need it – you can switch it off altogether during the day if you wish, or keep it on longer for especially cold days.

Bear in mind that any gas heater must have an exhaust to the exterior, and it is advisable to draw in fresh air from outside too. A tremendous amount of water is produced when natural gas burns, and condensation on the inside of a Copal shutter does nothing to extend its life. This means that if the heater is in an area with no outside walls – not uncommon in an industrial unit if you have an office in the front – then these facilities have to come through the roof, and this can be expensive. Otherwise, balanced flues are simple to install and are trouble free, and can be used for installing gas heaters in the front office, for instance. Electric heating, of course, has no such constraints, and heaters can be placed wherever you want.

Opinions vary, but I have found that unless you habitually photograph scantily clad models, the studio area only requires background heat. The general activity and modelling lamps from the flash can quickly bring the temperature up to comfortable levels, and beyond. The same holds true for the darkroom.

For the studio, if you choose electric heating, then one or two 3.4 kilowatt storage heaters will take the chill off quite nicely. Installed, they should cost between £300 and £500. Gas, on the other hand, will need a flue for exhaust, and most units are mounted high. There is the choice of convection or radiant heat; allow about £1,000 to install a suitable unit. A simple domestic electric convector heater will be fine in the darkroom, but hang it on wall brackets.

The office area requires full heating. There is little in this world more difficult than trying to be pleasant to visitors and polite and efficient on the phone while you are slowly freezing to death. Allow a full size storage heater if you are going the electric route at a cost of about £250, or a balanced flue gas unit at about £750 installed.

Both the gas and electricity companies have trained represen- tatives who will be only too pleased to come and visit you, and per- suade you that their system is best. I personally prefer electricity, but some of the bills can surprise. Don't forget that either system can be installed on a leasing arrangement, and that interest rates on these deals can often be lower than the bank can offer.

When you have made your heating decision, and, assuming you are starting with a bare shell, you next need to buy a box of black- board chalks, and mark the positions of each wall or partition on the floor. Take your time, walk around your plan and imagine it on a day when tempers are short, or when the studio is overflowing with products, people and equipment. If access to the darkroom, office, and exterior is easy and straightforward, and you have made each room sufficiently large to take the equipment you have chosen, then you can start thinking about building. This can cost as much as £20 per square foot if you bring in contractors to do this work for you, meaning that a modest office and single darkroom can cost you £5,000 or so, just for the walls. Unless you have rela- tions or other good contacts in the trade, go and buy a few tools and do it yourself, bringing in specialists for wiring and hanging doors when you need them.

You will need permission from your landlord, and this is best obtained as part of the negotiation for the lease. There should be no problem though, as you will not be knocking down existing walls, or altering the outside building in any way. Also, you should be aware that, strictly speaking, internal partitions in a "factory unit" are subject to building regulations. Whilst you do not have to have plans or work formally approved, the work should be done with these in mind.

It really is up to you how strictly you adhere to these regula- tions. Personally I have found the local city council most helpful in pointing out areas where you need to be careful. There are tables, for instance, defining the size of timber you can use to support a ceiling, depending upon the span. If you rigidly follow the rules you could end up using 2x8in beams at 18in centres to support plaster- board simply to keep out the light. You have to be intelligent about these things. A ceiling designed to support the weight of people

jumping up and down on top is a different animal to a light-tight cover for a darkroom.

Generally, you should use 2x4in stud and plate construction, with the studs at either 18in or 24in centres. This means that you lay a length of 2x4in rough sawn timber on the floor, and nail uprights into it every foot and a half or so. Make sure that you have a stud where you want to join your plasterboard panels, and measure the panels you intend to use – they are rarely exactly four feet wide, or mine never have been. Nail a length along the top, and you have the framework for your wall. Masonry bolts are used to fix the partitions to the breeze block wall inside the unit, and, if you are a "belt and braces" type like me, a masonry bolt every now and again into the floor doesn't hurt.

Where you want a door, use a "door kit" which consists of three pieces of timber which fit together to form a doorway. Whether you cut away the bottom plate at a doorway or leave it in position depends on the use – it is much easier to light-proof a door to a darkroom if you leave it in, but then you are constantly tripping over it.

Half way up each stud you should put horizontal strengtheners called "noggins". You should then support your ceiling beams on hangers which are available from your builders' merchant, and take 2in timber in a kind of stirrup support. Nail these in, and then put your lighting and power points into position. Wire these up if

Whilst you need a reasonable sized area for product photography, this little studio only measures twelve feet by eighteen, and yet can handle a wide variety of "pack shot" work

you know what you are doing; get your local electrician to do it if you don't. When these are in place, cover the frame with plaster-board, half-inch on the uprights, and three eighths on the ceiling (this can be fun – get a helper). Nail skirting board around the floor (this is called "pencil-round" in the trade because you pencil round it when you do corners), and buy lengths of architrave section for the doors when they are done.

Install your sink and plumbing at this stage. However, make sure that if you join your drain into the "manifold" in the loo, you put a "trap" at the loo end and at the sink end. If you don't do this, you will be greeted by sewage smells every time you go into the darkroom. Modern plastic fittings for drains and compression fit-tings for water mean this work is quite within most people's compe-tence.

Then install any water heaters you need. If these are of the electronic "pulse" type, you may find that everything in the studio "pulses" with them. Constantly flickering modelling lamps may not do too much for your concentration, and worse, this pulsing of the supply may affect the stabiliser on your enlarger. The solution is to have your electricity authority (or is it company now?) connect the water heater, and any other high current devices (such as room heaters if installed) to a separate phase of a three phase supply. You can then run your enlarger off a "clean" source. They some-times charge for this, but it is worth it.

Now, get the heating system you have chosen installed. Smooth off the gaps between the plasterboard with plasterboard tape, and you are ready to paint the walls. Bring in the joiner to hang doors (this really is a job I recommend you don't attempt), and the bare walls of your studio are complete. Tile the darkroom floor.

There is a lot you can do to make the reception area look attractive and opulent, cheaply. A ceiling which consists of white polystyrene sheets resting on planed and varnished white wood beams can look attractive, as can hessian pasted directly on top of plasterboard. Carpet tiles have the advantage of being relatively cheap and easily cleaned.

Mount some examples of your work on the walls. Cibachrome or reversal prints made from your trannies, mounted in borderless glass frames with a generous white or black border, are very effec-tive. Pop two comfortable chairs against the wall, and a plant of some description in the corner. A second-hand reception desk, suit-ably refurbished if necessary, and a coffee table with some recent photographic journals (*not* amateur ones!) complete a pleasant, professional reception area.

The rest of the office can be painted, and filled with good second-hand office furniture. There are some remarkable bargains to be had in this field, especially if you buy direct. A phone call to the maintenance or purchasing department of a nearby large company can often bring you a good four-drawer filing cabinet, a desk or two, and some chairs, for silly money. And you can tell them what you do, can't you!

Finally, bolt a Bowens "triple hook" system to the wall to hold your Colorama rolls, and build any benches you need for the studio area. Your insurance company will probably want you to change the locks on the doors to a five lever deadlock type, and now is as good a time to do this as any. Also, you may consider fitting some kind of burglar alarm system. However, insurance companies are not impressed with these unless they have an automatic dialling system through to a security desk somewhere. Direct lines to the local police station are rarely granted these days so you would have to subscribe to a security system, which can be expensive.

I recommend fitting a very visible self-contained alarm system, complete with foils, on windows in full view. If someone really wants to break in, they will, but the casual vandal will be deterred, and these systems are not expensive. You can install them yourself in many cases.

EQUIPMENT AND SERVICES

There is probably no activity that can compare with photography for avid collectors of equipment. I have seen seasoned professional photographers drool over the latest Sinar or Rolleiflex, and have looked inside camera cupboards full of lenses and accessories that have never been used in anger. Worse, I have been in camera stores and seen beginning professionals mortgage their houses (literally) to buy a camera system that was far beyond their needs. The very simplest bottom of the range product from a quality manufacturer would have been fine, and probably better suited to them to start off with.

We are all assailed with advertising that tells us we can't get a sharp picture unless we buy the latest super monorail at anything up to ten times the price of a perfectly acceptable simple studio camera. Lenses now are "super apochromatic" and absolutely "essential for the photographer who cares about quality". I even heard recently of a camera shop salesman describing a lens that has satisfied advertising photographers for the last twenty years as "sub-standard". One wonders just how photographers ten years ago managed to produce any work at all with such crude and inefficient equipment.

The hard commercial fact is that everyone is after your money, and it is obviously better to get you to pay £4,000 for a monorail than £400. The £4,000 job may have facilities for the busy photographer that the cheaper one lacks, but it won't necessarily take better photographs. Also, good photographic gear doesn't wear out that quickly, and the only way that the industry can continue to sell to you after your first purchase is to make you feel dissatisfied with your existing gear. They do this by the sowing seeds of doubt that your work with it may not be up to scratch because it does not incorporate the latest (expensive) mods.

Don't be fooled, don't be taken in. Photographers seem to have an inferiority complex regarding the quality of their work, usually totally unjustified, and some manufacturers and some dealers play on it. Cash is always a problem with a beginning business, so start off with only what is absolutely necessary. You can indulge in Rolls-Royce equipment when you are well and truly up and running in a few years time.

Choosing your dealer

Having said all that, you are still going to be spending several thousand pounds on capital gear. If you are happy with your first deal, you will probably want to buy all your materials as well from the same dealer. It makes good sense therefore to choose your dealer with some care, there is a lot more to this business than negotiating the best price. Look for these points:

● Good product knowledge

● Good stock

● Availability of rental gear

● A local rep "on the road"

Product knowledge

This is the most important requirement of any professional dealer. Many dealers take youngsters, give them a few catalogues, and expect them to answer technical questions on the phone from busy professional photographers. If you start to doubt the accuracy of the information you are getting, then you are wasting valuable time and money. Your salesman must know what he is talking about, and this knowledge comes from a combination of regular product training courses at the importers/manufacturers, and from several years experience of dealing with professional clients.

Total knowledge of the latest multi-mode 35mm auto-everything Niktax is not going to help you when you need to know how to un-jam a Hasselblad, or whether a 75mm Super Angulon needs a sunk or normal panel in a Cambo. Professional literature is not the most informative, and there is no substitute for practical experience. If you have ever tried to photograph a building and been unable to focus on it because you have the lens in the wrong panel, you are unlikely to forget the frustration of that moment.

Stock

Sales of professional gear represent a very small percentage of sales for the average dealer who handles both amateur and pro clients. Also, pro gear tends to be much more expensive, and many dealers rely on stock held by the importer for urgent needs. Whilst many dealers will admit readily to this practice, others will advertise that they hold comprehensive pro stocks. But all too often the particular item you want today is "temporarily out of stock".

You must deal with a dealer who has the goods on his shelves.

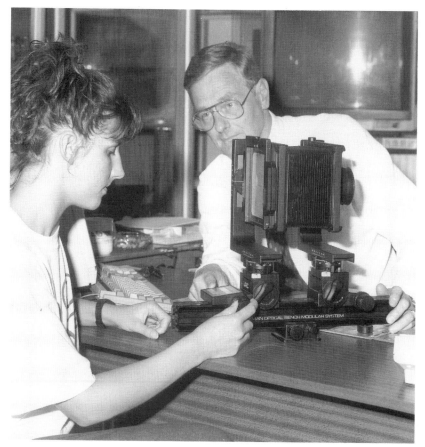

There is no substitute for an experienced salesman when buying professional gear. Photo courtesy KJP Nottingham

You need to unpack it, check it out, you need it replacing in a hurry if it doesn't work. Perhaps more importantly, the level of pro stock a dealer carries tells you a lot about his commitment to the professional market. Tens or hundreds of thousands of pounds worth of roll film gear, monorails, lenses etc. mean he is going to make sure you are happy with the service and will come back. The odd 500CM or F3 in a prominent position in the showcase does not necessarily mean a good level of such stock, or that the dealer particularly cares about whether you will come back or not. You also want to compare one model against another, touch it, play with it, before you decide. You can't do that with a catalogue, or worse, a phone call to the importer.

Rental facilities

Many photographers fill their cupboards with equipment that maybe, in a good year, might find itself needed at most once. Worse, these particular bits and pieces are usually horribly expensive, and just sit on the asset register adding to your depreciation and insurance costs. There is absolutely no shame in making a decision to only buy the equipment that you know will be in constant use, and use your dealers' rental facilities for everything else.

I have in front of me KJP's list of rental equipment, which covers 5x4in and 8x10in monorails; Pentax, Mamiya, Hasselblad and Bronica roll film gear; all the Nikon and Leica range; full studio lighting; down to the tripod, changing bag and flashmeter. At the time of writing, a Hasselblad 503CX with a 30mm Distagon and A12 back costs £26.50/day, for approximately £4,500 worth of gear. If you can plan it right, you can offer a roll film fish-eye advertising shot to your client on the Friday, shoot some stock for yourself at the weekend, and, providing you get the gear back by Monday morning, it will cost you less than £40. I use KJP's rental service a lot; I just wish I had started taking advantage of it sooner.

Your local rep

Many dealers claim that keeping a salesman on the road is expensive, and that they can offer better prices if they just maintain good stock and an efficient inside sales office. Whilst I appreciate the logic of this, the problems of buying pro gear generally do not revolve around price. Most dealers offer much the same prices anyway, and a couple of percent off the price does not make up for the service a local rep can provide.

When we set up our studio in the Midlands, the presence of a rep helped us enormously. We could make product decisions in the comfort of our own studio, try cameras and lighting out in their working environment. A local rep can also be quite knowledgeable about studio conditions and can offer valuable advice. He is also usually bang up to date on the latest products (and gossip), and when things go wrong he can get replacements to you in a hurry.

I remember shooting flowers in the middle of the summer when my flashmeter went wrong. The flowers were wilting with every minute, and if the local rep had not jumped in his car with a replacement, it would have meant either a reshoot at my expense, or a heavy film and processing bill. Once, we even had him doing pack shots with us when time was running out! Don't forget, however, that his primary purpose is to sell to you.

Final points

Finally, there are a few other details you should check on before making your dealer decision. Make sure your dealer has his own transport or has an arrangement with a courier firm. This service is either free or low cost, and it means that your goods will be travelling at the dealer's risk and not yours.

There is one other point that I feel very strongly about regarding staff in professional dealers. Most are practising amateur photographers, but some run little photo businesses on the side. I remember one day when I was just starting up, visiting a pro dealer, when the phone rang from a local businessman looking for a photographer on an urgent basis. Instead of recommending any one of six competent photographers in the area, and even whilst I stood at the counter with my hand in the air, a member of staff took the commission. When I argued that I thought the dealer was there to sell the equipment but it was my job to take the pics, the salesman said he felt that the job really was too small to interest a full time professional.

I have never done business with that particular dealer since. I don't see why photo dealers should make a profit out of selling expensive gear, and then take the bread out of their customers' mouths. Certain enlightened dealers will not hire salesmen who are part time photographers, and some regard this practice as grounds for dismissal. Sadly, there are others who feel it is fair game.

What you really need

Its time now to get down to the nitty gritty and look at what equipment you really need to survive in this business. You will need to be able to work in three formats, 35mm, roll film and 5x4in sheet film, and we have looked briefly at the kind of gear you need in each category. We will now go into a little greater detail, looking at the kind of work each camera system is going to have to produce, together with some ideas on what you should consider.

35mm

Unless your market needs a lot of location work, you will only use 35mm occasionally. Recording newsworthy happenings at your clients' will be one use, in-plant photographs for slide displays will be another. It makes little sense to spend thousands of pounds on a format that may only be used once a month or less. You probably already own a 35mm outfit; the chances are that this will be fine.

If you were starting from scratch, then I would recommend one of the fully manual models, like the Nikon FM2, or one of the stronger "plastic" automatics with a full manual override, like the Canon T90. Autofocus is not particularly useful, but TTL flash can be helpful for the "grip and grin" type PR pics, as can a depth of field preview for in-plant interior shots. One of my favourites, the Olympus OM1, is an excellent camera for this kind of work, and good second-hand ones can still be found, as can the TTL flash equipped OM2s.

You do not need a battery of lenses either. Depending on your personal preferences, you can either go for a 24/35/85mm combination, or a 24/50/90mm line up, which would be my own choice. You will need speed, so prime lenses are better than zooms. Also, interior shots will not tolerate the distortion present in most wide angle zooms, and primes are cheaper anyway. A small flash unit completes the outfit (you can borrow the studio's lightmeter).

Roll film

Your roll film camera will be your "workhorse", so choose it with care – it is going to make most of your money for you. This camera will be used mainly for product shots for brochures, and the designer (your client) will require the maximum area of transparency. This is the time where you must ignore the discipline of "filling the frame". More often than not, the size of the image on the film will be similar to that of a 35mm transparency – the "air" round it is needed for text, graphics or even just to extend to the edge of the paper as a "bleed". The brochure or ad designer may not even know whether he wants a portrait or landscape format at the time the pics are taken, and you must leave enough space on the tranny for him to make that decision.

For this reason, the 6x6cm format is less popular with graphic designers than the 6x7cm or 6x8cm formats. The 6x4.5cm camera, whilst an excellent tool for location work, is viewed as being little better than 35mm in the studio. As weight and bulk are of little importance when the camera is fixed to a stand in the studio, a good 6x7cm or 6x8cm outfit should be your choice.

Most designers I know don't like to look through a viewfinder and much prefer to view the image on a ground glass screen, and I must admit that composition, for me at any rate, is easier when I can stand back that little bit and see the image from a distance. This means using the waist level finder instead of a prism, which is fine for landscape pics, but presents a problem when the camera has to be turned on its side for portrait format shots. The revolving back fitted to the Mamiya RB67 and RZ67, and lately the Fuji GX680, neatly solves the problem as did the old quarter-plate reflexes of yesteryear.

The RB67 has been the war-horse of many commercial photographers, and many of us have made lots of money with the good old "clunker". I understand the Fuji GX680 is developing a similar following; I personally have not used one, but it looks a fine camera.

My recommendation would be for an RB67, now updated as the RB67 SD. This is one area where I would be very careful about buying second-hand. RBs tend to go on for ever, and usually only get disposed of at the end of a very long and active professional life. Unless you can find an amateur-owned one that has only had a few

The latest version of the old faithful RB67, the SD

rolls of film through, buy a new one. There are some minor problems with the RB, such as little springs falling out of the revolving back, and some bits wear in the roll film back, but these things can be fixed very quickly. Generally, they are extraordinarily reliable.

As far as lenses are concerned, in the studio you will use a slightly longer than "standard" focal length, and Mamiya make a very fine 127mm lens. At the time of writing I understand that Mamiya are redesigning and updating the lenses for the RB67, but I have had no complaints with the old 127. The other lens you will need is the 180mm f4.5, a longer focal length for smaller products. It is also a fine lens, and has been retained in the new range. Unless you take your RB out of the studio, you won't need any other lenses.

Buy a spare roll film back. With only ten exposures on a roll of film, you always seem to have to stop and reload when things are going well – two backs means 20 exposures at a time, which makes much more sense. One accessory which is not used enough is the bellows lens hood. Light striking the lens surfaces at sharp angles gets scattered around the interior of the lens, and always degrades the final image. If you restrict the light entering the lens to only that which is required for the image, then you will optimise quality. If you don't believe me, look at the lens hoods on professional movie cameras.

Finally, you will need that passport to bankruptcy, the Polaroid back. I have seen the floor covered with Polaroids before many photographers will press the button, and I wonder whether they are all being charged to the client. The Polaroid is a final check before you shoot to make sure that your lighting balance is right, and that you have not done anything stupid like leave the shutter sync on "M" instead of "X" (If you have not yet done this, you will – we all have). Also, use Polaroid type 664 black and white film – not only is it cheaper than the colour, but it will accurately reproduce the contrast and tones you get with E6 colour.

Sheet film

I wish I had a fiver for every time I have heard a photographer argue that he could take equally good pictures with his Hasselblad as so-and-so took with a monorail. I don't know whether it is a desire to make life difficult for oneself, or just basic fear of the thing, but mention of "five-four" soon brings out some partisan views.

And yet, with a little knowledge, a monorail camera solves many of the fundamental problems facing a commercial photographer, such as increasing insufficient depth of field, or correcting perspective because of a non-ideal camera position. Take the little time it needs to learn how to use a monorail (it is all in Appendix B), and you will find you have a photographic tool that will never let you down.

You will use the 5x4 mainly for still life advertising shots, although there will be occasions when you can use it to solve problems. I once had to use it in photographing a cat running through a sliding patio door – the designer insisted on a particular perspective for the patio door frame – and a rising front was the only way. On another occasion we used sheet film to provide a large area of tone above the image to drop catalogue text into – we'll go into these uses in Chapter 7.

A monorail camera consists of two brackets which slide along a piece of tubing, one which carries a lens and shutter, the other carrying a focusing screen which can be moved out of the way to insert a film holder. A bellows between the two brackets keeps out the light. The brackets, or "standards" as they are called, allow the lens, or focussing screen, to move up, down and sideways, and also to rotate in two different planes.

The difference between a £500 Cambo SC2 camera and a £3,500 Sinar P2 is simply in the mechanical construction of this piece of kit. At the bottom end of the price bracket, every adjustment or "movement" has to be set by unlocking, resetting the position, and relocking. At the other end of the scale, every movement is geared, and the construction is such that rotational movements take place as closely as possible around the optical axis of the lens or film. Whilst these refinements do help, they are by no means necessary, and identical pics can be taken with either camera – it just takes longer with the simpler one.

The Toyo 45C Monorail, an excellent first large format studio camera

There is no shortage of good monorail cameras at the budget end of the scale, with models by Cambo, Toyo, and Arca Swiss springing to mind. Also, because the thing just doesn't wear out, this is one area where you can buy second-hand with reasonable confidence. The Cambo SC2 at £500 new is a very flexible piece of kit, very well made, and is often offered second-hand at £300 or so. The cheaper Toyo models are a little more delicately made, and have geared movements. The Horseman is a good camera, and delightful to use, but more money.

Check also whether you really need sunken panels or WA bellows if you are using a 90mm lens. Some models are usable with the standard panels or bellows, and that can save you anything up to £150.

Don't forget also, that lenses for large format have standard mounts – Holes No. 0, 1, 2, and 3. Change your camera, but keep all your lenses to mount in the new camera's panels. This means that up front, whilst you are trying to save money, you can buy good lenses for an inexpensive camera and upgrade later without losing a small fortune.

When choosing lenses, a decision often made these days is to ignore the standard 150mm lens, and go for a 180 or 210 instead. This certainly gives a little more breathing space between you and the product. A 90mm wide angle complements the longer lens nicely, being useful both in the studio and on location for interiors and architecture. Lenses are available from Schneider, Rodenstock and Nikon, and are bought complete with shutters, either the Japanese Copal type, or the more expensive Synchro-Compur from Germany. Whilst Schneider claim that they are the best, I have used all three manufacturers' lenses, and have had excellent results from all of them.

What is important to remember is that, all other things being equal, the more expensive lenses are so because of their increased angle of view or coverage. Large format lenses are designed to cover a larger area than the film so that you can raise, lower and swing the lens and still have image on the film. If you like to apply lots of movement, then you want a lens with lots of coverage, and naturally lenses with lots of coverage are more expensive. However, the quality of image within the coverage of any lens is virtually identical. You would be hard-pressed to tell the difference between a standard Symmar S with a 70 degree coverage at about £300, and a Super Symmar HM with 80 degrees coverage at nearly £700, unless you exceeded the 70 degree figure. If you don't need to drive at 180 m.p.h. you don't need a Ferrari, and in our situation we will not need large movements, so a "standard" quality of Sironar, Symmar or Nikkor will be just fine.

When you come to fit the 90mm wide angle, you will realise there is an important difference between large format wide angle lenses and the wides you may be used to on reflexes. A lens designed to be used on a reflex camera must clear the mirror when it flips up. This means that a number of compromises must be made in its design, and most lenses of this type are in fact reversed telephotos. With the monorail however, there is no such constraint, and the lens can be designed with the proper lens/film distance appropriate to its focal length. The result of all this is that the lens ends up much closer to the film, so much so that in many cameras the standard bellows becomes so tightly compressed that movements become difficult to set.

There are two solutions to this problem. One is to fit the lens in a special wide angle "sunken" panel which allows the lens to be nearer the film than it would be in a normal panel, and the other is to use a special extra-flexible "wide angle" bellows, commonly known as a "bag" bellows. With a 90mm, most of the time you will only need one of these solutions, but there are cameras around where you will need both, especially if you ever add a 75mm lens to your outfit.

One point to watch, however, is to make sure that you buy both lenses from the same manufacturer. Occasionally, you will use them both on the same job, and, as different manufacturers use different coatings, the colour rendering of each lens can be different. Whilst in most cases the difference will be small, wait until you photograph a room set for a wallpaper manufacturer – different colour renditions will not go down well!

Sironars are made by Rodenstock, and their wide angles are called Grandagons; Symmars are made by Schneider with Super Angulons as their wides, and Nikon wide angles are called SWs.

The only other accessories you need for your monorail are several double dark slides, a focusing cloth, a ground glass magnifier (don't get one stronger than x6 or you will spend your time trying to focus the grain on the ground glass) and the ubiquitous Polaroid back, (the 545) about which you have already been warned. Try and adapt the bellows lens hood from the RB to start off with – "compendium" lens hoods for monorails are wickedly expensive.

Before we leave cameras, one solution for product photography is a 5x4in monorail fitted with a 120 roll film back, giving 6x7cm transparencies. This adapter is certainly cheaper than a separate roll film camera, but is much slower in use. However it does give you movements on roll film, and this can be very useful when you need to increase depth of field.

A combination which I have used extensively is the Toyo roll film slider mounted on a Toyo G monorail fitted with a 210mm lens. The roll film adapter used my RB67 backs, and the 210mm lens meant that the bellows were reasonably extended allowing quite large movements. The slider meant that I could focus on a bright Fresnel screen, and to take the pic all I had to do was close the camera shutter, slide the back into position and squeeze the cable release. All sheath removing and replacing was done automatically by the sliding back. I would think this adapter would work with the Toyo C camera just as well.

I personally don't think this combination fully replaces a roll film reflex, but I know of several people who do all their roll film studio work with a similar set up. Some monorail cameras also have an adapter to attach a Hasselblad camera body in place of the film back. This is also a useful gadget, but limits you to 6x6cm instead of 6x7cm or 6x9cm trannies. It also assumes you own a Hasselblad camera, whereas the slider gadget just requires a standard fitting roll film back, like the Mamiya or Horseman, for instance.

Lighting

I once visited a small studio in London shortly after the lighting salesman had been there. The studio was about 12x18ft, and I counted over 20,000 joules worth of flash power packs, and that was before I started on the monobloc units in the corner. The photographer, who was well into damage limitation on his bank account, confided that he hadn't realised that lighting was so expensive.

When we had finished looking at the products he was going to photograph, and the film formats he was going to use, we ended up with two 1,500 joule packs, three heads and a couple of 500 joule monoblocs for location work, which could double as fills in the studio if required. Even this level of power I regarded as generous, but I left him with a phone call to make, and a few less money problems.

Even in our 24x30ft studio, I have never needed more than four heads and 3,000 joules. I think the problem is that it is so easy these days to over-light a set. Fill lights should be used to gently lighten shadows, not completely eliminate them. There is only one sun after all; there should be only one key light. Again, we'll go into this in Chapter 7, but when buying lighting, you should start off with a couple of 1,250 or 1,500 joule power packs with multiple outlets, three heads, each capable of taking the full power of one pack, a couple of softboxes, a couple of good solid booms, a couple of standard lighting stands, and three large umbrellas – white/silver reversible.

Whose equipment to buy? Electronic flash equipment does go wrong, often quite violently, and the quality of after sales service and repairs is more important to me than either price or small differences in specification. Everyone has their own experiences with flash equipment, and has a horror story or two to tell. Mine involves a 1,800 joule unit gently on fire after a minor explosion, situated between me and the door, with the client, a major mainframe computer manufacturer, due to arrive any moment to art direct a brochure shoot. It also involves the managing director of this particular flash manufacturer finding the experience amusing. I don't use his products any more.

For the last eight years I have used Bowens lighting – Quadmatics, Monolites and Prolites – not only because I like the equipment, but also because of the level of service a UK-based manufacturer can give if they want to. On one occasion when I had a problem occur during a particularly important shoot, I phoned the factory at 5pm on a Friday evening. A director phoned me back from his home twenty minutes later, had a unit specially prepared for me on the Monday morning and "Red Starred" to me at lunch time, so I was back in business in the afternoon with only half a day lost. I wonder how I would have managed with the "send it back to us and we'll look at it" attitude.

Before you decide on a particular brand of gear, check on the level of service you will be offered, and, if the equipment is imported, what level of authority the importer has regarding replacement of faulty items. Also, check the country of manufacture – it is not unknown for equipment to be manufactured in the Far East, then shipped to another country before being imported to the UK. When you can talk to senior people at the manufacturer, things tend to get done much more quickly. The greater the distance between you and where the thing is made, the more problems you are likely to have in sorting out technical trouble.

The last absolutely essential item is a good flashmeter. I have tried most of them, and the best I have used was the older Minolta Flashmeter 3. I upgraded to the current (at the time of writing) Flashmeter 4, which I didn't care for at first – but I am learning to use all the additional facilities now. It costs nearly £500, but is worth every penny.

Another studio accessory you will wonder how you ever did without is the counter-balanced camera stand. These exist in all forms, some hydraulically damped, some even motorised, but a simple rigid stand, preferably designed for one format size larger than the biggest you will normally use will be fine. Mine was bought second-hand for about £300, an R R Beard stand made for 5x7in cameras. The ease with which you can put your camera exactly where you want it has to be experienced to be believed – you will never wrestle with a tripod in the studio again. Looks impressive too.

The last thing you need to buy at this stage is some form of suspension system for background rolls. These are available in half width and full width (9ft), and a restricted choice is available in 12ft width. A very useful system is the "triple hook" arrangement screwed to the wall about 10ft above the floor. This will allow you to have three of your most used colours available immediately, with a simple chain drive used for lifting and lowering. Make sure your studio steps are high enough to allow you to change rolls easily.

The darkroom

That about does it for the studio. We'll now look at the darkroom. You will certainly need a darkroom, and, if you offer the right facilities, you will have a definite edge over competitors who use an outside lab for all processing. By all means use an outside pro lab for colour printing, and for any extra-large E6 or black and white runs. But the ability to hand transparencies direct to your client as he relaxes with a cup of coffee after a difficult shoot should never be underestimated. And it's not difficult.

Most of the horror stories that abound when you talk about E6 processing come from small capacity "dip and dunk" machines. These small processors often contain less than five or ten litres of chemistry, and extreme care is necessary to prevent contamination of one bath with another. The E6 process is incredibly sensitive to this contamination, particularly bits of first developer in the reversal bath, and anything in the colour developer.

Consistency of agitation is also critical – I heard once of an experiment in a tank line processor where Ektachrome could be shifted from a blue cast to a yellow one simply by altering the size of the nitrogen bubbles used for agitation.

Luckily for us there is a solution to both problems in the use of small rotary discard machines. These processors work on the principle of using only a small quantity of chemistry in a rotating drum, which is then discarded, having been used once only. The agitation is easily standardised by fixing the rotation speed of the drum, and contamination is virtually impossible. Temperature control problems are solved by using preheated chemicals, while the drum revolves in an accurately controlled water bath. The only other variable is the time for each process, and, depending on the model you buy, this can be completely preprogrammed and automatic, or can be timed with a clock.

There seems to be an increasing choice of small processors like this on the market, and you should look around before making your choice. Do not, however, choose a processor until you have seen it process a batch of films, preferably ones you have shot yourself. This facility should be available at any manufacturer or importer; if it isn't, don't choose that processor. Any manufacturer or importer should be constantly trying out new materials and chemistry on his equipment. Only this way can he advise you on how to

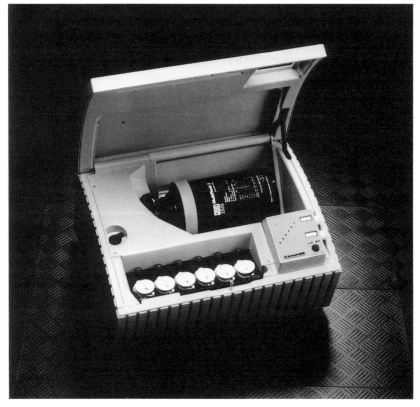

The Jobo Autolab 1000, a compact self-contained rotary film processor

achieve the best results with the film you use.

I personally have had excellent results with Jobo processors, imported by Introphoto in Maidenhead. These processors range from small, amateur, manual models up to fully computer-controlled automatic professional machines. If you have the time, then a manual model will cost you in the order of £600, or if you like to leave the machine "doing its thing", there is an automatic stand alone processor for about £2,000.

One of the advantages of the "large drum" type of processor such as the Jobo is that you can do the occasional print in them as well. Whilst I certainly would not recommend a Jobo as a "line" print processor, it is ideal when a client wants a Cibachrome or "R" type print in a hurry. The Jobo CPA and ATL models go up to 20x24in, certainly big enough for the designer who wants a print to make up into a visual for his client. The ability to pull one of these prints off in an hour or so, at an appropriate rush fee, enhances your credibility with your client as well as your bank balance.

Enlargers

You are also going to need an enlarger. Like cameras these things come in all sizes and prices, and, like cameras, there are some good value models at the bottom of the price range. A good enlarger, like a De Vere or Durst Laborator, tends to last a long time because of its built in rigidity, and there are some excellent second-hand bargains around. You are going to use your enlarger to produce black and white prints, duplicate transparencies, the odd Ciba or R type print, and the rare C type neg/pos print, in that order of volume and importance.

You should buy one with a colour head as this will enable you to use variable contrast papers, and the diffuse lighting on a dichroic head suppresses dust and dirt on the negatives. The maximum neg size should be 5x4in.

Don't bother with condenser heads, the dust problem will drive you to drink, and don't bother with cold cathode heads, they are fragile and only usable with black and white materials. Finally, the neg carriers should be glassless for all sizes (see condenser heads above), and the lenses should be beyond reproach. Rodenstock and Schneider are the standards.

In addition to a second-hand De Vere or Durst at around the £1,000 mark, there is an excellent Japanese enlarger that can be had new for much the same price. I have used an LPL 5x4in enlarger solely for tranny duping for several years with excellent results. A constant exposure Multigrade filter module is also available for an extra £200, which allows you to dial in the grade of paper you need and certainly speeds things up. If you want to buy new, this is an excellent piece of kit.

Choosing a lab

By now, you should have all the major items you require for your studio, and you will need some time to "shake it all down". However, while you are doing this, and before you open your doors for trade, there are a few other things you can be getting on with. Firstly, although you may have your own "mini" processing facilities, there are tasks which you will want to entrust to a professional colour lab.

The first of these is standard C type printing. Unless you have clients that are willing to pay at the top end of the "hand print" price list, you cannot make money doing your own colour printing. You have to use a lab, and you will also find, as you travel around, that different labs have different ideas about print quality and style.

A lab that has a high percentage of social work will use low contrast paper, and may have only limited stocks of the "snappy" glossy paper that you need for your PR print runs. If you use a high contrast film similar to the late lamented Kodak VCS emulsion or it's successor VHC, then the lab's printers may not be fine-tuned to this type of film, and machine prints will certainly show it.

Visit the labs in your area, explain to them the services you will require, and find out if they have a collection and delivery service. Set up some mock pack shots using products bought from your local supermarket and send them off for machine printing. If you have some reservations about the results you are getting, go back to the lab and explain what you are looking for. There are some labs that "can do no wrong" and "its never their fault", and naturally you cross these off your list. Normally, however, a lab wants your business, especially in machine printing, and will go a long way to accommodate you.

Couriers

You are also going to have to find yourself a courier service. These days, anyone whose taxi firm isn't doing as well as it should goes into this business, attracted by the profits of 30p a mile and above for 300 mile round trips. But the fact is, only a company that is specifically set up as a courier with a number of cars, vans and bikes can give you the service you need.

In the advertising world everyone from the Board of Directors of the client company downwards underestimates the time it takes to produce good creative pictures and copy. Budgets are invariably late in getting approval. By the time you see the brief, the separations were required last week and the ad should have appeared last month. The cost of a motorbike to take trannies or visuals halfway across the country is but nought to the problems you will have if you miss a press deadline. You mark it up and put it on the bill anyway.

Choose someone who is reliable by reputation (check with other clients), and open a monthly account.

Model agencies

Another area with its fair share of cowboy operators is the model agency business, and again you need to have good contacts with the right people in this area. Many agencies are little more than a couple of "entrepreneurs" exploiting local girls; others have more shady backgrounds. You should deal with a well established agency experienced in supplying models for commercial photography. One way of making sure that you are talking to the right agency is to ensure that they are members of the Association of Model Agents. Members are vetted, and have to show that their only income is from commissions on bookings.

Many agencies show the Department of Employment licence number prominently on their literature – this simply means they are registered and is no guarantee of quality or integrity. Ask for the names of a couple of clients and give them a call. If the agency checks out, ask for a selection of "comp cards" for your files; then you will be ready when your client needs a model.

The computer

Most small businesses these days consider themselves incomplete without "the PC", and whilst yesterday's status symbol was the portable telephone today's successful executive is not complete without a leather satchel containing a portable lap-top computer, complete with several megabytes of memory and 40-odd megabytes of hard disk drive. I wonder what extraordinary tasks are necessary for these paragons of industry to perform as they carry around computing power that only a few years ago required rooms full of equipment.

Visiting "professional" computer stores, I get the impression that the small computer business is even worse than the pro camera business in many ways. So many reasons can be found to encourage we mere mortals to part with our hard-earned cash. We tend to forget that not so long ago we all happily managed with card indexes, hand-written ledgers and old, second-hand office typewriters.

The truth is that most small businesses can benefit enormously from the most basic of computer installations. Used sensibly, the average small PC or Amstrad PCW is more than adequate for our needs. Listen to the computer shop salesman though, and we are talking about "hard disks" and "twin drives" and "expanded

RAM", all of which is gilding on an already much-gilded lily. These things aren't cheap any more either. Today, you are much more likely to be offered an installation costing £1,500 or more, than the humble PCW at about £300 plus VAT.

Frankly, the time wasted in getting small computers up to speed can be out of all proportion to their usefulness. A PC is a great help, but only in a very elementary capacity.

Before we decided that our business was best run on a manual ledger system, we ran a full accounts package on an Amstrad 464 computer with two floppy drives and Quest software. It worked fine. However, I don't recommend putting your accounts on to a computer, at least for the first few years. As technology in this area evolves, anything you buy now will be totally out of date in no time.

All you really need is a little machine that will write invoices, produce the odd letter, and run a simple spreadsheet program to help your cash flow and planning process. An Amstrad PCW or basic PC will be fine for this. You need one disk drive, between 256k and 512k RAM, and a printer of sorts.

Because we also run a picture library, our computer is an old Epson PC with a hard disk, which we needed to store details of several thousand colour transparencies. However, all the applications described here are possible on a basic Amstrad PC with one 5.25in floppy drive. If you prefer the PCW route, the Amstrad PCW 9512 is an excellent machine.

The 9512 has the advantage of coming with a daisy-wheel printer as part of the package. This gives a very professional image to your letters and invoices, which look as though they have been typed on an expensive electric typewriter. You should be able to obtain all you need, computer or computer/printer plus software, for less than £600 plus VAT for the PCW route, about £100 more for the PC option.

The sales estimate form

This spreadsheet application started out as an automatic invoicing program. It has proved so useful as a pure estimating tool that it has not yet been finished. I am sure that only a little work is needed to take the data and have this program print invoices and statements. On the other hand, you may be happy just to use it to estimate quotes and as an aid to invoice preparation. One advantage to just using it as an aid is that you can "tweak" the figures a little if you want to.

The form itself, shown opposite, is self-explanatory.

Coupled to a daisy-wheel printer with a simple word processing package, a personal computer can give your correspondence a very professional appearance. A spreadsheet program is invaluable in planning and reporting.

```
                     Estimate: For internal use only

Estimate for:      ABC Advertising Ltd, Job 123     Date: 1/04/1992
===============================================================================
                   Qty    Unit pr      Ext      G.P.%      Charge
OPERATING:         ---    -------      ---      -----      ------
No of days          2     £300.00   £600.00        0      £600.00
No of 1/2 days      0     £200.00     £0.00        0        £0.00

FILM:
EPN 120            15      £2.87     £43.05       33       £64.57
RDP 120             0      £2.40      £0.00       33        £0.00
RDP 35              0      £4.21      £0.00       33        £0.00
RVP 35              0      £4.61      £0.00       33        £0.00
SO366               0      £3.75      £0.00       33        £0.00
RDP 54             20      £1.16     £23.20       33       £34.80
FP4 35              0      £2.45      £0.00       33        £0.00
Polaroids, Colour   0      £0.95      £0.00       35        £0.00
Polaroids, B&W      6      £0.82      £4.92       35        £7.57

PROCESSING:
120 E6             15      £2.45     £36.75       33       £54.85
35 E6, unmounted           £3.15      £0.00       33        £0.00
35 E6, mounted      0      £5.00      £0.00       33        £0.00
54 E6              20      £1.55     £31.00       33       £46.27
35 C41                     £2.00      £0.00       33        £0.00
B&W                 0      £1.50      £0.00       33        £0.00

PRINTS:
Machine             0      £0.00      £0.00       33        £0.00
Hand                0      £0.00      £0.00       35        £0.00
Other               0      £0.00      £0.00       35        £0.00

OTHER PHOTOGRAPHIC:
Rainbow B/G         1     £28.50     £28.50       35       £43.85
1/2 Colorama        0     £18.52      £0.00       35        £0.00
Other                                 £0.00                 £0.00

MISCELLANEOUS:
Trav time (hrs)     0     £20.00      £0.00        0        £0.00
Mileage (miles)     0      £0.30      £0.00        0        £0.00
Couriers                              £0.00       20        £0.00
Sundries                              £9.50       20       £11.88
Postage & Carr                        £0.00       10        £0.00

SUMMARY:                             Cost:    Profit:     Charge:
--------                             -----    -------     -------
Time, Operating:                     £0.00    £600.00     £600.00
Time, Travelling:                    £0.00      £0.00       £0.00
Film/Proc/Pols/Other              £167.42     £84.48     £251.90
Prints                               £0.00      £0.00       £0.00
Mileage                              £0.00      £0.00       £0.00
Couriers                             £0.00      £0.00       £0.00
Sundries                             £9.50      £2.38      £11.88
Postage & Carr                          0          0           0

         Totals:                  £176.92    £686.86     £863.78
                                 ---------------------------------
Job Gross Profit:        79.52%                                 0
```

*The sales
estimate form*

But leave it at that, at least for the first few years. More complicated software packages to help you "run your company" can take weeks if not months to install, and your time is better spent in getting clients through the door and pics sold. In the next chapter we'll start doing just that.

MARKETING AND SELLING

By now, you should have your studio operational in the sense that all building work is long finished, and all lighting gear is delivered, installed and tested. You should be familiar with all your camera gear, and be able to shoot and process E6 film with reasonable ease. You should also have the printing side of your darkroom operational; certainly black and white, possibly Ciba or R types as well. You feel that you are now ready to go and get the clients and start making money.

But just as a Frenchman once said that a nation gets the government it deserves, so does a business get the customers it deserves. Right from the start you must apply the correct rules as to who you are going to sell to, and what products you are going to market.

I visited a trade show recently, and whilst waiting for a salesman to show me some new equipment I overheard a conversation between two professional photographers, discussing a new studio that was being set up in their town. "There really is no need to worry", said the older of the two, "it's just one of those amateur turned pro operations – you know, a bloke walks in and asks how much for a portrait, and is told: 'would twenty five quid be OK?'."

Professional photography has its fair share of cowboys, but at the other end of the scale successful commercial photographers tend to respect others who run good professional studios. Also, you can be pretty sure that the opinion of an established, respected photographer about your operation is very likely to be similar to that of a design studio or ad agency. Both are in the creative media business, and they both tend to think the same way. You can take heart that if you have been used to cut-throat or questionable business dealings in a previous occupation, you will not generally find your new competition indulging in the same game.

Good photographers are for the most part nice people, and if you find that you are competing with the Arthur Daley type, then you should take a second look at the market you are addressing. Get a reputation for good work and professional conduct, and you will be surprised at the number of friends you make amongst "the competition". They will often refer work to you that they can't handle, and will expect the same in return from you.

Image is all important, and you are laying the foundation for that now. Resist the temptation to make "a quick tenner"; it will save you thousands in the long run.

Ethics

Now is perhaps the time to discuss business morals in general.

A long time ago, I was involved with a small company bidding to supply components to one of the biggest computer manufacturers in the world. All the technical people had satisfied the client's requirements, and the sales people had arrived at a quotation which they felt would have the edge on the competition. The bid was presented and left with the prospective client, whilst everyone held their breath. A week later, we had a phone call from the client requesting a factory visit, and, if possible, could they meet our accounts people? Totally confused, we fixed a date, planned a factory tour, and arranged lunch with the financial controller. At the end of the day, before we drove the visitors to the airport, the company was told that the bid had been accepted and a contract would be issued in due course.

After all the congratulations had died down, we asked "why meet the accountants?" We were told that the client liked our product and our company. They wanted us to be happy with them as a client, and therefore the deal had to be as right for us as much as for them. They wanted to see that this order would fit into the plant without major problems, and that the price enabled us to make a good return. "We don't think you are diddling us," said the chief negotiator, "we want to make sure we are not diddling you – after all, we are all only here for mutual benefit".

That little episode taught me a lot about dealings in business. Successful companies and businesses generally remain so because their clients feel they are paying a fair price for an acceptable product. Clients of successful businesses stay clients because they are reasonable in their demands, and fulfil their commitments promptly in return. Long term relationships are built up, and life is great. The "I can always get it cheaper" or "I really screwed them into the ground" attitude belongs more on the second-hand car lot than in the creation and development of a professional commercial photographic practice. Don't ever diddle your clients, and only let a client do it to you once.

Checking out your clients

Who should your clients be? Broadly, there are two main groups: those who are the "end users" of photography, and those who are commissioning photography as part of a sale to a third party. The first group contains the companies who are producing their own advertising and brochure material in-house, more often than not in the retail trade, whilst the other consists of ad agencies and graphic designers.

Taking end users or "direct" clients first, many companies feel they can handle the work of producing catalogues and ads themselves. Some make a very good job of it; others, particularly when it comes to advertising, would be much better off entrusting the job to an agency. This work originates in the marketing department of the company, and your first approach should go as high as possible. Firstly though, do a little checking on the company.

You need to have an idea of what they have been used to in the past, and a phone call to the marketing director's secretary requesting a copy of their latest sales brochure is the first step. If she asks why you need it, tell her who and what you are and that you would like to put a presentation together for her boss. You never know, she may volunteer information that is useful to you – I was once told that a company had "terrible problems" with their current photographer (happily unnamed). Another told me that they dealt with a studio some 40 miles distant, and if they could deal with a local photographer, so much the better.

Many secretaries have time on their hands and will often talk to you quite freely about what you should do to please their boss. You will also find out whether the photography is commissioned direct, or whether an agency is involved. If so, you will usually get the name of the agency. Also ask for a copy of the last annual report; you may have to talk to the chief accountant's or MD's secretary for this.

When all this bumpf lands on your doorstep, study it carefully and try to get a feeling for the company and what it does. If it is selling to retail outlets, then generally their requirements will be for product photographs for a comprehensive trade catalogue, on a limited budget. If they sell direct to their clients then they will require sales brochure photography of a more comprehensive nature, and may be happy to pay more for "product in use" shots as well as the straight shots described above. If they do their own advertising (rare), then you have to move another step up the quality (and cost) ladder.

Direct accounts

Look at the photography, and try and decide how you would tackle it. Then, if possible, get hold of some of the product and shoot it, your way, but in the same style as the brochure. If the product is readily available in the local stores, buy some. If it is not, then phone the marketing director and say you would like to present your studio to the company by shooting some transparencies of their products, free of charge, and could you please borrow some. I have never known anyone say no to that offer. When you have produced a few shots in the "house style", shoot some more with your own, hopefully different, ideas. In Chapter 7 you will find ways of making "the pack shot" that little bit different. But make sure that if you present a new idea, you are able to shoot hundreds of trannies in the same way – you never know, the client may love it. In addition, shoot some black and white, and produce a few of the best 10x8s you have ever done.

Mount the transparencies in thick black mounting board, with an aperture cut out in the middle, using a 45 degree mat cutter. This gives a thin white line around the transparency, and finishes off your work in a most attractive manner. Mount the 10x8in prints on the same size of board as the transparencies; I like 12x15in. If the transparencies are roll film, then mount two per board, but no more. 5x4in trannies should have a board to themselves. Make sure you have a label on each board with your name, address and phone number. *Do not* put "Copyright Joe Blow" on it.

Type out your rates, produce a covering letter, and make an appointment to see the great man himself (or, increasingly likely these days, the great woman). Take along your light box with an extension lead. When ushered into the presence, explain that you have just opened a new commercial studio, and wish to present some examples of your work. Explain also that you have attempted to follow the house style in some shots, but have additionally shot some product as if you had been given a completely open brief. Plug in your light box, place the mounted boards on it, and listen. Don't babble. And don't talk about technicalities. The last thing your

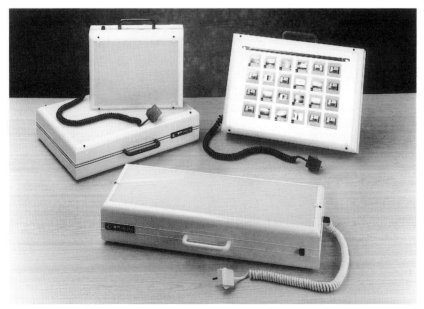

A good light box is an essential investment. DW Viewboxes have a wide range

client wants to know is which lens was used, or whether this film is better than that and so on. I have watched more people talk themselves out of work than the other way round.

Keep it strictly professional. Expect questions about your day rate, and your turn-round time. Don't forget to mention that you process transparencies in your own lab ("E6 processing" is double Dutch to a businessman), and casually toss the black and whites on the table. Expect, and be able, to quote for PR runs of up to 100 5x7in or 10x8in prints. If your contact wants to "show these to the MD" it is a good sign, but make a date to phone them back to see how it went. "Maybe I can call you at the end of next week" is always a good thing to say, especially if a request has been made to "think about it". Don't be pushy, but don't leave without a reason to renew the contact. Leave your rate card and the covering letter with the transparencies. And for goodness sake wear a suit, especially if you are a member of the fairer sex.

I have found this approach works very well, and neatly gets over the problem of a thin or non-existent portfolio whilst at the the same time creating one. It often results in a trial commission, which usually involves photographing a "difficult" product, like chrome, or matt leather, or translucent plastic kitchenware. But no-one said it was going to be easy, did they?

Selling to agencies

Tackling the agencies is a little more difficult. Bear in mind that most ad agencies have photographers knocking on their doors on almost a daily basis, and as a result they tend to have a dismissive attitude towards you at first. Don't be concerned about this; it is their built-in filter to stop people wasting their time. You will find that the attitude changes when they realise you are in fact serious about the business and that you can offer the kind of service they require from a photographic studio.

There are two ways to approach these people – the first is to start by offering them a dupe tranny and black and white print service, the other is to go straight in and sell photography. Which you choose depends on the state of your portfolio. I have found that if you offer a lab service for dupes and prints, you are very likely to come away with an order on your first visit and have started dealings with the client there and then. The down side of this approach is that they may come to regard you only as a lab service, and it may be difficult to persuade them to give you photographic work later.

The other approach is to go straight in and offer your portfolio for consideration for studio photography. Don't forget to mention that you do your own transparency processing, dupe production, and black and white. This approach is fine, but, if the agency

Advertising agencies are not always found in steel and chrome monstrosities. This small building near Peterborough houses one of the area's leading media companies

already has a close working arrangement with a photographer, it is more difficult to get in than taking the lab services route.

My advice is to get a small portfolio together – some of the shots you did for the direct accounts will do for a start. Also shoot some pictures of your own, with as much variety as you can. The kind of subjects you should consider are new buildings, with a deep blue sky and fluffy white clouds, framed with tree branches. If there aren't any on site, I'll tell you how to put some there in Chapter 9. Find an attractive model, pop a leather jacket on her shoulders and shoot her on roll film in a woodland scene. Show you understand fill flash principles by results.

In the studio, make an attractive still life with some cheese, pickles, bread and a mug of beer. Shoot some glassware with both high key and low key lighting. Buy (or make) a small light tent and shoot some attractive porcelain plates (your local shop will lend you some in exchange for a print or two).

Photograph a tea set with a chrome tea pot or kettle. Shoot some of these in black and white and colour neg as well, and use 5x4 wherever it is practical. Then look at Chapter 9 and produce dupes of most of the shots you have taken, especially the ones with delicate tones and colours, such as the glassware and porcelain.

Mount all the trannies in board as before, but leave the sheet film notch marks visible so that the client can see it really is a dupe when it is a dupe, and that you haven't just shot twice in the camera. Again, type out your rates, attach to a covering letter, and make an appointment to see the art director of the agency.

When you are granted an interview, take your portfolio and letter, and introduce yourself and your business briefly. Admit that you have shot the portfolio for the meeting, and that you have included dupes and prints to demonstrate the quality of your lab work. If you intend to sell Cibas or R types, then include one of those. Don't waffle, and don't try to blind them with science – they've heard it all before. If some of your work is adversely criticised, try to adopt a positive approach to the criticism. If you end up working with them, the agency is going to want you to take pics their way. A stroppy photographer is the last thing they want with press deadlines coming and going and clients changing their mind at the last minute.

Try and show some humility without being servile. You can prove your own particular theories when you know the agency better. If you handle yourself right, you should receive a trial commission. Again, wear a suit.

Other marketing methods

What are the other ways of shouting "Here I am"?

A mailing can work well if it is targeted correctly. A simple, brief letter with a 5x7in machine print of a suitable subject and with your name printed in (your local pro lab can do this very cheaply) will at least get your name on file, and possibly may generate a phone call to you. Resist the temptation to photograph a scantily clad nymph – a shot of a food mixer will do you far more good.

Advertising in the local paper is cheap and is used by many, but I have found the people I am after seldom read it, and I personally feel that commercial photography is out of place cheek by jowl with the local plumber or electrician.

The local business magazine, however, is more suitable for our purposes. If you can write well, or know a journalist who presumably can, why not write a press release announcing your arrival in the business community? Getting it published may involve a discussion with the editor and ad manager; a half or quarter page ad in the issue concerned will certainly oil the wheels. Don't forget that these magazines desperately need advertising revenue. Sometimes you may be lucky and have a freelance journalist do the whole thing for you. It will cost you a couple of hundred pounds or so, plus the cost of the ad if you have to buy one, but it will certainly generate some enquiries.

Some photographers swear by paid ads in media directories, and certainly this advertising is worthwhile if you intend to cast your net on nationwide waters. However it is less useful if you plan only to operate locally, and it is quite expensive. It is worth mentioning at this point that if you become a corporate member of the British Institute of Professional Photography, your name will be included in the ads they place in the local Yellow Pages, and you will also be included in the directory they publish every year. You can get a couple of contacts every month from this source alone.

Finally, there is the "open day", where you invite anyone interested to visit your studio and have a drink and a chat. I must admit to little enthusiasm for these dos, as much from the host's point of view as from the guests'. They certainly bring out the competition in hordes, as well as large quantities of "photo buyers", usually with hollow legs. As PR exercises they can possibly be justified if you make sure there are a few journalists around, but as a way of generating business, I have yet to be associated with one that worked.

Vetting your customers

As you are doing all these good things, try to evaluate the quality of your prospective clients as well, and avoid some of the more obvious trouble zones.

Anyone can start up as a graphic designer or ad agency. All it requires is a small office, a desk, drawing board, and a nice letter heading. They can then commission thousands of pounds worth of photography, repro and print, and then go swiftly down the Swannee when they cannot finance the business they have taken on.

When you open an account with an equipment supplier you are vetted thoroughly before a single filter or roll of film is dispatched to you, and yet photographers grant enormous amounts of credit to the most flimsy of businesses.

Credit checking of new clients is a very "iffy" business, and a bank reference really does not tell you anything unless it is firmly negative. The only real course of action is to keep your eyes open during your early contact, to see if the agency is reasonably well run and that they have several clients of quality. Many so-called ad agencies finance their operations entirely from the commission they receive on space bookings. If you are involved with one of these then be careful – the end, when it comes, is swift and brutal. A good ad agency lives on payment by clients for creative work, often passing on any space commission to the client. These agencies have the budget to pay properly for the services they require, like photography, typesetting and repro, and tend to have been around for a while.

Pricing

We have mentioned rate cards, but not how you should arrive at your pricing structure. You can get books which contain guidelines, but rather than accept these blindly you should calculate what you actually need to charge before you go into print on rates. Also, when you start up, it will be expected – at least by the ad agencies – that your scale of fees will start at the low end. This is a very good policy. Remember, you can always increase your day rate with honour, but a photographer who decreases it is already doomed.

A studio operating normally should be "booked" for between two and three days per week. Less than that will mean you have difficulty in recovering your overhead costs, and more than that will mean you have more work than you can handle on your own. You need time to tidy up the place, try out new things, do some lab work, or simply take advantage of a lull in activity to relax a little. Three days booked per week (I like to choose Tuesday, Wednesday and Thursday), is about as much as you can continue week after week, month after month.

This, if you allow for three weeks holiday a year, gives you a total of 49 x three working days per year, or 147 days. Divide your projected turnover by 147, and you have the amount of invoicing you require per day to meet your plan.

Looking at Table 2 in Chapter 2, your second year turnover is £45,000. Dividing this by 147 gives just over £300 per day invoicing, for the three days of each week. This daily figure will include materials and mark-up, so your minimum day rate will be more like £260 to £275. Having done this calculation, you can set your day rate where you wish – you now know where you stand, and how much you have in hand.

The day rate only provides for your presence and expertise. You also need to recover from your clients the cost of materials and services. A simple way is to merely charge materials and processing on a "per tranny" basis, making sure the cost is sufficient to cover your costs and give a little profit as well. This is the method favoured by many photographers, and I use it myself on small jobs. My current rate for trannies is £10 each for 35mm and roll film, and £15 each for 5x4. Any Polaroids are charged at cost plus a small mark-up. A typical small job priced like this would be five product shots taken in half a day, with perhaps two Polaroids. Using a day rate of £300, the bill would look like this:

    1/2 day photography at 60% of day rate: £180
    5 6x7cm colour transparencies @ £10 ea: £50
    2 Polaroids @ £1.25 ea: £2.50

    Total: £232.50 + VAT

On larger jobs, I charge actual materials and processing costs plus an appropriate profit. It is not unknown for a trade catalogue shoot to produce over a hundred roll film trannies in a couple of days, using 30 rolls of film costing £125 processed. The bill for something like this would be:

    2 days photography of your products
    and the supply of 100 6x7cm transparencies: £600.00
    Photographic materials and processing for the above: £195.00

    Total: £795.00 + VAT

Priced on a "per tranny" basis, the bill would be double at £1,600. We'll look at estimating larger jobs later on, but this illustrates how additional profits are made in addition to the day rate.

Using the figures above, if you wanted to start at say £275 per day, you can afford to do it, and then gently ease your fees up as you become known and develop a reputation.

However, don't go into print on the "time and materials" basis formally. Just make sure that when you discuss larger jobs with clients, they are aware that you can price in this manner.

Handling the objections

I am always bemused that a client, perfectly prepared to pay £20 an hour or more to have the oil changed in his car, demurs at £35 an hour for professional photographic services. Their accountant will charge anything from £60 an hour upwards, and solicitors breathe in similarly rarefied air. And yet they will pay £1,000 – £1,500 a day for a "London Studio". 'Tis a crazy world, but you have to be ready for these objections. After all, George in Quality Control is really into photography, wins competitions at the camera club, and has ever such a good camera, and he'd do it on Saturday morning for a few rolls of film...

Luckily, those of us who work mainly for agencies are rarely confronted with these arguments, but quite senior executives in direct industrial accounts will often talk like this. Confronting it as nonsense will do you no good, because, most of the time, these people genuinely believe that George in QC could do the job. Some amateur photographers are indeed capable of producing pro quality trannies, and George may just be one of them.

The only way I know of countering this attitude is to initially agree with most of the objections, but gently sow seeds of doubt. Yes, an amateur can produce very pleasing pics of the product, but will they be suitable for four-colour separations and printing? Will it be done quickly? I have seen amateur photographers anguish all day over one simple pack shot, when the average pro will run it off in fifteen minutes or less. Will he have the experience to match the product with the background or setting, and quickly? Will he remember to have the product looking to the right on a left hand page and vice versa? Can the client be sure enough of the photos to allow the only example of the product to be flown to the USA before the film is processed? Will the amateur still be fiddling with a camera that he only bought last week when the heat from the lamps has wilted the flowers beyond redemption?

The professional assures reliability, and the only way I know to counter "George in QC" is to admit that George might be able to provide the pics, but that *you* will provide them on time, on the right film, with the right lighting, and with the right exposure. And that is what costs the money.

The "I could have this done in London for only a few hundred pounds more" gambit is more difficult to counter. Many clients seem to feel that there is a David Bailey or a Lichfield in every West End studio, and that having it done in London is an immediate guarantee of superiority. Whilst it is true that many of the best of us are found in London, many studios there are run by ordinary mortals, but with extraordinarily high overheads resulting in similarly high day rates. You can't rent anything in London these days under £25/square foot, and that immediately contributes £250 to £300 a day to the day rate for quite a modest studio.

You have to explain gently that, unless your client is really after a "name", they will get the same quality of work from you as they would in London, but that there they will probably have to pay twice as much for it. Most see the light eventually, but you may have to grit your teeth and watch the plum, profitable jobs go to London whilst you are left with the rubbish. Local ad agencies suffer from this perhaps more than photographers. Sometimes you may have to make a difficult decision and drop the client.

Image – or how others see you

Photographers share with ad agencies the need to comfort their clients and make them feel confident in their choice of creative service. I suppose it all comes back to price again – a client who is welcomed in a luxurious reception area and served coffee in the best Wedgwood, is led to feel that maybe their money is being spent wisely in having such an obviously successful company handle his account. Whilst I suspect that there is much truth in this cynical view, the more perceptive of your clients should also feel that the care that is lavished on the coffee ceremony is probably also being applied to the tranny processing, and that business in general is done on a high level of professional competence.

I was privileged recently to be "a fly on the wall" in a meeting where an ad agency had just visited a local commercial studio. "No way I'd use them," said the senior creative director, "the studio was in a total mess, it was like a pigsty, equipment all over the place, cables all over the floor, wastepaper bins overflowing." First impressions had killed that studio's chances that day, and for quite some time to come.

Another new studio never got off the ground because the owner's seven year old daughter had the run of the place! Remember that your visitors have just left the comfort of their senior executive offices and rosewood furniture, via their air-conditioned BMW or Jaguar, to visit your converted industrial unit. Have the place clean, tidy, and give them the best chairs you can afford. And the Wedgwood coffee cups.

The "image" thing must go all the way through. Some photographers are proud of their old faithful cameras, battered and worn as they may be. But in the commercial studio this will not earn you any kudos. Keep your gear in good condition externally as well as internally. Keep lighting cables neatly cleated in position. Mains wiring should not be via a multiplicity of extensions on the floor. Keep the focusing cloth draped over the monorail – it keeps dust out of the bellows. Every week, give the studio a thorough clean and remove all the dirt. Empty all the bins regularly, and keep the floor free from Polaroid backing sheets – horrible if you get one on the sole of your shoe; worse if your client does.

Image considerations should be everywhere. A red velvet jacket may impress in the social field – it implies the wearer is an artist. But in the commercial world, wear the same as your client, be it a suit, or blazer and flannels, or neat sweater and slacks. Clean shoes and everything else will make your client comfortable in your presence and feel at home in your studio. If your partner doubles as receptionist, then these disciplines apply even more stringently.

Keep the inside and outside of your car clean – you never know when you may have to run a client to the station, or back to their office for a mislaid visual, and they may not have their own car. Having your client wait while you clear lighting stands and magazines off the floor won't do a lot for you.

Stationery

Your stationery is your ambassador outside the studio, and yet so many people give it little attention. Some photographers' letter headings look little better than photocopies, and any attempt at good design is noticeable by its absence. A curled-up 35mm film in heavy black, smudged line drawings of Hasselblads, statements like "photography for the discerning", are just tacky, and have no place on a successful commercial photographer's letter heading.

Fortunately, good taste is usually just down the road at your local ad agency or designer. Have them design a stationery set specifically for you, comprising letter headings, visiting cards and "with compliments" sheets. Allow them to choose the typefaces and the paper. Conqueror is a good old war horse, but there are other papers just as good. Let them use their normal printer. Your business is taking pics, theirs is creating images – let them do their thing for you; it won't cost a fortune.

The telephone

Finally, we should talk about that awful instrument, the telephone. I personally hate the thing, and will go to any lengths to avoid using it. I do not believe that any other method of communication is so capable of giving the wrong impression. A good telephone manner is a gift from on high, but it can be learned. Take the following examples:

Example 1

"Ring Ring.."

"Hello.."

"Is that Blankframe Studios?"

"Yes."

"Can I speak to Mr Blankframe please?"

"Well, he was around a moment ago, hang on a minute..."

Time...

Time...

"No I can't find him – could you ring back?"

"Well, this is John Rogers here from Rogers Associates, he was going to call me with some prices today but I have only just got back to my office..."

"Ooh, I don't know about that, you'll have to call back."

Example 2

"Ring Ring.."

"Good afternoon, Blankframe Studios, may I help you?"

"May I speak to Mr Blankframe please?"

"May I know who is calling please?"

"Rogers from Rogers Associates."

"Oh yes Mr Rogers, Mr Blankframe is shooting at the moment, but I have the prices you wanted. Should I read them to you and confirm by fax?"

'Nuff said.

CARING FOR YOUR BUSINESS

This is the most important chapter in the whole book; please don't neglect it.

You have your studio organised, clients are beginning to come to you, you are beginning to get an idea of the different kinds of work that make up your chosen business. Large invoices are now going out in the post at the end of each week. All of a sudden you own your own business, you are independent, all your worries are over. That holiday in the south of France now looks more like a reality than a dream. You relax.

The sad truth is that the seeds of disaster are often sown at this point, by over-confidence, and by neglect of the disciplines of running a business. This chapter is about what you have to do to allow your business to continue, to grow a little, to survive.

There are some ground rules you have to apply to the day-to-day management of your business, and there are some guidelines in handling the major projects your studio will be asked to handle. We'll start with the general everyday disciplines, in particular, cash planning, expenses and stock control.

Forecasting

Many moons ago, when you started up the business, you produced a cash flow forecast, both for the bank and to calculate what facilities you would require. But by now it is probably not worth the paper it is written on, so much has changed. Some things have cost more than planned, maybe a few have cost less, purchasing decisions have been altered – all kinds of things have happened. And yet the authorised overdraft at the bank is the same, and your drawings are still the same. Do you really know what your cash position will be next week, or next month, or even three months from now?

Well, you need to. More businesses go down the tubes because of a lack of cash than for any other reason, no matter how healthy the order book or invoicing.

To start with, you need to bring your cash flow forecast bang up to date, and use it as the sole management tool for your day-to-day operations. Think of your business as a fast car travelling down a motorway at night, with the cash flow forecast as your headlights. If it is up to date and accurate, then your way ahead is brilliantly lit for hundreds of yards. If you have ignored it, then you are truly in the dark, and you will crash into the first obstacle that comes your way.

If you entered the cash flow forecast on your PC, then all you need to do now is modify it slightly to include the names of your clients in the "receipts" section. Line 12 on the earlier example's "from sales" should now be a total made up of all your outstanding invoices, or "receivables" as they are called.

Estimate when each of your invoices is due for payment – a good rule of thumb is that it will be paid at the beginning of the second month following invoicing. Thus, an invoice issued by you at the end of February should be paid in the first week of April. Similarly, an invoice written by you on the first of March will not be paid until the fifth or sixth of May. You are granting your clients up to ten weeks credit, free of charge.

When you have entered all your invoices in this way, look at the expense side of the forecast. Drawings, rent and rates are unlikely to have changed, but materials, lab services and stationery will certainly be different. Go through the form, altering everything that either has changed or you think is likely to change, and recalculate.

Make sure the overdraft figure agrees with your bank statement at the beginning, and then look three months ahead. You will soon know if you are using more or less cash than planned, and you need to get this information to your bank manager quickly if you are going to need more facilities than have already been arranged.

Recalculate this form every Friday, and you won't go far wrong. You can also see the effect on your bank balance when Jones & Jones is a month late in paying their bill.

Which business is going to get favourable treatment from their bank in the following two examples: business A which asks for an extension on their overdraft for 30 days from now because Jones & Jones is late paying their bill, or business B which just lets their overdraft limit pass by, forcing the manager to pick up the phone to find out what on earth is going on?

Remember that if you make a habit of abusing your bank facilities, there will come a point when your manager just bounces your cheques. If the bounced cheque is to your materials supplier, then you won't be able to obtain film for that major shoot you just booked for next week. For many businesses a serious financial crisis would probably be just round the corner at this point, but it needn't be so, if you just keep a close eye on your cash as I've described.

Every month, produce a "hard copy" of your cash flow forecast on your printer and send it to your bank manager. Include a couple of sentences on how things are going, mention any problems you have foreseen, and any particular successes you may have had. Don't make it a long screed, but just enough to reassure the bank that the business is in good hands and you know what you are doing.

You cannot do anything to remedy a situation unless you know where you stand, and you don't know that until you get into the habit of regularly running this little program through your computer.

Improving your cash flow

Now, how can you improve the cash flow situation? Obviously the easiest way is to get your clients to pay up sooner, and we'll look at that a little later.

But there are other ways of improving your cash flow. Do you have a monthly account with your film and camera supplier? Is it "30 days" or "net monthly"? There is up to an extra 30 days credit if you choose the latter.

Do you plan your purchases to fall into next month's payment dates, or do you just pick up the phone when you think you should buy more film? A few moments thought can often delay the due date for payment by 30 days, without any real hardship to the business.

Do you pay cash for your petrol, or do you have a monthly slate at the garage?

Do you pay your insurance premiums in one payment, in advance? Most insurance companies allow monthly payments of large premiums at less than the bank rate of interest and it certainly is worth investigating these.

Attention to stock levels also directly affects cash flow. Do you really need the fridge packed with film? There are very few places in the UK where you can't get pro film delivered at a couple of days notice, and most discount schemes start at ten rolls of film or ten boxes. Also, quantity discounts don't make sense if you have to buy three months supply in one go. A pro studio has to carry enough stock to service the urgent booking, but I have known small studios sit on thousands of pounds worth of film, paper and chemicals and then wonder why they had a cash problem. It is a pernicious fact that once you establish a high stock level of materials, you tend to keep it at that level.

Whilst all the action above can have a positive effect on cash flow, if you can make genuine economies and not spend as much, then you will help both your cash and your profit.

Photo studios tend to go from one minor crisis to another – film is delivered late, the new lens doesn't fit, flash equipment blows up.

Under these circumstances, to advise delaying long distance phone calls until after 1.00 p.m. may seem as though priorities are all wrong. But the telephone is a major expense these days, and bills of up to £500 per quarter are all too easy to run up.

There are ways of containing it. Firstly, if you phone a company and the switchboard operator puts you on hold for more than a couple of minutes, hang up and call again. No point in paying prime long distance rates whilst your contact is being chased in the warehouse. Buy a fax machine – these cost only a few hundred pounds these days, and a message on an A4 sheet takes less than a minute to transmit. Curiously enough, most people will reply to your fax with a long distance phone call (well, its their money).

All of these actions affect your overhead spend, and you do need to keep up the pressure on this steady outflow of money.

Costing

Other periods of major expense will be when your studio is booked on a major shoot. Here, it is critical that attention is paid to all expenses, and that all chargeable costs are in fact charged to the client. Errors usually start at the estimating stage.

Firstly, if for marketing reasons you decide to charge less than the calculated day rate, then you must treat the difference between what the rate is and what it should be as a marketing expense. This is a legitimate ploy, but like any expense it is a direct cost against your business and you should attempt to reduce it as soon as possible.

You should start to think about charging a standard day rate when you have done about six months trading, and an increase of ten to fifteen per cent can normally be achieved without too many tears. This gives you an idea of the maximum discount you can apply to the calculated rate initially, if you want to be "straight and level" within six to nine months or so.

The next problem is that the costs of the shoot are often incorrectly estimated. The estimate form already mentioned is a great help in making sure you have not missed anything. Again this is a simple spreadsheet application – it only demands about an hour to program, and five minutes or so to run. It jogs the memory so that every item is included and a correct mark up is applied to purchases (see Chapter 5).

When the job is done, make sure that all materials are booked out in one form or another. Just helping yourself to materials from the fridge is an excellent way of making sure they end up being given to the client free of charge. A detailed job sheet is not really necessary if you already have an estimate form run off, but you do need to have a sheet of paper listing all the film, background rolls and other materials used. And don't forget petty cash items like payment for the pizzas at lunchtime, taxi fares, etc.

Invoicing

On the day following the shoot, you should get together the original estimate form and the piece of paper that served as the "job sheet". Now add any other details that are relevant to that particular job, like courier bookings and outside processing. Rerun the estimate form with the updated information, making sure you have the actual costs for the bought-in services such as the lab or the courier. Phone them up and make sure you have the correct amount of their invoice to you, even if they haven't raised it yet. Enter the details on the estimate form, and calculate the final invoice price to your client.

I have always meant to amend my "estimate" spreadsheet so that it prints the invoice as well; one of these days I'll get around to it. Until then, my better half takes all the details from the estimate form and produces the invoice.

Send the invoice off in the post the day that the agency, or the company that commissioned the photography, accepts the transparencies. Don't wait for your suppliers' invoices to come in; get your invoice out fast. Occasionally, you will come across an agency that asks that the invoice be delayed until their client has approved the trannies. What they are in effect saying is that they want you to underwrite their art direction of your photography. Refuse – your customer is the agency, and if they have misinterpreted their client's instructions it is hardly your fault.

One agency tried that one out on me recently. When I informed them that we didn't work like that, they told me they didn't think it would wash, but thought they'd try it on anyway!

On your invoice make sure your terms of payment are clearly stated, and ensure that the client knows who to make the cheque out to and what address to send it to. There are some customers who will go to any lengths to delay payment, and you want to avoid statements like "we didn't know what your terms were" or "we didn't know who to make it out to". Don't give the client any excuse for not paying you as promptly as possible.

Give your invoice a reference number. Accountants prefer you to number all invoices consecutively from 001 upwards; this simplifies their checking procedures at the end of the year when they do your accounts. We don't do this, because it immediately tells your clients how much business you are doing, and more importantly, how many other invoices you have written between consecutive jobs with them.

If you have only worked for one client during a particular month (it happens), the last thing you want is for them to know.

We use a reference number which gives the total number of invoices per client. For instance, the twentieth invoice we send to Smith, Jones & Wright will have the reference number SJW 020. We don't mind telling our clients how much business *they* have done with us.

Enter the amount of the expected cheque, inclusive of VAT, into your cash flow forecast in the appropriate month, and note the invoice amount and date in your sales ledger (of which more shortly).

It is perhaps appropriate at this point to talk about the husband/wife team, and how this really works in the small photographic business. Running any business requires production, marketing and administration skills, and it is always better if production is kept separate from the other two. In a two person team, one should accept the production role (photography, lab work, etc) and the other should look after the administration side and day-to-day marketing. Apart from not getting in each other's hair, this has some positive operational advantages, one of which we are about to discuss when we talk about getting our money in quickly.

Managing your clients

If running out of cash is the chief reason for companies failing, then not getting in the money owed to you quickly enough is the chief reason for running out of cash.

Small businesses seem to adopt a very coy attitude to the large company next door which is slowly squeezing the lifeblood out of them as they withhold payments. "We need their business", I am often told. "We don't want to upset them, they may go elsewhere" is another oft-expressed fear. I reply that indeed the best thing that could happen is for these clients to go to your most feared competitor. They will then clog up his cash flow, perhaps forcing him out of business. Attitudes to cash collection tend to change under these circumstances.

There is no shame in insisting that one partner in a business deal keeps to their side of the agreement, and yet so many people shy away from adopting a firm attitude. This is what we do:

We send our invoice by post (then it can't be lost in the car, or left in a briefcase) promptly, as soon as work is approved. Then, in the middle of the month before the bill is due to be paid, we send a statement of account. This is simply a document which records payments and invoices over the last three months or so. It reminds accounts departments that invoices are due for payment. On the last Friday of the month, my wife telephones everyone who is due to make payments, politely asking that they "don't forget us" this month.

This very simple procedure works. Clients know that we will chase payments when they become due, and it is very rare for us not to obtain a commitment to pay from the end of month phone call.

A commitment to pay is what you are looking for. If the payment is not made when promised, you can quickly phone and accuse the client of not keeping their word. My wife does this whilst I am still photographing products with the art director of the agency, or discussing the next shoot. It means that she can have a jolly old ding-dong about late payments whilst I can enjoy the best of relations with the client elsewhere. My relationship is not spoilt, and my "admin manager/cash collector" can chase to her heart's content without fear of upsetting the client.

Base things like money are seldom mentioned at the "creative" level. However, if my wife is having a real problem getting the payment, then a quiet word from me in an art director's ear is usually enough to sort things out quickly.

From time to time you may be told that your bill will be settled when your client's account is settled. This procedure merely transfers all the cash flow problems of your client's business to your own, and you have enough of your own thank you very much. Unless the delay is only for a few days, and you know the client well, don't accept this. Gently point out that their cash flow problems are their problems, and should not become yours. You will be surprised how much a gentle but firm attitude works – especially if someone other than the photographer is doing the talking.

If you follow these guidelines, then you should not have too many problems getting the money in. We have very little in the way of bad debts because we are firm in our approach to the cash problem and our clients are aware of our policy. Without exception, the companies I know that do suffer in this regard have a half-hearted, almost servile approach to their debtors, who naturally hold on to their money as long as possible.

When things go wrong

From time to time, you will be faced with a situation where matters are getting out of hand and you need to act very quickly to protect your money. For me, the biggest problem is in deciding when the situation is serious, or whether it is merely a temporary "glitch". You don't want to endanger a relationship that took a long time to build up because you are overhasty.

We apply some rules. Rule One says that if a promise has been deliberately broken, then the situation is serious. Broken promises to me mean a promised cheque overdue by more than ten days or so, or a statement that a cheque is in the post when it patently is not.

Excuses we have heard which are rarely to be taken seriously:

"The books are with the accountant and we can't do anything until we get them back."

"The MD only writes cheques every third Thursday in the month, and you just missed this run."

"Our terms are 120 days, didn't anyone tell you?"

"We've run out of cheques and are waiting for a new cheque book."

"Our cheques need two signatures, and the other one is away in the USA on business."

Some companies honestly think that some people believe that lot.

Rule Two says that if a cheque bounces, the situation is serious. I have not yet met a bank manager who will bounce a cheque without first discussing the situation with the customer. You can generally assume that relationships between your client and their bank are pretty bad when cheques bounce, and that is not good news for you. The only exception that I know of is when your client changes banks with some unpresented cheques in the system. However, your client will be able to tell you this, and it is very easy to check with one phone call.

Rule Three says that if the quality of the photography is questioned for the first time when the invoice is overdue, then the situation is serious. You will get something like: "Well, we didn't like it to start off with, but we thought that if we changed things round a little, we could use it." If you didn't like it to start off with, you would have said so up front Sunshine.

Finally, Rule Four states that if the client asks for an invoice to be redirected somewhere else then you are on very sticky ground, and if "somewhere else" doesn't want to accept the invoice, then the situation is serious.

In all of the above cases, you run the very real risk of never getting paid, and you must act quickly.

Chasing debts

There are a host of collection agencies who will seek to convince you that they can collect all your overdue bills and "problem accounts". Be wary of those which simply send letters threatening County Court action, and charge you accordingly. Whilst the threat of County Court action may make a few debtors pick up their cheque books, it will only make others smile, and anyway, you can just as easily threaten court action as anyone else, and it only costs a first class stamp.

Successful collection of debts should not need to include the County Court, which should really only be used as a last resort. We were privileged to experience a "professional debtor" at work a couple of years ago, skilfully using the County Court to delay payment of one of our invoices for over a year. It is not an experience we would like to repeat.

The client was a retailer who had heard of our reputation for producing reasonably good work with her kind of product. She wanted work "of the very highest quality" to illustrate an article she was writing for a glossy home interest magazine. The lady came to us with the recommendation of one of our best clients. As a result, we didn't bother with our normal checking procedure, which only involves a phone call or two to previous suppliers anyway. In addition, our client was "running out of time" and we agreed to do the work on Good Friday, and produce the trannies "same day".

The work involved setting up and photographing several formal still life arrangements. By the time everything was arranged and photographed to the client's satisfaction, we had gone through a day. When the trannies were processed our client noticed she had omitted some products on one of the arrangements. We came in the following morning and re-shot that particular piece. The client left delighted with the trannies, and we invoiced for one and "a bit" studio days at standard rate.

When the bill fell due, we made our normal phone call, to be advised that the publisher of the magazine was settling the invoice, and hadn't we already been paid? We called the magazine and were told, as we thought, that photography costs were the responsibility of the contributor. We knew at that point we were going to have a fight on our hands for the money. We decided to apply the County Court procedure immediately.

Not being too familiar with the actual procedure, we decided to take some advice from a solicitor operating the "half hour of legal advice for a fiver" scheme. This has to be the best value for money short of a legal friend in the pub. The procedure was explained to us, and as we parted with our fiver, we left feeling we would have our cash within a few weeks. Nothing was further from the truth.

The first thing you do with the small claims procedure is to issue a seven day notice that you intend to take the case to the County Court. When this notice had expired, we applied to the local court for a hearing. In due course, a summons was issued which our client simply ignored. A new date was set, which our client ignored again, but at this hearing, judgement was made in our favour, in absentia. Theoretically, the debtor has a period of time in which to pay up before the judgement is registered against his or her name. Naturally, our client ignored this notice period.

We were now some five months away from the date the work was done, and not much nearer our money.

The next procedure usually is to "enforce the judgement", which means sending in the bailiffs. Our client, however, had nothing of value in the house that was not held in trust for someone else, or was not on HP. We did not discover this for some time, because the bailiffs have to be granted access to the premises, and as the bailiffs must give notice of their impending visit, it is convenient for the debtor to be out when they call. In our case, several abortive visits were made before access was gained. We were now nine months down the line, and about £50 in fees poorer.

The next thing we were advised to do by the County Court (they are incredibly helpful by the way), was to invite our client to court so that a court examination could be made of her means so that an attachment order of some kind could be made. As you have probably guessed, our client did not deign to attend the first appointment.

When the second appointment was made, the client visited the court the day before the due date, with a promise to pay within a day or so. The court promptly suspended activities for 14 days in fairness to the client. Naturally, no payment was made, and by the time a new appointment was made for the second visit, we were now a year down the line. The client ignored the second appointment too. A third appointment was duly made; this appointment has to be kept otherwise the client is held in contempt of court, can be arrested and, in some cases, sentenced to a prison term.

At this point my wife lost patience, and started to do what we should have done in the beginning. She telephoned the client every day, at work and at home, until we got a commitment and a cheque. It took ten days, and it didn't bounce.

This case is extreme, but it does show what can happen if you put too much faith in the County Court system. We would only refer the most extreme case now. The lessons we learned were that there are "professional debtors" around, but that if faced with one you mustn't give up – you will get your money eventually. The other is that confronted with the same situation today, we would go direct to the "examination of means" as soon as judgement had been entered. We would have saved six months in the case above.

Far better is to continually press for payment yourself. Remember that it is illegal in this country to harass a debtor, but asking for a payment commitment, and phoning again when that commitment is not kept, is not harassment. Also, try and get something on account. If they can't pay all of it, then get some of it.

If all of this unpleasant stuff is not to your taste then there are collection facilities available which do work. The above example shows that the "solicitor's letter for £25" approach is not going to help you much. Effective help is going to cost much more than this, but you may be able to recover something from the debtor.

The appropriately named Dun and Bradstreet has a collection service which (I can assure from personal experience) does work. They charge a fee proportional to the time a debt is outstanding, and their method consists of talking to your debtor and coaxing the money out of them. If their normal methods fail and the case has to go to court, then their fee is dramatically reduced. This means that every effort is made to obtain payment quickly without recourse to legal proceedings. Their telephone number is in the back of this book under "Useful Addresses".

Finally, before we leave this subject, remember that a client who does not pay their bills is not worth having. We tell these people that we have an arrangement with our bank manager – he doesn't take photographs and we don't lend money. You don't need these problems, there are plenty of good, paying customers around that you would be wiser spending your time with. We, in our time, have refused to work for several companies, some of them household names, because of their poor record in paying bills. Maybe if more people did this they would alter their policy – but there always seems to be someone around who will accept 180 day terms.

Essential records and accounts

Because the Inland Revenue and Customs and Excise trust you, and in order that they continue to do so, you have to keep accurate records of your affairs. These are not complicated, and consist of three main books which you must keep: a record of your purchases, known fancifully as the "Purchase Ledger"; a record of your sales, the "Sales Ledger"; and a book which records the passage of payments in and out of your bank, the "Cash Book".

Before you leap out and buy beautifully bound, pre-printed ledgers, note that I use standard hardback plain ruled books, bought for a few pounds at the local stationer.

We'll deal with the purchase ledger first, as this seems to cause most problems. Remember, your purchase ledger covers your purchases of film, equipment, repairs, petrol, entertainment, everything.

You'll need to rule ten columns, across two pages. From left to right, they are the date the purchase took place, a brief description of the purchase, the supplier's name, and their invoice number if it exists. The next two columns are used to enter the VAT-free price of the purchase. We use two columns to distinguish between capital items and all others. It helps a little at the end of the year to keep these two separate. The next column is for the VAT charged, then the total of the price plus the VAT. The next column gives the method of payment, i.e. "by cheque", and the number. The final column is the date paid. We tend to add up the totals on each page as we go along; this helps the VAT return preparation.

The only other rule we have is to start a new double page at the beginning of each month.

Collect your invoices on a week by week basis, and fill in your ledger every Friday afternoon. If you have a computer you may be tempted to put your ledgers on a spreadsheet. This does have the advantage of being able to split up your purchase types more easily, i.e. you can have a column for stock, a column for car expenses, etc. We have found that it takes longer to do this than to simply pick up a pen. It does take longer at the end of the year to do the accounts, but I still think the pen and book method is better. It does not tie up the computer either if your partner is writing letters or invoices on it.

The sales ledger is similar, and in fact we use the same book as the purchase ledger, working from the back forward. At the end of the year, we then have one book containing purchase and sales figures that can be archived with the invoices and copy invoices. We then start a new book for the following year.

The columns in our sales ledger are the date of invoice, a description of the work carried out, the client's name, and the invoice number. We use two columns to record the invoice amount, differentiating between photographic work and the disposal of an unwanted asset. The next column is for VAT charged, and the next for the invoice price inclusive of VAT. The final column is for the date the client settles his account. Nine columns in all. We fill in the sales ledger each time we send out an invoice.

The third record you need to keep is a record of bank transactions, commonly known as the "Cash Book". This can be a simple standard type cash book, or you can rule your own lines in a plain book as with the ledgers. We have seven columns in ours: the date, the name of the drawer/payee (we use To/From), the cheque number, the amount in separate debit/credit columns, a narrow column for reconciliation ticks (of which more later), and the balance.

How does all this work, and how much time does it take? The day-to-day administration of a small business is really quite simple, and there are only two dangers. The first is trying to over-complicate it, usually by trying to adapt ready made bookkeeping systems to your business, and the other is by neglecting your admin "chores" and getting behind. This is how we operate:

Every day, when we receive the mail, we split it into cheques and everything else. "Everything else" gets put into a folder for attention on Friday afternoon. We then find the copy invoice for each of the cheques we have received, and write on this copy the date paid and the cheque number. The same information goes into the sales ledger.

At lunchtime the cheques go into the bank, with the entries added to the cash book. We do this every day; there is no point in having cheques lying around for days. You never know, there might be less money in the client's account than they have written cheques for, and it's first come first served with most banks.

Every time we send out a sales invoice, we enter the details into our sales ledger, and on the day-to-day list of outstanding invoices ("accounts receivable") we keep pinned up on the wall.

At the end of every week, we enter all the bills we have received into the purchase ledger, including any cash (i.e. not on account) purchases made during the week. We also update the cash flow forecast on the computer so that we know we have the money to pay account bills when they become due.

Finally, at the end of the month, which for us tends to be the first week of the following month, we get together all the bills due for payment. Then we check with the cash flow and the cash book to be sure that there is enough money to pay them (there will be if you have followed all the good advice here), and we write out the cheques.

For each invoice we pay, we write on the invoice the amount of the cheque, the number and the date. We attach a compliments slip to the cheque, writing on it "In payment of your invoice(s) No. so and so", pop it into an envelope and send it by first class post. Don't wait to be chased – you can hardly complain about late payers if you are one yourself.

We then file the invoices in the purchase invoice file for posterity, and enter the payment details into the columns provided in the purchase ledger, updating the cash book at the same time.

This takes my good lady wife about half an hour a day on average, and a couple of hours on a Friday afternoon while I sweep up the studio or clean the darkroom. The books are in an up-to-date condition should the VAT people want to look, and when the end of the year comes the preparation of our annual accounts is a doddle.

The only other tasks during the year are the preparation of the quarterly VAT return, and reconciliation of the bank statement when it plops through the post every month.

The VAT return

These days the small business has a number of choices regarding the payment of VAT. The choices vary almost every month, from payment of VAT upon payment of invoice to a single yearly payment. You should check with your local Customs and Excise office for the most up-to-date options, but frankly, for our kind of business, preparing a quarterly return is such a simple procedure that I cannot understand all the fuss some people make over it.

Add up all your purchase invoices over the period. If you have totted up each page as we do, all you have to do is add each page together. Similarly, add up all the VAT on each page. Don't forget you must not have included the VAT on any non-allowable items such as entertainment. You now have the value of your inputs, and the tax you are reclaiming, boxes 2 and 5 on the VAT return form.

Now for outputs, or sales. Turn to your sales ledger, and add up all the total sales invoices and VAT as before. Until recently, you had to come to an agreement with your VAT inspector regarding the recovery of VAT on the private use of petrol (or diesel) in your car. Now you simply pay a fixed amount every quarter for private use, having reclaimed all the VAT paid on fuel in your input section. This payment, which varies depending on the size of the engine, is simply added to your output tax figure. You now have boxes 1 and 5 completed. The difference, box 3, is simply box 1 minus box 2, positive or negative depending on whether you pay the VATman, or he pays you.

Photocopy your return, send it off with your cheque if you owe, in plenty of time. What's the fuss all about?

Bank reconciliation

The bank reconciliation is really a check that you have included everything in your cash book, and a check that your bank has not made a mistake (rare).

Go through each credit/debit on the bank statement, find the same one in your cash book, and put a tick in the reconciliation column in your cash book and against the entry on the bank statement. Any items without ticks in the cash book haven't reached the bank yet, and any items without ticks in your bank statement have been overlooked by you. This is also the time to enter bank charges and commission in your cash book. Don't forget to reconcile your bank statement with your cash book. It is a monthly check that you are where you think you are financially, and gives great peace of mind (or should).

That is all you need to do to keep your business well cared for and squeaky clean through the year, and it represents about five hours of work a week.

Next, we'll look at the preparation of the annual accounts so you know how well you are doing. The Inland Revenue has more than a passing interest in these as well, as has your bank manager.

The annual accounts

As soon as possible after the end of your financial year, you should prepare your annual accounts. Many people entrust this job to a firm of chartered or certified accountants, but there is no obligation for you to do so, and the task is very straightforward. Doing it yourself will save you anything up to £1,000, and that's not bad for a weekend's work, is it?

As already mentioned, if you do decide to go it alone, you should have access to a tax "guru" to fine-tune your accounts, and help prepare your "tax computation", which is really what all this is about.

Before we go into the actual preparation, why are these accounts necessary in the first place? Your relationship with the bank is such that your manager is happy with regular monthly reports and cash flow predictions - the money is coming in all right, therefore you must be doing all right.

The fact is, until you do a full set of accounts at the end of the year, you don't *know* whether you are doing all right. Cash can be coming in well, and yet you may be losing money on each sale. You have to go through this procedure to find out exactly how your business is doing. Our friends in the Inland Revenue are also quite interested in your progress, as they will be very happy to extract the requisite amount of income tax from your hard earned cash if you are doing really well.

The first document you have to prepare is your profit and loss statement for the year, known as your "Trading and Profit and Loss Account". A fictitious example is shown below. You will see

```
Fred Bloggs Trading as Blankframe Photography
23 New Street, Telford, Staffs.
Trading and Profit & Loss Account for year ending 30th April 1992
                                          This year:
                                          30.04.92
                                                    19,050
Work Done

Opening Stock                                250
Add Purchases                              6,500
                                           6,750
Less Closing Stock                         1,250
                                                     5,500
Gross Profit:                                       13,550
Sundry Income:                                         108
                                                    13,658
                                                    ======

Less Expenses:

Wages                                      2,000
Motor & travel expenses                    1,250
Car lease
Repairs & renewals                           500
Rent                                       4,500
Rates                                      1,200
Light & heat                               1,000
Telephone & telex                          1,000
Printing, stationery, post & advertising:    600
Bank charges                                 250
Bank interest                                400
Bank loan interest                         1,250
Insurance                                    720
Equipment hire
Bad debts
Depreciation                               3,000
Entertainment                                250
Accounting fees

Sundries                                     100
                                                    18,020

Net Profit/(Loss) for year:                         (4,362)
```

Example: Trading and Profit & Loss Account

that it is not dissimilar to the document you produced eons ago for your bank manager, discussed in chapter 2. If you have taken your PC home for the weekend, it is quite useful to build up these forms on a spreadsheet, and the job will be a little easier next year.

The first figure you need to get is the total of all your photographic work done in the year, less VAT. You will now see the sense in having two columns in the sales ledger, one for photo work and the other for sales of surplus equipment. For now, we are only interested in the total value of your photographic work, both studio and laboratory, and we take this total directly out of the sales ledger, and enter it as "Work Done".

You next need to know the direct costs that can be applied to this work done. The rules are that materials and purchases directly related to each job are counted as direct costs (or "cost of sales" in accounting parlance). The obvious ones are film, paper and chemicals, background rolls, and any other materials that you keep in stock or "inventory". To find out what these costs are through the year, simply add up all your purchases of these materials out of your purchase ledger. You may, however, have started the year with some materials in the fridge and studio, and you should have a list of these items somewhere, with their value.

Accountants go into raptures when you mention inventory valuation. All we simpler beings need to know is that you should value these items at the lower of either their actual cost or their current value. Do the same calculation for the stock you have left at the end of the year, and hey presto, you have "Opening Stock", "Purchases", and "Closing Stock".

However, you need to modify the "Purchases" figure, because you will have had to buy certain additional items and services specifically for each shoot. Here you add all your model costs, processing costs, couriers, taxis, meals – anything that was specifically related to the shoot in hand and therefore are true costs of doing the job. You can now work out the gross profit, which is the profit you have made on the work done before you apply your day-to-day or "Overhead" costs.

Gross profit equals work done, less net purchases. Net purchases equal opening stock plus materials purchased plus direct costs less closing stock. Gross profit is your principal income, but you do add another line here, "Sundry Income". This item can cover a multitude of sins, but generally it is for anything you can't find a home for elsewhere.

Summing up, using our fictitious business, you did £19,050 worth of business (no VAT remember), your direct costs on those sales was £5,500, and as a result your gross profit was £13,550. Not bad for a first year.

We have looked at the income, now we look at where all the hard-earned cash went – the expenses.

Firstly, you are allowed to hire your partner in a husband/wife business providing his/her wages fall below the threshold for PAYE or National Insurance. It is currently at about £2,350/year, and is allowed as a genuine expense providing your partner does do some useful work. You are, by the way, supposed to actually part with the money. I have inserted £2,000 as "wages". Most of the expense headings are self-explanatory, and you need to go through your purchase ledger to tot up each type. Don't forget items that will not normally appear in your purchase ledger, like rent and insurance premiums paid by direct debit.

Two lines which require a little explanation are "Repairs and Renewals" and "Depreciation". Let's take "Repairs and Renewals" first. "Repairs" are self-explanatory. "Renewals" is a catch-all heading for low cost bits and bobs that have virtually no resale value. Developing tanks, thermometers, odd filters and the like, all come under this heading.

"Depreciation" is mentioned in Chapter 2, and is essentially your estimate of how much you need to set aside each year to replace your major capital assets. The Inland Revenue won't allow depreciation as a valid expense, so it has to be taken out before you do the tax calculation. Nevertheless, you should estimate it the best you can because it is a real cost of doing business. A brief

```
Fred Bloggs trading as Blankframe Photography
Balance Sheet as at 30th April 1992

Fixed Assets:

   per Schedule                          15,000

Current Assets:

   Debtors                     4,000
   Cash in hand                  250
   Stock                       1,250

                               5,500
                               =====
Current Liabilities:

   Sundry Creditors and Accruals  2,500
   HM Customs & Excise
   Bank Overdraft              4,000
                               6,500
                               =====
Net Current Liabilities:                 (1,000)
Net Assets/C Liabilities:                 14,000
                                          ======
Financed by:

   Capital Account,
   Balance as of 1st May 1991            20,862
   Cash introduced

                                         20,862
Less:                                    ======

   Net Loss for year          4,362
   Drawings                   9,000
                                         13,362
                                         ======

Balance carried forward:                  7,500

Bank Loan:                                 6,500

                                          14,000
                                          ======
```

Example:
Balance Sheet

method of calculation is given in Chapter 2.

And that is your P&L, as it is usually known. Wasn't too difficult, was it? You lost a few thousand, but you started a new business, and a result like this will normally be accepted by the Inland Revenue for the first year or two. In terms of your annual accounts, you have now done most of the work. You now need to look at the "Balance Sheet".

This is a statement of the "net worth" of your business, and is an analysis of what you own, what you owe, what you are owed, and how much money you have put into the business. The Inland Revenue don't hold too much store by it, but most bank managers love it. I personally don't get too excited about balance sheets either – you tend to know if you are heavily in debt without all of this palaver, but, you have to do it.

Doing a balance sheet is rather like putting down any number, and altering it until it fits. You start off with what you know, and add the rest. I use a PC spreadsheet program. A typical example is shown opposite.

Firstly, look at your "Fixed Assets". These are the items known as "Capital Items": cameras, enlargers, lighting, any item in your depreciation calculation. Also, you need to include improvements you have made to your industrial unit at a real valuation. If you sweated and did it yourself for £5,000, but it would have cost £10,000 for a contractor to do it, then put £10,000 in the asset value. Your labour is definitely worth something, and you would have had to pay labour had you hired a contractor to do it.

When you have added up all your fixed assets, take off depreciation that would apply at the date the balance sheet is prepared. A rule often used is to apply a full year's depreciation to any part of the year in which the asset was acquired. In other words, if you are depreciating a Nikon F4 over five years with a nil residual value, then you value it at 80% of it's purchase price whether you bought it on the first day of the year or the last.

This gives you the first figure on the balance sheet – "Fixed Assets: per schedule" (this just means that you attach a list). The figure I have used is £15,000. Fixed assets means that these are items which are not constantly changing. Assets which do change are called "Current Assets", and include "Debtors", "Cash in hand", and "Stock".

Debtors, the first entry, is simply the sum of all unpaid sales invoices on the date that the balance sheet was prepared, not including VAT. Cash in hand is any positive balance in the petty cash or the bank account, and stock is your materials inventory on the date concerned. On our example, £4,000 is owing to us for work done, we have £250 in a tin box under the bed, and we have £1250 worth of film, paper and other stock. Up to now, all this is your wealth, your assets in the business.

Now we start to look at the liabilities to balance off the assets. This is your debt, so to speak. As before, we look at them in turn, only we take the current liabilities first.

The first heading is "Sundry Creditors and Accruals". Forget accruals; put in here all the money you owe to suppliers that has been invoiced by them – unpaid electricity bills etc. We owe £2,500 in this area. The next heading is HM Customs and Excise. Put in here any VAT due but not paid. Finally, find out what your bank overdraft was on the date and pop the figure in, £4,000 in our case. Total the three items.

Now subtract the current liabilities total from the current assets total, and you have net current liabilities, which should normally be positive in favour of your current assets, but in our start-up situation is £1,000 negative. Then add in your fixed assets, and you have the net balance, in the column marked "Net Assets/Current Liabilities", of a very healthy £14,000.

Against all this you have now to allow for the drawings you have made against the business, the profit or loss you have made during the year, and any cash you have put into the business. You also add the balance of any fixed term bank loan.

In other words, where has the money come from to finance these net assets? We know you have put money in, and we know that you went to the bank for a loan. If it were easy to establish exactly how much money you have personally put in (the "Capital Account"), you would take this amount of money (£20,862 in our case), take off the net loss for the year and your drawings at £750/month, and have a balance of £7,500 as shown under "balance carried forward". Add the bank loan as a source of money at £6,500, and you end up with the same figure as we had under "Net Assets/Current Liabilities", of £14,000.

Simple. In practice, however, it is not so easy and you have to mess around and work backwards to get the £20,862 figure. The formulae to use, with my workings out, are here:

Capital Account - (Drawings + Loss) = Balance C/F

Balance C/F + bank loan = Net Assets/Current Liabilities

In the above, we know the drawings, the year's loss, the bank loan balance and the net assets/current liabilities. We can therefore rewrite the formulae as:

Capital Account – (£9,000 + £4,362) = Balance C/F

Balance C/F + £6,500 = £14,000

It is easy now, the balance C/F equals £7,500, and therefore:

Capital Account – £13,362 = £7,500
or:
Capital Account = £20,862

We can now add in all the figures to give the completed balance sheet. I don't know whether this is an approved way accounting-wise, but it is the way I've always done it with no problems.

The only thing that you need to do now is account properly for your fixed assets, your cameras, lenses, enlargers, computer, etc. Although the taxman is not interested in your depreciation from a profit and loss account point of view, "the Revenue" (as they tend to be called) does get interested when you sell an asset at anything other than your depreciated value.

If you have a Nikon F4 that you bought last year for £1,000, and thought it would last five years, then at the end of last year it would have been in your books at £800, and this year at £600. If you find someone willing to pay you £900 for it, then you have made £300 profit over the depreciated value. The Revenue expect you to pay tax on that, and you must add this item to your tax computation.

Similarly, if you can only sell your F4 for £500, then you have made a loss of £100, and you can add that to your tax computation. Generally these things tend to cancel out, but sometimes they don't, so be aware of the implications.

As mentioned above, the Revenue don't take into account depreciation in the profit calculation, nor will they allow entertainment. Also, if a business asset can be used for private use, they expect you to pay a proportion of it by not allowing the full expense in the tax computation. They are quite reasonable though, and if you genuinely only use a car for one sixth of the time privately, then they will allow five/sixths of motoring expenses on the tax computation.

The Revenue, because they don't allow depreciation on assets, do have a tax allowance scheme known as "Capital Allowances". They will allow you to set 25% of the value of your assets in any year against income.

The way this works is that, say, in year one you acquire capital items worth £15,000. At the end of the year, you claim 25% (£3,750) as capital allowances in that year. At the beginning of the following year, you start the year with a "pool" value of £15,000 less 25%, or £11,250. Add to that any assets you buy during the second year at their cost price net of VAT, and subtract any assets you disposed of during the same year at the actual disposal price. This gives you your new pool value upon which you calculate your new 25% capital allowance.

Bear in mind that you cannot pool any car that has private

```
Fred Bloggs trading as Blankframe Photography:

Your Reference: 444/333111

Income tax computations 1991/92:
=================================

LOSS per Accounts:                              4,362

ADD: Depreciation:              3,000
     Entertaining:                250
     Motor expenses, £1250 x 1/5  250


                                                3,500
                                _____

Adjusted Loss carried forward:                    862
                                                  =====

Capital Allowances:

Pool:
=====
                 Brought Forward:             11,000
                      Additions:                 nil
                      Disposals:                 nil

          Capital Allowance, 25%:              2,750

                 Carried Forward:              8,250
                 ===============                =====
```

Example:
Tax Computation

use. It must be dealt with as an individual item. Also the capital allowances due must be restricted to account for that private use. This is one area where you must take appropriate advice.

An example of a typical tax computation is shown above. Note the reduction in motoring expenses for private use, and the fact that the whole of the depreciation has been deducted from the loss. The capital allowance calculation follows. Note that you do not have to claim capital allowances in the actual year – because of the pool system you can postpone the claim to a more advantageous year if you wish.

In total, the tax loss carried forward for the year's trading is £3,612 including capital allowances. Under certain circumstances, this tax loss can be used to generate a refund of tax previously paid, and you are then rewarded with a handsome cheque.

Warning!

Please note that this computation has been included only as an example, based on the situation at the time of writing. As tax laws change continuously, you must always discuss your situation with your tax consultant before finalising and submitting any figures.

All you need to do now is assemble your P&L, balance sheet

and tax computation, and, with the following letter (or similar), send the total package to your local tax inspector:

```
H.M. Inspector of Taxes,
Bigtown 3rd District,
1 City Road,
Worcester

August 12th 1992

Your Ref: 444/333111


Dear Sirs,

     Fred Bloggs, T/A Blankframe Photography

I enclose my accounts and tax computation for
1991/92 which I trust you will find in order.

               Yours faithfully,



               Fred Bloggs
```

And you can go away and relax.

THE PHOTOGRAPHY

At last we are getting into what this business is all about – taking photographs. In this chapter we will be looking at the different kinds of work you will be asked to do in the studio and outside, together with some advice on how to handle some of the more tricky situations. The difference between brochure and advertising photography is often poorly understood, and we will spend some time on that subject. We'll also look at the skills you'll need to develop in dealing with people as well – clients, art directors and the models you may employ.

When you are commissioned for photography, you must always ask what it is going to be used for. Studio work may be used for retail brochures, trade brochures, press releases, local and national advertising, point of sale displays, retail flysheets, exhibitions, reception displays, packaging – the list goes on, and each application requires a different approach. There is a similar list of end uses for location photography, which we will look at later. Meanwhile, let's first look at the "pack shot", mainly used for press releases and trade catalogues.

The pack shot

The principle use of the pack shot is to inform, not to sell. The trade brochure is used by retailers when ordering new stock, while the press release is for reproduction in the "new products" sections of trade oriented magazines. Its purpose is to tempt the reader to send off for more information.

The photographic difference between these uses is that generally the trade brochure shot is taken on reversal transparency film for colour reproduction, while the press release pic is taken on black and white neg film for prints. Colour prints are occasionally requested by agencies, the reason being that some magazines like to make the choice between colour and black and white pages at the last moment, and it is possible to get both from a print even if quality is not all it should be.

The basic set-up for both types of shot is the same, and you will find that the majority of these photographs are taken using what is variously described as a "product table", "shooting table", or "scoop". If you are very rich, you can buy one of these tables from several manufacturers with prices ranging from a couple of hundred pounds up to over six hundred. Or, for about £30 and an hour or two of your time, you can make one.

The "Tinsley" product table is shown below, and is designed around the use of standard graduated backgrounds available from Wiggins Teape (Rainbow) and KJP (Colorshade). The table is usually lit from above with a single light source, usually a 500 watt second flash head fitted with a one metre square softbox unit. A Bowens Quadmatic head or Prolite 82 or 100 fitted with a Wafer 100 works just fine, and gives between f22 and f32 on Fujichrome 100.

When putting together the set above, it is important to remember that the pack shot has to be cheap and cheerful and yet accurately represent the pack, and sometimes its contents. It needs to be quick to shoot, and therefore only one light should be involved in the set. My own record was over a hundred of these in a day, on different backgrounds, but I was using a motorised camera and had "helpers" from the client unpacking, polishing and repacking the products.

One of the greatest aids available today is the graduated background. This is a sheet of painted plastic material which goes from pure white in the foreground to a colour at the top when mounted on the product table. Anyone who has tried to light a product from above on to a plain coloured background will know that the lower half of the pack will show a strong cast from the background roll, so you must then spend valuable time bringing in more lights or reflectors to throw white light into the affected area.

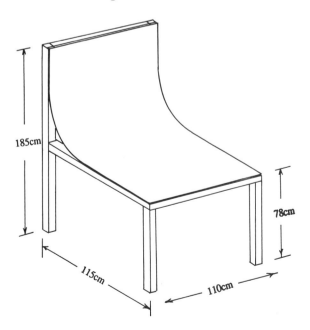

An easy "build it yourself" product table

*A product
table in use*

The graduates eliminate this problem, throwing white light up at the front, and allowing quite a lot of freedom in positioning the product. These backgrounds are available in all colours, some with grid lines for those that like that kind of thing. Every studio should have a selection – they are virtually indestructible and easily cleaned with Jif or something like it. Usually you can shoot most subjects without using reflectors, and with the main light either over the top of the subject, or – my preference – slightly behind the product, bringing in a hint of backlighting.

Sometimes you may be asked to shoot a range of products on the same tranny. The subjects could be different sized flower pots, or the same product in different colours. Use your noodle when arranging them. If they are different colours, make sure all the products receive the same intensity of light. You can turn a bright blue into a dark purple simply by placing it in shadow. If they are different sizes then make sure your arrangement shows the difference properly.

I remember being involved in an invoicing dispute between a client and a studio where a photographer had carefully arranged five different sizes of container – smallest at the front and largest at the rear. The tranny was extremely attractive and the arrangement artistic, but he had shot it with a longish lens (I think 200mm on 6x6), which resulted in the rear product looking only a little bigger than the one in front. In fact the rear container was some 12ft high and the front one just a couple of inches tall. The client complained that the shot didn't demonstrate the range of sizes correctly. I had to agree.

Another thing to watch on pack shots is the use of props. Personally, unless the client really insists, I don't use them. It is all too easy to produce confusion as to what exactly is being promoted. The only justification is if a prop is necessary to prove a particular sales point – a tiny silicon chip on a ruler or on the end of one's finger is fair game; a bowl of flowers at the back of a set of industrial grinding wheels is not. Don't laugh, I've seen it – honestly.

In pack shots, keep it simple, don't make life difficult for yourself. Try other backgrounds by all means if you want to be a little different. Metal plates, ceramic tiles, and textured glass will all give quite a variety of effects, and can all be lit easily with one softbox. If the client wants to go further in "creativity" then there are other techniques described in Chapter 8, but they all cost more money, and for a trade catalogue, are they worth the candle? Remember, the pack shot is used to inform and to show a product to its best advantage. Mood creation belongs in advertising, not the trade catalogue.

There is a great temptation when you are asked to do press release pics as well as trannies for a catalogue, just to pop some black and white film into a back and shoot using exactly the same set-up as for the transparencies. I have come to grief doing this on more than one occasion because I have forgotten that blue prints light on monochrome, and that a shiny black product against a bright red background will end up as an indistinguishable black blob on the print. Unless you are bang up to date on the way your particular film reproduces colour, then use a graduated white to grey background for black and white, and be generous on the exposure. It will be that much easier to print.

In these shots, you will find that the involvement of your client in the shooting is minimal. If the account is direct, then you will probably be dealing with the product manager or assistant, and they usually have more important things to do than sit around your studio and supervise a fairly straightforward shoot. If your client is an agency, then again, the art director for the account will simply want to approve (or specify) the backgrounds for each group of products, stay around until he/she is satisfied that you know what you are doing, and then get out of your way.

You will normally have access to a "visual". This is prepared by the agency to give the client an idea of the final result, and is also used to obtain authority to proceed with the next steps in production. It can be anything from a sketch on the back of an envelope to a beautifully prepared and coloured mock-up of the catalogue page(s).

The visual will tell you whether the pic has to be shot vertically or horizontally (portrait or landscape), how much "air" there should be around the product, whether the pic extends right to the edge of the page (a bleed), or whether it is framed. Also it should show any particular detail the designer wants included, for instance, whether the cable runs from left to right or vice versa on a telephone shot. You should also know from the visual whether the shot is to be used on a left or right hand page of the brochure. Don't ever have products looking out of a brochure – introspection is the norm.

Do not ignore implicit instructions in the visual if they are present. Many designers like total control over the photograph, and in many ways you are merely a technician converting their wishes into a transparency. Other designers favour the team approach with both parties contributing creatively. You will learn as you go on how each designer likes to work with you, and over the years a mutual understanding develops. Do not forget, however, that the designer is the boss – and unless they ask you to do something which is photographically unwise or even impossible, then you should give them what they want, or risk having to reshoot the whole thing.

I remember shooting a retail catalogue with a designer who had very firm ideas on what he wanted. I felt that the camera angle we were using was totally wrong, and I spent some time trying to explain that when the pic was reduced to two dimensions on the paper, the perspective would be a little strong. I argued at some length, proving my point with a Polaroid, but to no avail. Finally the designer turned to me and said "look, you're only here to press the button – just do it please". When I had exposed the dark slides, I turned to the designer with a smile, and told him that that comment would cost him £50 on the bill. He apologised, and yet strictly speaking he was right to insist on getting what he wanted, though the method was wrong. He paid up, and we're still friends.

Before we leave the trade catalogue illustration, there is one important technical point. Make sure that all the transparencies on a particular page match each other for colour and density. If the lighting or background roll hasn't been changed then you won't have a problem, but if there have been changes, then make sure you bracket your exposures by half stop intervals. For trade catalogues, at the colour separation stage, transparencies for a particular page are often scanned together for economy, so individual adjustments of colour or density are not possible. If you always give your designer enough bracketing to allow them to select a page of trannies that look attractive together, you will have a friend for life.

Clients also tend to be very loyal to a photographer who can handle this work quietly and efficiently. In many companies the job of producing the catalogue is a thankless task, given to a fairly junior person either on the product manager's staff or in the marketing services department. Unfortunately, the more senior people in the company don't often appreciate the vast amount of work that has to go into a production of this nature, from initial selection of the products through design, photography, typesetting and colour separations, to final printing. The result is that impossible timetables are set and your contact is often working under extreme pressure. The more quietly and quickly you get on with the job and help them out, the more likely you are to retain the account on a long term basis.

You will find that the pack shot and the press release picture form a large percentage of your studio work, and, once you have your technique standardised, will be some of the most profitable work you undertake. Many photographers specialise in this kind of work, and it definitely has its merits. Most of it is unsupervised and you can work at your own pace, providing that you do not actually waste clients' chargeable time.

Advertising

Up to now you could consider the photography we've discussed as being "internal". We have not yet addressed the final user, or the final buyer of the products we are helping to promote. The pack shot is aimed at someone still in the selling chain, a wholesaler or retailer or rep of some kind. The photography has had to help someone make a purchase decision, but the decision is one of choice – whether to stock ABC Toys Ltd's products or maybe XYZ Ltd's offerings. The decision to buy someone's toys to resell has already been made; it is up to the catalogue to demonstrate ABC Toys' superior range and quality. The end user has not yet been addressed, and photography to attract the punter on the street is a very different proposition.

Advertising photography is about creating desires, moods, comforting people who have already made brand choices, sowing doubt in those who (according to the advertiser) have made the wrong brand choice. It is the advertising agency that produces the ideas about a theme or campaign, and the photographer helps them create the images which express these ideas. Your combined offering is placed before the end user in the form of a newspaper or magazine advertisement, and you know how successful you have been by the resultant sales, particularly in the direct response type of ad.

If you regularly work with a successful agency in this field this work can be highly stimulating and rewarding. If, on the other hand, you spend time putting tacky ad pics together for the local businessman who feels that ad agencies are a waste of money, then it can be soul destroying. This is not the place to argue the case for the existence of ad agencies, but the number of smart, intelligent businessmen who will employ expert help in all other areas, but feel they can handle their own advertising, never fails to amaze me.

Local newspapers also frequently offer to "put something together for nothing", and that is about what the end result is worth. The newspaper or magazine collects its several hundred pounds space fee, but the resultant ad has about as much client appeal as the local church gazette small ads produced on Fred's old spirit duplicator.

Art direction

Recently I was renewing my car insurance and was shopping around, as my normal broker was being particularly unsympathetic about the loading on the premium because my car was a "turbo", despite the fact that the "turbo" was connected to a diesel engine.

Not getting anywhere with him, I popped next door to a new broker who had just set up in town. The offices were well designed, the staff courteous and well trained, the computer installation looked as though it had been installed by an expert, but the shop was empty. My insurance problem was sorted in very short order (without a loaded premium), and whilst my lady wife was writing the man a cheque, I noticed, proudly displayed on the wall, quite the worst set of newspaper ads I have seen for a long time. Complete with pointing fingers and a multiplicity of typefaces, they looked like the first efforts of novice art students learning how to use a process camera.

When I gently suggested that maybe the company could do with a change of ad agency, the salesman confided to me in very hushed tones that "the boss" did all the ads himself – he didn't like to waste money on agencies. When I replied that his company seemed to have everything going for it – pleasant environment, skilled staff, up-market image – and that some good advertising would bring the volume of work they so desperately needed, I was greeted with a shrug of the shoulders. "You won't convince him", I was told.

On the other hand, a designer came to my studio with a brief he had obtained for the opening of a new store selling leather furniture. Instead of the standard top-lit shot of a sofa in the middle of a carpet that everybody uses, he wanted to sell the "feel" of soft leather, create an almost sexual desire to possess and touch it. The client had been difficult to persuade to place even a couple of column inches in the local rag, yet here the designer was putting together a creative ad with expensive photography, including a model.

The designer knew exactly what he wanted. Only half the sofa should show, with the most attractive pair of legs we could find, sideways on, complete with satin tights. The bottom three inches of a pleated skirt showed, the pleats being held together with double-sided tape. Shiny leather shoes, a piece of soft carpet and a totally black background completed the pic. The copy ran "Leather: natural, sensual and warm". The sexual overtones were obvious, and yet it was done in exquisite taste.

The advertisement ran full page in black and white on the Thursday and Friday evenings immediately before the shop opening. The client was horrified with the bill, but only until one hour after the shop had opened. That exercise so convinced him of the value of good advertising that he now runs one of the most successful ad agencies in the area, in partnership with the designer of the ad!

This demonstrates the difference between photography to inform and photography to persuade. Unfortunately, there are still a number of people around who do not know the difference, and some of them work in the ad creation business. A good advertising photograph does not have to show the product clearly; in fact many do not show the product at all.

I have been privileged to work alongside some incredibly skilful people in the ad business, and the converse, some inept designers who really should stick to pasting up text for magazine pages. Thinking of a theme for a series of advertisements is a marketing skill, designing the ads themselves is a graphic design skill, and the two qualities don't necessarily go together. Occasionally they do, and when that happens, photography for advertising is stimulating. You take the rough with the smooth, the good with the bad, but remember, too many bad 'uns don't do your portfolio any good.

Before we leave these examples and look at how an advertising shoot is put together, we'll look at one more ad in the furniture business. The client was a French manufacturer of quality furniture. The theme developed by the agency was the longevity of style and quality of the workmanship, such that the furniture, although wickedly expensive, would last for generation after generation. It was a short step from there to develop a picture idea of a little girl visiting grandparents. Because of the French origins of the furniture, the stylist gave the little girl's clothes a Gallic style.

The only props were a lamp and a bowl of plastic grapes. The little girl sat on a chair, with just the edge of a dining table lit. The first black and white ad worked tremendously, and later the campaign was run in colour in the "quality" general interest magazines. I still prefer the original mono pic, which is described in Appendix A.

Any similarity in style detected here between this pic and the

LEATHER.

NATURAL, SENSUAL & WARM.

Into-Leather brings leather furnishing into a new-day of
style. a dawning of colour and comfort chosen
from the most imaginative of Europe's designer-
craftsmen. In our studio you'll find a friendly
word on hand to advise on the right grade
of leather, the care of furnishings and even
the advantages of our interest free credit — all from people
who care about you and leather.
Into-Leather. A warm welcome to a leather alternative.

now OPEN

into-Leather

Market St., Whittlesey. (0733) 202600   LEATHER FOR LIVING

HANDMADE LUXURIOUS SUITES FROM £995.00

- 60 DIFFERENT DESIGNS
- 50 STRIKING COLOURS
- IN 5 GRADES OF LEATHER
- 12 MONTHS INTEREST FREE CREDIT
  0% APR. Written details on request.
- 2-SEATERS FROM £415
- from houseproud

"Legs". I believe that a good monochrome picture will beat a good colour one every time

"legs" shot is totally intentional; they were both designed by the same art director.

A skilled art director, experienced in supervising photography, is a godsend on an advertising shoot. They are the "master of ceremonies" so to speak, whilst you interpret their ideas and sketches, and produce the transparency. It is your job to make it happen.

120

The advertising shoot

Your first contact with the agency will be when the art director is firming up their ideas for the shot or shots. Usually they will ask if a particular effect can be obtained easily, and what would be involved timewise and costwise to produce it. Once they know that these vague ideas are feasible they will come back with more concrete ideas and proposals, and maybe a visual of sorts, although at this stage it is probably still on the back of a fag packet.

It is at this point that you commit yourself to doing the photography, and to a rough budget of costs. Here many photographers make enormous mistakes, both in their estimates of how long the thing will take and about what is possible and what isn't. I personally know of no more soulless occupation than to go through a couple of days' photography knowing that I have goofed in the estimate and will probably lose money on the job.

Taking the cost factor first, don't be afraid to quote what you really are comfortable with. If you feel that you would like half a day to try out a new technique before the actual shoot, then build it in. No agency is going to expect you to know everything, or to have tried everything. If a special lens or format would suit the project, then build in the cost of renting gear in addition to your normal day rate. Don't forget that you will probably have to build a special set for the shot and take it down again afterwards. Quote for the labour and materials cost in set building, plus a fee for tying up the studio while the set is built and struck afterwards. I use half the normal hourly rate for this. (A tame chippie is a godsend for a photo studio, and fortunately most of us know one.)

If models are going to be involved, then make sure you are quoting from their latest rates, and don't forget travel expenses and the time fee whilst travelling.

Finally, don't forget film and processing costs, including Polaroids. Use the little estimating form in Chapter 4; it is a useful checklist. When you have totted everything up, build in a small contingency, and tell the agency you have done so. Don't worry about the final amount; remember a full page colour ad in one of the quality home interest magazines can cost from a couple of thousand pounds up to five times that amount and more, per insertion. The chances are that there will be multiple insertions in several different magazines. Make sure you cover everything, and then let the agency know your figure. They can then build your estimate into their quote to the client.

In addition to the estimate of cost, you have to make sure that you can really come up with the goods photographically. Most designers take a short course in photography during their training, but this is one area where a little knowledge can be dangerous. Make sure that what is being asked of you is possible. Some designers believe that a monorail camera can make everything sharp in three dimensions at once, and that you can alter perspective at the same time. If your art director is asking you to alter the laws of physics, then tell them so – they'll respect you for it. Try, however, to suggest an alternative that is possible and that comes close to their original idea. Make sure that when you have finished the "technical" discussion, you both know what you are going to produce.

Sometimes, you will be asked to do something which is "borderline" technically. However, as long as you point out the hazards, there is no reason why you should not go to, and beyond, the limits of film and equipment.

One case in point is the contrast range permissible on a piece of transparency film for repro. All the textbooks advise that a certain lighting ratio must not be exceeded if the film is to register all detail in both highlights and shadows, and the figure of 1:32 or five stops is given. Some repro houses go further and reckon that 1:5 or two and a half stops is all that they can handle. I personally feel that placing a restriction of that nature on the lighting, whilst OK for the pack shot, is unacceptable when a specific effect is being sought. Reducing the lighting contrast to 1:5 would certainly (for me at any rate) produce flat, lifeless pictures, although some would say technically perfect.

Providing you warn the art director that detail will be lost in the shadows or highlights, and they understand what is going to happen, go ahead and light it the way you want. I have overexposed bits of trannies substantially when a specific effect has been needed, and left dark areas totally obscure when that has been needed too. If the repro house moans, then no-one said it was going to be easy for them either.

When you both are agreed on the shot, the art director will go away and produce the agency's quote for the client. Occasionally, if a special effect is being sought, they may commission a trial shoot in order to judge for themselves whether they want to go further with the idea, and sometimes to give the client an idea of the effect in question. You can add the cost of this trial shoot to the final invoice, though I always try to keep the charge down for this kind of work.

Be prepared for a little wait. Clients don't seem to like giving the go-ahead on advertising shoots until about a week before press date. Most agencies don't finalise the design of an ad until they have the tranny, or at least a Polaroid. They then need a few days to complete design, obtain separations and Cromalins (more about that later), finalise copy, and have everything approved by the client before sending it all off to the magazines. When you get the go-ahead, you may have no more than a couple of days' notice to organise the whole thing.

The most important thing to remember is that your most precious commodity is time. Use motorbikes, couriers – anything that will save you an hour or two. If models are required, and the agency asks you to book them, then make sure the comp cards you have are up to date, or have the latest ones couriered to you if not. A couple of years may make quite a difference to that sweet little girl you have chosen. Make sure the client is happy with your choice of model before booking. Again, bike comp cards round the country if necessary. *Don't* put them in the post.

Make sure you have the right backgrounds available if you use them, and (don't smile) make sure you have enough film in the fridge.

Generally, the art director will leave the choice of format and film to you, and the golden rule here is to use the largest format that is practical under the circumstances. Advertising still-life shots should always be taken on sheet film, and if the subject contains a large area of plain tone then you should consider hiring or borrowing 10x8in equipment. Typical subjects for this treatment would be glasses of wine or beer, food and flowers. You would not normally shoot children or pets on sheet film, although I was once forced into it. Shots with models are usually better handled on the roll film reflex.

As far as film is concerned, a slow 100 ISO daylight reversal stock should be your choice. I find that my clients like the colour of Fuji RDP stock, although I personally think it comes on a bit strong at times and prefer Kodak EPN. It is your choice, however.

When the great day comes, make sure everything is organised. If models are travelling by rail, have a taxi at the station to collect them – you don't want them wandering around the countryside looking for a wrongly understood address. Ensure there is enough car parking for the client, the art director, an assistant. Phone your local courier company and warn them they may have to go and buy a piece of ribbon or a roll of double-sided tape that someone "forgot". Have the coffee pot full.

Usually, the client will be present during the shoot, at least part of the time, and this can be as much a good thing as a bad one. A client used to commissioning advertising will generally just ensure that the shoot is proceeding according to the approved ideas, usually, but not always, represented by the visual. If a minor modification has to be made for practical reasons, then it is handy to have the client on hand to approve it.

On the other hand some clients may take an active part in the shoot, even to the point of interference, on the spur of the moment altering decisions taken weeks before. If this happens, leave the client in the hands of the art director; don't enter the discussion. The art director knows the client, and is quite able to defend his position without any assistance from you. If the client wants substantial changes, it will usually mean a reshoot, and the ad agency is best at renegotiating the fee.

The retail brochure

It is difficult to categorise photography for retail catalogues. The obvious first requirement is to show the product clearly. But there can also be a requirement, additional to the pack shot approach, to put the product in context – a selection of garden accessories spread out on a lawn on location, or a collection of household utensils with a kitchen background.

From the photographer's point of view the disciplines are very similar to advertising photography. Most shoots are art-directed, and many involve models, and much that has been said regarding the actual production of advertising photography can be applied to this field. However, because the theme in these pics is much looser, there is more room for the photographer to add his own two-penn'orth of creative ideas.

The shoots tend to be longer, and require more organisation than the two or three pic advertising shoots already described, especially if a client's entire product line is going to be photographed. You will require a large area to store products, and need to make sure you know what you have shot and what has yet to be dealt with. Other than this, if you can handle the logistics of most ad shoots, you should have no problems with shooting the average catalogue.

Before we leave studio photography to move on to location work, there is one point that should be made. For most clients these sessions in the studio photographing this year's products or this month's ads, whilst certainly a change of scene, are not great moments of excitement. To a few others, however, it is like entering a great new fantasy world, and occasionally people can forget themselves and be silly (especially when models wearing very little are involved).

The "air hostess" approach of making light of it usually works here, but occasionally things can get out of hand. Your loyalty at that point is to the model and not the client, and you have to be firm, sometimes to the point of clearing the studio of non-essential people. Remember, you are not running a soft-porn show, and if you allow a model to be embarrassed in your studio, you will find it very difficult to book through that agency in future.

Location work

You can be asked to work out of your studio environment for a variety of reasons – clothing catalogue shots are usually taken outdoors these days; businessmen may want interior shots of their offices and factories; sometimes products cannot be taken off premises and pack shots have to be taken in a corner of the ware-house.

However, most of your location work requests will be for PR work. When I was on the other side of the fence, public relations work was a very serious business, vying for importance with the advertising budget. Public relations is the art of polishing a company's image in the environment, making it look like a good citizen, competent in it's operations, the ideal choice of company "to do business with". Good photography plays a tremendous part in a public relations campaign, showing tasteful architecture, clean, efficient assembly lines, and a content and efficient workforce. Good PR can put a company on the map and create market leader-ship as fast as any other marketing tool.

Why then, do most people regard PR photography as no more than the "grip and grin" award presentation pics for the local rag? It seems, also, that to be a PR "consultant" all you have to do is write the occasional press release, get some form of picture taken (the cheaper the better), mail them off to magazines and newspa-pers, and present the unfortunate client with a huge bill.

True PR photography is handled in much the same way as an advertising shoot. An agency will have planned a campaign, and will wish to discuss set-up shots to be taken in the factory, in the offices, perhaps even in the premises of their client's customers. Each shot will be planned, and you will be expected to take the same care creatively and technically as you would with an advertis-ing shoot in the studio. Equipment needs, however, are different.

You will need a wide-angle roll film facility, and portable monobloc flash units, with two or three heads and at least 500 joules per head. A good, solid tripod like the Manfrotto Tri-aut will keep you firmly on the ground.

The main skill you will need to acquire is that of balancing flash with ambient light, the secret being to keep the flash discreet. Bleached-out faces and dark backgrounds are not the sign of a pro-fessional commercial photographer, and are quite easily avoided if you use the "analyse" facility of the Minolta Flashmeter 4. Balance your lights so that the flash intensity is at least one stop down, and do a check with Polaroids every time. If you find that exposure times start to extend, and you are into reciprocity failure problems, then light the furthest wall away from you, either with some more flash, or a couple of quartz floods, either with or without daylight filters. It is surprising just how much a light wall at the end bright-ens up a dull shot, even if it is lit with unfiltered tungsten light.

In PR photography always try to place an effective symbol, rel-evant to the client's business, in the picture, and have the people in the shot actively involved in doing something. For example, if the shot is of a new instrument being used in a lab in an oil refinery, make sure someone is operating the instrument correctly, with background views of the refinery visible out of a window behind them.

Above all, take your time and look at the background. Remove anything which is untidy or that could confuse. If the shot is going to be used prominently, or in an annual report, suggest that you use a professional model instead of Fred in his lab coat. Treat the shot as seriously as you would the most prestigious advertising photograph. Good PR photography should be a long way away from the flash-on-camera grip and grin shot.

Other location work follows the principles laid down for studio photography. Clothing is one major subject that readily lends itself to the "outdoor" treatment, and sports and leisurewear catalogues are now usually shot outside. However, do try to plan the shoot with the agency beforehand.

When you have selected the location, find out where the sun will be through the day, and plan each shot accordingly. Move around – don't take every photo straight into the sun with fill flash; it is an interesting technique but very easily overdone. Remember to "warm up" shots taken in the shade with 81 series filters. Take some side-lit shots without reflectors, and let the shadows go. Make the photography a little bit different – your client will like it and re-book you.

And finally, if it is pouring with rain, go ahead and shoot it anyway. You will be surprised what Fuji film and rotten weather can produce. My last (at the time of writing) clothing shoot took place in near blizzard conditions in Covent Garden; the pics certainly were different ...

ADVANCED TECHNIQUES

When you do a lot of work for one client, the standard treatment for pack shots can start to pall. The client begins to make tactful remarks like "I saw a really different pic in so and so's catalogue the other day...". I would not recommend playing around with the techniques in this chapter for the odd catalogue illustration, but when you are doing hundreds or even thousands of illustrations for one client over a year or so, you have to look further than the graduated backdrop.

Problems arise when you have to build repeatability into the set. If you have a client with a large trade catalogue, you will be taking pics throughout the year to slot in with those taken maybe a year or so before. A pic taken on a Colorshade white/red sheet No.3 in January will look the same as a pic taken on the same sheet in July. When you leave this standard set-up, you must make sure you can repeat the transparency at any time.

If you are going to try some "wild" effects, make sure you make very copious notes on the set, and a Polaroid of the set itself is useful. Hang on to one of the original trannies if you can. It can prevent unpleasant arguments in the future: "you know George, I'm sure that colour was richer before ..."

Having given that important caveat, there is another. How you improve a transparency's impact depends a lot on the end use of the picture. In advertising photography, the sky really is the limit, and you, and the art director, can give full rein to your wildest ideas. But in brochure photography, you have to keep your feet on the ground. Remember that at the end of the day the product has to be recognisable. This is especially important in mail order catalogues; the end customer is making a purchase decision based on your photograph. You will get few good marks if the product returns rate is high because "it isn't like the picture".

Taking brochure photography first then, how do we make our pics that little bit different?

I like to think of a picture being made up of three variables – lighting, set and background. When we use a product table with a Colorshade background roll and a softbox, we give ourselves little room to manoeuvre. We could move the light source forward or back, we can position the product forward or behind the point where the colour changes to white, but our options are limited. We have defined lighting, set and background. For straight pack shots, this formula has the distinct advantage of simplicity, speed of operation and repeatability. But when we want to be a little more "creative", we must think in terms of lighting, set and background separately.

Lighting

The first variable is lighting, and here, contrary to the opinions of many, I don't think you have a great deal of scope for really "different" shots.

There are a number of clichés, such as honeycombed heads fitted with colour gels, usually combined with a black background, a treatment often used for hi-tech products such as hi-fi equipment. Another is lighting the set through a scrim fitted with black card cut in the shape of a casement window or leaves and branches, usually used for homely products such as wine or cheese.

Don't ignore these techniques – everyone uses them – and you will be expected to be able to set them up on demand. I still maintain, however, that if you really want something different, you have to look at the set or the background first, and adjust the lighting to give whatever effect you are seeking.

The set

Moving on to the set, this can be anything from a plain Colorama roll to bottom-lit Perspex using colour filters. The set is the support for the product, and it is a good idea to replace the hardboard support on the product table with either a piece of 6mm plate glass or 5mm opal Perspex sheet. This will allow you to bottom-light the set easily, and in the case of the Perspex you will be able to curve the sheet upwards, providing a scoop.

If the products you photograph are heavy (like car batteries for instance) make sure your support is adequate, or brace the support from underneath. If the brace is directly under the product, you won't see it on the finished tranny.

You can achieve even, intense lighting under a translucent sheet by lining the base of the product table with two inch polystyrene insulating board. This creates a giant light-mixing box which you can light from behind using a standard flash head. If you build the set like the sketch below, by using two filters on the flash reflector, you can create bottom lighting of one colour whilst providing a back-lit background of another, with the two colours merging.

An interesting technique using bottom-lit Perspex starts off with the set above, using coloured light under the panel. The

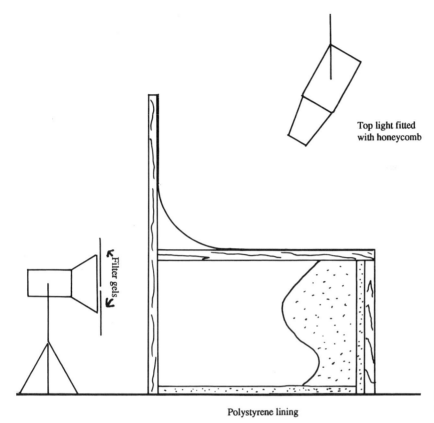

Top light fitted
with honeycomb

Filter gels

Polystyrene lining

*Studio fixture for
"bottom" lighting*

product is then lit from above using a spot or honeycombed flash. This gives a circle of white light around the product alone. The resultant tranny shows the product against a deeply saturated colour background, and the top lighting shows the brilliance of the pack printing to great advantage. The contrast of the top white light to the bottom coloured light makes the pack look clean and bright. Also, there is no colour spilling into the white areas of the product as you would have if you simply positioned the product on a sheet of coloured paper.

This basic set is very versatile. By replacing the Perspex above with plate glass (remember, *always* have the edges ground and polished; fingers come off very easily otherwise), you can introduce a grid pattern using card strips. A packaging shot using this technique, which is easy to set up, is described in the "examples" section later on.

Take a base plate of glass, then a coloured foil, then strips of coloured card, finishing off with a piece of glass on top. You can now place your product on a two-colour set, but with the intensity of each of the colours variable. If you wish, you can replace the strips with a sheet of card with holes punched in it. The card colour will lighten with the overhead product lighting, and the "grid"

Pack shot using bottom lit technique

colour will vary with the power of the bottom flash.

You can use this technique with any background treatment you fancy. But be prepared to spend a lot on Polaroids balancing up the lighting; there is a lot of trial and error in getting it right.

The copy stand set-up

If you have invested in a good, tall camera stand, you can use this set to give two-dimensional objects a bit of a "lift". The standard technique for photographing flat copy is to tape a piece of graduated background to the copy stand easel, light it from both sides, and shoot away. Great for simple pack shots, but often, if the client wants something different, he doesn't get it.

Rest the copy on a sheet of glass. Light it from either side as if it were a copy stand easel, and position the camera over the set. Then, add a creative background under the glass. Crumple some kitchen foil and light it with a filtered flash head. Keep it slightly out of focus (you can control depth of field by moving the back-

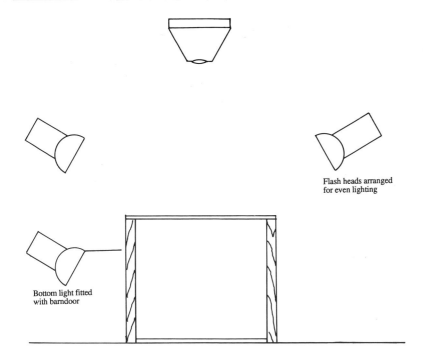

Flash heads arranged
for even lighting

Bottom light fitted
with barndoor

*Studio fixture for
"copystand"
lighting*

ground up and down as well as with the lens). You are now starting to give the client something a little different.

Another starting point for experiment is to cover the glass with black paper and punch a few small holes in it. Place little bits of coloured gel behind the holes, and pop a star filter on the lens. You could replace the black paper with a dark midnight blue foil, and have a night sky with twinkling stars.

You can also use the standard table as a support for the product in front of a standard background. A simple Colorshade sheet hung vertically behind the table and lit from below can give a very attractive background, especially if the surface under the product is fairly neutral. Standard matt laminates are easily obtained, and you can improve the lustre by giving it a quick going over with furniture polish.

Glass can be useful, but be careful with mirrors. The standard mirror gives a double reflection, one from the surface of the glass, another from the reflective coating under the glass, and I find the result disturbing. If you need the "hard" reflection you get from a mirror, then you can buy a mirror with the reflective coating on the top surface, but they are not cheap, and the coating is fragile.

Black and white backgrounds

Before we leave the set – or what we put the things on – there are two other little tricks of the trade which are handy to know.

If you use the bottom-lit Perspex surface as is, and simply

place the product on top, then you get an excellent "white-out" shot, with the product appearing to float in space. This technique is excellent for black and white product shots for magazine press releases. I find that when many monochrome prints are reproduced, unless the prints are screened with skill, the background comes out as a most unappealing, dirty grey tone. We can also help things along by producing no tone at all in the background of our prints, and this technique certainly helps.

The opposite of this technique is to shoot on black velvet to enhance the colour of a product. I like black backgrounds. The problem with them is that they often come out a horrible dark blue/green colour on transparency film. So I use genuine black velvet. It costs a small fortune, but it is the only kind that works.

Velvet has a "grain", so make sure the matt side is towards you. Brush the velvet towards the camera, and light any way you choose. Underexpose the film by a half or one stop, and push the processing by at least one stop. This increases the contrast so that you get a deep, dense black, equal to the film's maximum "Dmax". You have to experiment a little, and sometimes you will get a colour shift towards the yellow as you push process. A 2.5cc or 5cc gelatine filter in front of the lens will usually bring things back to normal. I bracket exposures around half a stop underexposure, and push the E6 by one whole stop. I then get gorgeous blacks, especially on Fuji film.

One practical advantage of this technique is that a designer can drop reversed-out text straight on to the tranny, if you have left enough room. They save money in repro costs, and this is one more reason why they will prefer to come to you again in the future. We will take a look at repro techniques and problems in Chapter 10.

I try to make life as easy as possible for my clients. If it involves extra work, then charge for it, but a little understanding of their problems, as well as their wishes, will be seen as a gift beyond measure, well worth the extra cost of dealing with you.

Front projection

Any discussion of backgrounds always includes a heated debate on front projection techniques. Front pro seems to have periods of popularity followed by a couple of years of derision in the trade. It is then rediscovered, with every dealer in the land offering a special "new" package.

I am a great believer in front projection as a creative tool, but it needs to be fully understood. You really do need to know what is going on, and to be in control of the situation. Many of the problems associated with front projection arise from a lack of appreciation of how the thing works, and what can upset it.

Many photographers still have painfully fresh memories of a recent period of intense activity in the front projection field. Portrait studios were being sold underpowered units at high prices, with the promise of high profits. Clients, it was claimed, would pay premium prices for pics of themselves relaxing in front of the Eiffel Tower or the Pyramids. But this kind of thing always looks false and contrived. The clients, far from viewing it as a premium service, regarded it as "trick" photography, and were not prepared to pay much for it.

If the exercise had any value, it was to confirm the continuing market for high quality, "straight" portraiture in the eyes of the high street punter, and the latest generation of front pro units designed for the social photographer do take account of this. These units are capable of producing softly lit portraiture using believable domestic backgrounds. They are, however, outside the scope of this book.

Front pro is not a replacement for a Colorama roll, but should be viewed as an integral part of the creation of a good commercial photograph. To do this, you must know how it works.

If you get a projector, focus an image on a standard projection screen, then place an object between the screen and the projector, you will see an image of the slide reflected from the object as well as from the screen. Many creative pics have been put together using this technique, which relies on the fact that a model's tummy will reflect a 35mm slide almost as well as a normal projection screen.

If you now replace the projection screen with a high efficiency glass-beaded cine screen, you will see that the image reflected by the screen is much brighter than before, whilst the reflection on the model's anatomy remains the same. In fact, it appears less bright because the eye compensates for the increased brightness of the screen. If now you imagine that you could have a screen much brighter than the cine screen, then you would get to the point where the screen image was so brilliant that you would not see the image on the model at all. This is the principle front projection uses.

A front projection screen has a reflectivity so high that it exceeds any normal subject, producing an image several hundred times as bright as the one on our model's torso, or on any other object for that matter. It therefore follows that if you photograph anything sitting in front of an illuminated front pro screen, it will appear as a silhouette until it is lit separately.

The front pro screen is a very special piece of equipment, and is certainly not cheap. It consists of a metallised coating containing microscopic glass prisms on a black paper or plastic base. Normally, the projector used to produce the screen image is at right angles to it, and the reflectivity of the screen falls off as you move

The Hensel Vario Compact 3 front pro unit

from side to side. However, the high performance of the screen is such that any stray light falling on it from the side will degrade the projected image substantially, and this limits what you can and cannot do with the subject lighting. Once you understand this fully, you should have no problem with front pro.

Some workers with front pro use black curtains or screens to keep the product lighting off the screen surface. I have never found these totally effective, but it is worthwhile having a couple of 8x4ft

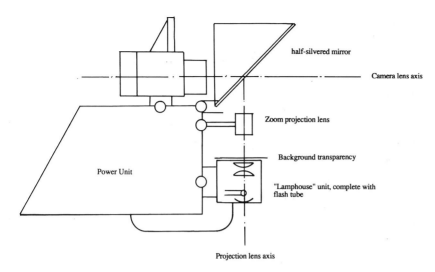

half-silvered mirror

Camera lens axis

Zoom projection lens

Background transparency

Power Unit

"Lamphouse" unit, complete with flash tube

Projection lens axis

Front pro unit diagram

panels painted black to move around the set in some shots. Also, there is a technique using black net (looks like ladies' tights material) in front of the screen. In conjunction with the right type of screen this can be useful, but it is a technique more suited to the portrait studio. Our application is best served with the standard screen without any additions.

Before we look at practical applications, lets look at a typical front pro unit, as illustrated below.

The unit shown is the Hensel Vario-compact 3 unit, primarily designed for roll film cameras. I personally use the larger Super Compact 2 unit as it is more suitable for use with sheet film, but both units are very similar. The unit allows a camera to combine the image from the projection screen on to the image of an object placed between the camera and the screen.

The camera is mounted on a rigid rail on top of the unit, and looks at the screen through a half-silvered mirror placed exactly at 45 degrees to the optical axis of the camera lens. Under the camera there is an electronic flash power pack which feeds the flash head, mounted under the mirror. This head uses a small flash tube/modelling lamp combination in an arrangement very similar to the normal slide projector lamp/condenser assembly. On top of this head is a slide carrier that holds the transparency used for the background, either 35mm or 6x6cm. The projection lens sits between the slide and the mirror, and is usually a fairly high quality zoom projector lens that covers the 6x6cm format.

This assembly needs to be adjusted so that the axis of the projection lens is exactly superimposed on the axis of the camera lens. The Hensel unit has a spot in the centre of the projection lens, making alignment a five minute job. This alignment procedure

assumes that the camera lens iris when closed down is exactly con-
centric with the lens axis itself. Some workers have had lenses
modified to ensure this, but I don't bother – I have had no problems
with the Bronica, Mamiya or Schneider lenses I have used, and I
frankly doubt whether going to such lengths is necessary.

However, you do need to think carefully about the focal length
of the camera lens you use. If the projected image on the screen
needs the projection lens at the long end of its zoom, then a wide
lens on the camera will cover more than the image on the screen.
Similarly, if you are showing all of a 6x6cm slide with a wide
setting on the projection lens, then a longish lens on the camera
will only show part of the screen image.

A little common sense is all that is needed, but I find that a
slightly longer than standard lens on the camera is best. On the
RB67, the 127mm lens fits beautifully, as does the 105mm Zen-
zanon on the Bronnie SQA. On 5x4in, a 180mm or 210mm fits best,
and on the rare occasions when I have used 8x10in on front pro,
the 360mm Symmar worked well.

Once you have made the format/lens choice (most of my work is
done with an RB67/127mm combination), you need to have a
Polaroid back handy. No-one has yet calibrated a flashmeter to
work with the average front pro screen, and using Polaroids is the
only way I know of getting the screen/object lighting ratio right.

We will leave the technical aspects for a little while and think
about what you can do with this wonderful tool.

Using front pro

When you receive your brand new front pro unit, you will probably
find a set of standard slides for "backgrounds". These are good for
experimenting, and useful for the simpler catalogue shots. To
exploit the unit properly though, you need to produce background
slides specifically for each shot. Let's look at two examples of how
this can be done in practice.

One of the most useful props you can make for yourself is a
glass product support. This is a piece of 4mm float glass about 3ft
square, fixed in a frame between two uprights in a "swing" mount
similar to a dressing table mirror. You can then glue or Blu-tack
products to this piece of glass, swing it slightly to remove reflections, and shoot the background through it. The background slide
can then be shot to complement the main product, and the subject
and background combined using the front pro unit.

Our first example used this fixture to produce a shot for the
front cover of an instrument company's brochure. This client was
"direct"; there was no agency between him and myself. Previous
covers had always featured piles of electronic equipment on a
blue Colorama roll, and I wanted to offer him something a little

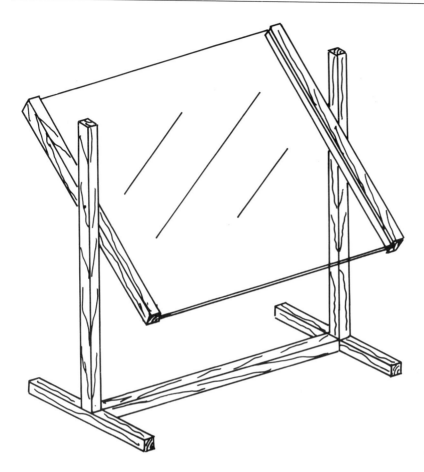

*Front pro
product fixture*

different. I asked not to be briefed on the shot, but to submit a tranny for his approval.

After establishing that one of his company's strengths was in circuit board production, I borrowed some completed circuit boards to find an "interesting" one. When I did, I shot the reverse of the board on 6x6cm using the copy stand to produce the background slide.

Then I mounted the board on my "dressing table" sheet of float glass with plenty of Blu-tack, and lit it from above with a Bowens Mistylite. To stop light from the softbox spilling onto the screen, I hung a foot or so of black paper behind the light using those incredibly useful double clips that Bowens sell for a fiver. I kept the screen about six feet behind the product, and balanced up both light sources.

By varying the background focus simply by de-focusing the slide with the projection lens, I produced a selection of trannies for the client's approval. The camera used was a Bronica SQA fitted with a 150mm lens.

The second example comes under the heading of "standard

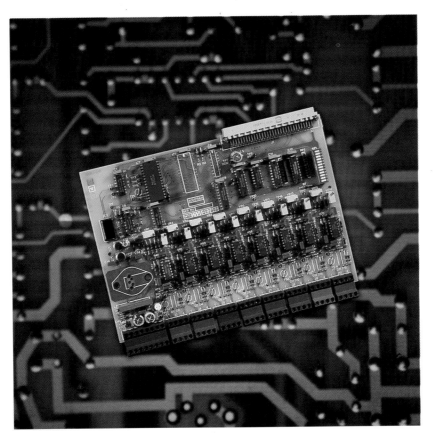

Front pro circuit board shot using fixture

background" shots, and describes the production of a series of brochure pics, taken to a definite budget.

One of the advantages of front pro is that you can easily lift a product shot away from the "graduated backdrop" type of pic into something much more interesting. You may not use the creative possibilities fully, but if the client is pleased with both the results and the bill, then we have done our work well.

In this case the products were quite intricate alloy and steel castings. Previously we had done quite a complex front pro pic for this client on 5x4, but this time he wanted some simple A4 brochure pages – interesting, but low cost. Both his agency and myself jointly came up with the idea of shooting his product against simple geometric grids on a black background. The product would sit on the same piece of boilerplate we had used for the complex shot.

The designer went away and produced a series of grids drawn on art board. I photographed these on the copy camera on 5x4in lith film, but with an image size of 2in square for the Hensel unit. These were processed and mounted in a 6x6cm glass slide mount along with yellow, red and blue coloured foils. (I have never yet succeeded in producing a lith neg that hasn't got the measles, no matter what dev I try, but spotting was kept to a minimum for cost reasons.)

These backgrounds were then put in the front projection unit, the projection lens set for image size and focus, and the camera/subject distance fixed.

At this point, the first limiting factor for front pro has to be considered, and that is power. In this particular set up, the background needed to be sharp. Physically, it was difficult to get the product less than about five feet away from the screen. Also, if I were any closer than that, it would have been difficult to light the product without light spilling onto the front pro screen. Any such spill would have resulted in a nasty grey background instead of a dense black. The lighting arrangement is shown below:

The product lighting consisted of two Quadmatic heads fitted with louvres and barn doors to contain light spillage. One was fitted with a coloured gel filter. The depth of field requirements meant shooting at at least f22 on the Mamiya 127mm lens on 100 ISO film. This meant that the Hensel was at about three-quarter power, and the Quads were running at about 500 joules each. The balance was set up with Polaroid type 669 film.

This example shows how important it is to have a front pro unit with adequate power. Light spillage from the product lighting means that you have to move the subject away from the screen. The more you move it away, the more depth of field you need in

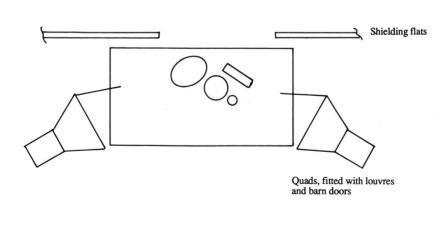

Front pro screen

"Castings" studio set-up

Shielding flats

Quads, fitted with louvres and barn doors

Front pro unit

"Castings"
transparency

order to keep the background sharp. The more depth of field required the smaller the stop. The smaller the stop, the more power you need in the front pro unit.

Before we bought our Hensel unit, we had other units demonstrated in our studio. The common fault with almost all of them was that they were underpowered. By the time I had the set right, I needed about f16 on the camera lens, but the front pro unit needed f8 or f11. One much vaunted unit gave up the ghost at f5.6. It has since ceased production. However, back to our castings.

We had everything working right by about 10.00 a.m. on the day of the shoot, when our client arrived with a truckload of castings. We shot no less than forty odd products in about sixteen groups, making sure that the filtered Quad had the complementary colour of the background slide – yellow with blue, cyan with red, magenta with green.

We finished at about four in the afternoon, and, for a price not too much more than standard pack shots, a delighted client went away with some quite snappy trannies, even if you could see the designer's slips with the pen, and the odd spot or two.

Front pro technique is excellent for shooting engineering products. Other examples might be water company products shot against a reservoir, or oil industry safety equipment taken against the refinery "flare".

It's useful for other subjects too. We once shot the pack of a football game using an action soccer picture as background. You just have to think a little. If your design agency clients know what you can do with this gear, they will have as many ideas as you. Imagination is a great thing in this business.

Is it worth it?

Before we leave this section, a word will not go amiss on the subject of money. It is very easy with techniques like front pro to waste incredible amounts of time and film. If you are happy to increase your own knowledge at your own expense, using a customer's requirement, all well and good. It is possible, however, to spend days producing something that your client positively dislikes, and end up with no pay for much work.

With front pro, and indeed most kinds of experimental photography, you must make some arrangement about fees before you start. Most ad agencies will be quite happy to fund a day or so of fooling around if there is a reasonable chance of getting something useful at the end of it. My guide is that I will ask for funding for experiments if I believe the exercise is worthwhile. But if I think it is really a waste of time then I dissuade the agency from thinking along those lines. To be worthwhile, an experimental shoot should at least produce a good idea for a shot (supported by a Polaroid or two).

LABORATORY SERVICES

In this chapter we'll look in the darkroom, and at some additional services that your studio should be able to offer.

Whilst your first mission is to operate a photographic studio, a fair percentage of your income can come from selling lab services. You need to have black and white and E6 services in-house to be able to respond well to your market in the first place. You may as well then use the investment you have made in enlargers and other laboratory equipment to offer other facilities to your clients. These can include duplicate transparencies, internegatives and copying services. Another good opportunity for additional profits is in mounting and lamination, so we'll take a look at that too.

Black and white

Whenever photographers get together, the subject of black and white always comes up. Many clients feel that monochrome should be cheaper than colour, and yet of course the reverse is true. But if they can get colour "done" at Boots in an hour, then why does it take so long for black and white? Why does it cost so much?

I have failed to convince really intelligent men that mono is done by hand, whereas runs of colour 5x7s are done automatically. Sloshing around in dishes or feeding individual sheets into a processor takes a lot longer than pressing a button and walking away. Yet every time I quote for a PR run of black and whites I get the feeling that my client really thinks he is being taken for a ride.

There is also another problem with monochrome. E6 processing has to be done in-house because the trannies are usually wanted in a hurry. With B&W there are normally a couple of days grace, time enough in theory to send the whole job to a pro lab. Unfortunately, results from most labs tend to be disappointing.

If you think about it though, it is fairly obvious that this should be so. There are lots of different combinations of emulsions and developers around. Most labs have a standard black and white processing procedure, "ten minutes in D76" being typical, and the chances are against this being optimum for your particular requirements. You will therefore start off with a non-ideal negative. Couple this with the fact that what pleases their printer as a monochrome print may not be what you are trying to achieve, and you have a recipe for disaster.

That this situation should prevail is as much the fault of photographers as anyone else. Black and white prints are usually used as press release product shots for magazines, and the "anything will do" attitude is common. The usual excuse for supplying rubbish tends to be that as the standards of screening halftones are so bad in many magazines, there is no point in producing a quality print.

In my opinion, that is all the more reason for taking care. Because the repro quality can be so bad we should do our utmost to produce prints that will survive the process. Our task is to operate within the environment rather than making an excuse out of it. However, the reality is that until photographers demand better monochrome quality from the labs, they will not get it. Unless you are lucky with a local lab, you are going to have to do it yourself (and have a price problem on your hands).

Black and white is generally shot on either 35mm or roll film, and, for the small studio, the larger versions of the amateur Paterson type tanks are about the best for processing. One that takes half a dozen spirals will generally be large enough for most of your needs.

Select your own film/developer combination, and learn to get the best out of it. I use Kodak T-Max 100 film developed in HC110 Dilution B. The important thing is to get to know one combination and stick with it, at least for all your studio product shots.

I personally find that most manufacturers' development instructions give me a very contrasty neg, so I have learned to underdevelop by about 10-15%, and overexpose if necessary to compensate. T-Max doesn't seem to need this overexposure; it gives negs that I like exposed at rated speed and developed for 90% of the recommended time. This gives me my "perfect" negative, one that will print on grade 3 paper, give bright whites, a full range of greys and a good solid black. A print like this will usually survive the poorest screening.

Spend some time getting your black and white right. It is going to be around for some time yet, and you might as well get it right from the start.

Try and curb any desire you may have to shoot on colour neg stock and print in black and white. Multicontrast papers do give an almost acceptable print from a colour neg, but the tonal values are all wrong. Printing times are also longer. Panchromatic papers are better, but can be difficult to handle. Our objective is to produce a negative that will enable us to produce a run of good snappy prints in the minimum of time. The only way I know to do that is to shoot on medium speed pan emulsion and develop gently.

Once you have your negative sorted, you will find that printing becomes quite easy. I use a colour head with the filtration set to give grade 3 on Ilford Multigrade paper. The quality of multicontrast papers is excellent these days, and you only have to stock one grade of paper. The other advantage of using a colour head is that small dust particles and some water drying marks disappear with the diffused light used. Again, it all saves you time and reduces the number of prints that end up in the dustbin.

You will find that after a while your negatives become so consistent that devices like enlarging exposure meters and test strips become unnecessary. When you can pop a negative into your glassless carrier and produce a good print first time, you know you are there.

Developing prints is a messy business, unless you really do a lot and can afford a dry-to-dry processor. There are cheaper alternatives to this excellent machine, but most of them tend to be "dry to slightly wet" rather than "dry to dry". I have still to find a better way of developing prints than processing a number of them back to back in dishes. On a good day, I can process getting on for a hundred prints in an hour, with very little waste. If you print 5x7s two at a time on 10x8, you are approaching two hundred prints an hour, and that is worth the mess I suppose.

Do give adequate fixing and washing – prints going brown on the process camera will not enhance your reputation. Also, don't leave resin-coated papers too long in the wash – they tend to fall apart at the edges. You will lose all the advantages of high speed processing if you have to trim every print.

One final word. Always evaluate your prints when they are dry. Many papers go darker on drying, and a print that looks a stunner in the fixer can look grey and dirty when dry. Check every now and again; it is worth it.

E6 processing

There is a lot of rubbish talked about E6 processing. Many view it as if it were some kind of secret, dangerous undertaking, only to be attempted by the very brave or very foolish. It is true that E6, in performing the reversal by chemical means, tends to be more tricky than the old E4 process. Nevertheless, a little care is all that is needed to produce good E6 time after time after time.

But why get involved anyway? Why not send it to your local lab?

If you are in the rare situation of having a client happy to wait two days or so for their trannies, then go ahead. If the lab has the right equipment and knows how to use it, then you will get consistent, good E6.

My own world, however, is a little different, and deadlines are usually such that the client wants the transparencies "on the day".

London studios can pop the film round the corner on a motorbike; we have to process it ourselves. Happily, there are some definite advantages. Firstly, we can satisfy this "wanted yesterday" requirement. Secondly, we can fine-tune our E6 to give the client bright, well-saturated transparencies that really stand out. Doing it yourself also means that if you want to be a little profligate on chemistry usage to optimise quality, you can. The cost increase is really insignificant compared to the final invoice price to your client.

The enemies of good E6 are inconsistent times and temperatures, and contamination between baths. Most problems can be laid at the door of either too cold a colour developer or contamination of the colour developer – with the first developer, for instance. We can eliminate both of these problems with the right processor. There are two types of small processor for film, the "dip and dunk", where you "dip" the film in each of the baths in turn, and the "rotary discard".

Looking at the dip and dunk type first, these come in all shapes and sizes. With some you have to do the dipping and dunking yourself, and with others the film is carried along on a kind of roller-coaster, getting dipped and dunked automatically. They range tremendously in size, from small mini units holding a couple of litres for each bath to monsters holding a thousand litres of chemistry. Although some people claim good results with the smaller units, the few times I have had film processed in them consistency has not been good. When the limits of inter-bath contamination are measured in parts per million, I reckon the bigger the processor the better. This is borne out by those leading E6 labs in the major cities which provide excellent and consistent E6 using large dip and dunkers.

The contamination problem is solved for us by using small rotary discard machines, as mentioned earlier. There are a number of these on the market but the principle in each machine is the same. A measured amount of fresh chemistry, prewarmed, is introduced to the film which is wound on spirals in a light-tight tank rotating in a thermostatically controlled water bath. After each process step, the bath is discarded, and the next introduced. Thus it is theoretically impossible to have contamination between baths providing the correct washes are carried out.

I have used Jobo machines to process film from 35mm to 10x8in sheet, and have found them to be reliable and consistent in use. Jobo's importers, Introphoto in Maidenhead, have a team of people who are well versed in E6 lore, and who solved all of my problems when I started using their machines.

With E6, you have a choice of chemistry. You can choose the traditional six baths, or a three bath process consisting of developer, combined reversal and colour developer, and bleach/fix. I have used both, and when we concentrated on Ektachrome 100 film in the studio, we found that the Photo Technology "Photochrome 3" three bath process worked well. In fact many of the illustrations in this book were processed this way.

When Fuji film started creeping into our lab, I found that the Agfa Process 44 six bath process gave me more neutral results. Don't forget that Agfa have developed a colour developer for rotary discard machines, CD ROT (presumably short for rotation). Even capricious films like Ektachrome 6121 duping stock can be quite happily "brewed" in this without problems.

Duplicate transparencies

When an ad is run for long periods, there is often a deterioration in the condition of the original transparency. Although in many ways modern scanning techniques produce outstanding colour separations, some repro houses seem to delight in soaking every tranny in oil. They then return it in a sticky mess, or damage it further by cleaning. It seems to be a variable feast. Some repro houses are excellent, scanning trannies many times with no ill effect, whilst other companies render them totally useless after only one scan. In the past couple of years we've had trannies folded in half, stapled, torn – you name the abuse. I suspect not all the damage comes from the repro house either!

All of this doesn't gladden the heart of a client who has paid upwards of £1,000 for a shot that probably cannot be repeated. With an ad these days running in upwards of eighteen or more different magazines and formats, the cost and time taken for outside lab produced dupes is often prohibitive.

The correct way to cover yourself is to shoot many sheets of film at each bracket, and I always try to do this. Unfortunately, there never seems to be enough time, and all too often you must agree to "dupe the original".

The photographer who keeps the original transparency on file, making dupes every time the agency produces a new ad, is providing a welcome service to the agency and client, as well as popping an additional £200 – £300 in his pocket. Also, if you goof (perish the thought) in filtration or exposure on the original, you can usually "tweak" the dupe to correct.

Reproduction quality 5x4in dupes are not difficult to produce with the simplest of equipment, and with Kodak's 6121 duping stock colour separations are excellent.

Dupes are made in the darkroom in much the same way as reversal colour prints, only using 5x4in sheet film, E6 processed. The enlarger can be quite a simple one, but make sure it will cover the largest size of tranny you are likely to dupe. I use an LPL 5x4, as it seems to produce nice bright dupes and has a light attenuator which I find useful.

You have the choice of various film stock. Standard camera films such as RFP, EPY or EPR give "snappy" dupes with high contrast. However, specialist duping films such as Kodak 6121 or Fuji CDU give soft results which are ideal for colour separations. Another reason for choosing the "soft" option is that these emulsions are also suitable for taking second generation dupes should someone lose the original.

The first thing to do is to calibrate the enlarger, both for exposure and filtration. If you use 6121 film then a "start" filtration is given with each batch. Buy plenty of film – a dozen boxes or so. It keeps indefinitely in the fridge, and you will be working longer with one batch. Set the start filtration on the colour head on your enlarger, and find a transparency in your files that has plenty of soft tones. I use a 6x7cm EPN tranny with a grey background and skin tone as an illustration here. Focus up on a sheet of white paper in a dark slide, and expose four sheets of film at ten seconds exposure at f8, f11, f22 and f32. Process reasonably quickly.

When the film is dry and on the light box, you should have one sheet that is near enough in density, but the wrong colour. From the colour ring-a-round illustrated, identify the colour cast approximately, and remove filtration (reversal remember...) to correct. Expose two more sheets of film at this new filtration with the previous exposure and at one stop less, keeping the ten second time constant. Process. With the help of a ring-a-round you should get there in four goes or so.

Then, write down the exposure and filtration in your log. Unless you deliberately want to change colours or density, this filtration and exposure will remain constant for dupes with your equipment and that batch of 6121.

And basically, that's it. There are some further things we can do though. Firstly, take the filtration on the enlarger head. Then subtract the "start" filtration on the film box. This gives you a correction to apply to any new batch. Typical results would be:

Enlarger setting: 60Y 0M 20C
Film box filtration: 40Y 0M 35C
Correction therefore: +20Y, 0M, -15C

This applies to any EPN original. Other E6 films will be very similar, but do allow for slight variations.

If you are going to duplicate different sizes of original, or crop heavily, you need to modify the standard exposure found above. At £12 or so the little Ilford EM10 exposure meter is great for this. Select a highlight area of the tranny (in the example shown here I used the vase on the table), put the measurement cell in position, set the lens at the exposure already found (f18 in my case), and

Original "EPN" 6x7cm transparency (above), 5x4in dupe (right)

rotate the calibration scale until the green light comes on. Note the number, in my case 25. The meter is now ready.

With 6121, always respect the 10 secs exposure, or recalibrate for a different time. Reciprocity failure shows itself by colour shifts, and I remember wasting days once until I read Kodak's notes.

Now, to dupe a tranny, pop the original in the carrier, emulsion down. Set the filtration on the head as described, frame and focus up. Select a highlight area with the EM10 meter and adjust the lens iris until the green light comes on. Expose at ten seconds and you have a repro quality dupe as soon as the E6 is done.

In addition to this service for your own trannies, ad agencies have a continuing need for good dupes, and the charge these days is anything from £15 to £25 a go. Once your gear is set up, you can make a substantial profit, not only from duping your own shots, but selling the service at an appropriate price.

Further applications

Making an exact copy is the normal function of a tranny duping service, but there are additional creative possibilities once this process is up and running. One of the simplest and possibly one of the most effective things you can do is combine transparencies. You

148

No Correction
+5M   +5C   +5Y   +5G   +5R   +5B
+10M +10C +10Y +10G +10R +10B
+20M +20C +20Y +20G +20R +20B

Colour ring-a-round to assist in dupe film calibration

can do this by putting both trannies in the enlarger, or by exposing several trannies separately on to one piece of film.

In the first instance, you can add a "frame" of leaves around a building photograph, especially effective if the building is one of the modern monstrosities we see creeping up everywhere. You can build up a library of tree and leaf frames, either on E6 film or lith film, which gives a black silhouette frame. Sandwich both trannies together, put them in the negative carrier, and expose once as for a standard dupe. The single exposure technique is used when you are combining the original transparency with a darker "mask".

Sometimes you may want to add white clouds to a featureless blue sky, or a moon to a dark night sky. This is done by making cloud trannies and moon trannies and simply exposing these on the dupe film after you have already exposed the original. It also works well for adding large images of the sun to back-lit landscapes. You can create quite interesting pics in the darkroom using bits and pieces from your transparency files, and your clients will use the service once they know it is there.

Another way you can create new images in the darkroom is to dupe trannies using special effects filters on the enlarger lens. Many picture libraries create some of their most popular images this way. They prefer their photographers to shoot "straight" in the field, leaving their technicians to produce creative trannies in the darkroom. The only limit to this is your own imagination.

The dupes described above are produced exclusively for colour separations and printing. However you will often be asked to dupe 35mm slides for projection, and, again, with the right gear and materials, this can be a very straightforward and profitable occupation.

There seems to be a proliferation of gadgets on the market to dupe 35mm to 35mm, some of them based on upside-down enlarger heads, but most people who regularly dupe slides use a Bowens Illumitran or similar machine. The Bowens Illumitran consists of a variable power flash generator; a mount to hold either the 35mm or roll film original; and a camera mount, complete with bellows, upon which you can pop any 35mm camera and an enlarging lens. There is a pre-flashing unit available for those that need it, but if you use specialist duping stock you will rarely use it, as contrast will not be a problem.

Calibration is very similar to the procedure used above with Kodak 6121 duping stock, except that you should use Ektachrome SO366 35mm film, available in 35mm cassettes. Filtration is added using normal colour printing filters, the cheapest being a set of Ilford Cibachrome filters, cut down to fit the Illumitran drawer. It is possible to calibrate in three runs.

If you manage to sell the whole film, you can produce 35mm dupes for about 25 pence each; they currently cost from £1.50 to £2.50 from pro labs. Quality is remarkably good. One client asked me to run off a 36 exp cassette of SO366 from one 35mm original tranny. I regularly see A4 ads produced from them, with excellent colour and sharpness.

Internegatives

Up to now, most of the work done in the lab has been for reproduction purposes. However, design studios and ad agencies also require work for intermediate stages, such as prints to use for visuals, or simply to have as reference while they design the ad or brochure page. From time to time you will be asked to produce prints from your trannies, and from other people's as well.

There are two ways to get a print from a tranny – you either take a standard EP2 print from an internegative, or you go direct using a reversal print process. My experience of direct reversal prints is that, unless the tranny is perfect, contrast is high and the colours never seem right. Because sometimes you have to work from an over or underexposed bracket, it can be a disappointing process. It is, however, a quick way to get a colour print from a tranny, and, if there is no time to do it properly, then a quick Ciba or Fuji/Kodak reversal print done in the Jobo will often do the trick.

But if you do have the time, then a good 5x4in internegative done from the tranny will give you a better, truer print. This also gives you the option of producing further quality prints simply and cheaply, either at the local lab, or in your own darkroom.

Kodak make a specific internegative material which is designed to be exposed using filtered light, which has variable contrast depending on the filtration. To use this material properly you have to have access to a densitometer. I have used it, and it gives excellent internegs, but I feel its use is more suited to the professional photofinishing lab than our little operation.

I generally use Kodak VPS sheet film, exposed in a Polaroid MP4 copy camera, with the transparency mounted in a Bowens Illumitran on the copy board. VPS is a gentle negative material, and I find this combination gives me a nice, bright print with good colour and without excessive contrast. Until I bought the MP4, I used Kodak VPL for internegs, exposed using an enlarger, with equally good results, but a little higher contrast. If I feel a tranny needs brightening up a little I still use this technique.

Occasionally a colour print comes into the repro chain. A typical example is when a company changes a logo and doesn't wish to photograph the whole range of products again. Another is when a distracting background needs to be changed or removed. Although many of these modifications can now be done at repro, often a large print will be taken off the transparency. This is then airbrushed, and either copied back on to transparency film for scanning or scanned direct. The internegative route is the only real way to do this.

By the way, don't give your client a print smaller than 20x16in; I normally give 20x 24in.

In addition to colour internegs, often a client will wish to send out a mailing of monochrome press release shots when they only have a colour tranny. For years I overexposed slow 5x4in black and white sheet film, underdeveloping it in dishes in the dark. Now I use Polaroid type 54 film, which has a reusable negative. I expose

*Bowens
Illumitran,
complete with
contrast
control unit*

it in the Polaroid MP4 camera with the tranny in the Illumitran. Polaroid recommend that you use a solution of sodium sulphite to clear the gunge off the negative, but I use warm water and a little careful rubbing with a finger or two. Contrast control is easy – if you need more, you leave the pack a little longer before tearing it apart; less, you leave it less time.

Prints produced from these Polaroid negs are excellent, they print on grade 2 paper, and have fine grain. I use them up to and including 10x8in with no problems at all.

Colour printing

Although many magazines and newspapers now favour the use of colour prints, the commercial world, thank goodness, has not succumbed – yet. You do see excellent repro taken from prints from time to time, usually in articles illustrating new scanning techniques. Unfortunately the normal quality of colour repro using colour prints is nowhere near as good as transparency originated work. It is true that for a press photographer there are more advantages in using Ektapress than Ektachrome, but for our sort of work, unless a client specifically insists upon prints, you should always give them a transparency for repro.

Producing colour prints is also a time consuming and expensive business, and this is one area where you really shouldn't get involved. Find a lab that produces good machine prints and send the work to them. Mark up their prices to your client – we work on a minimum of 33.3% gross profit, and there are occasions when a 50% gross profit or more can be justified.

When you shoot film destined for machine printing, take care that you frame the shot correctly. You will often be asked for A4 prints – when they are to be used in a salesman's presenter, for instance. If you are shooting on 6x6cm or 6x7cm, make sure that you have an image on the negative that will fit the A4 format. Machine printers can't crop selectively, and if you've framed it wrongly, you are going to have to pay for hand prints. I use a paper mask on the ground glass, or a 645 back, sometimes both. This is one area where the 645 camera is useful in the commercial studio.

When you send your negatives for machine printing, insist on two test prints for approval. No matter how good your lab is (and there are some very good machine prints around these days) you must protect yourself from the client that "doesn't like the colour" of the couple of hundred A4 glossy prints you place on their desk. Before you order the run from the lab, give the client one of the test prints, and let them see you also have a copy. The test prints also ensure that the lab produces the run to the same quality, but I have found that this is less of a problem than a capricious client.

Copying

One of the most useful pieces of equipment you can have in your studio is a good copying stand. Unfortunately, good ones don't come cheaply, and less than good ones are totally useless. Unless the copying stand you are looking at can take an RB67 fitted with an extension tube and a 127mm lens, walk away from it.

Most photographers I know either adapt an old half-plate enlarger, or use something like the Polaroid MP4. Modifying old enlargers is fine if you have the time, but the MP4 is a complete copying system, and if you buy the right bits, it can save a tremendous amount of time while giving you consistent results. New, they cost a small fortune, but good second-hand ones can be found. Expect to pay upwards of five or six hundred pounds for the basic kit, and add a little more depending on the accessories supplied.

The MP4 comes in two versions of column and baseboard, standard and XL. If you go for the XL then you will never run out of column height. It consists of a standard copying easel and column, but instead of a camera bracket, it comes complete with its own 5x4in camera with interchangeable lenses. The standard lens is a 135mm enlarging lens complete in shutter, and covers 5x4.

You normally have the choice of using a Polaroid 545 holder or standard double dark slides. A reflex hood is provided for focusing, and you have a choice of screens. Lighting is provided by means of four 150w lamps on two rather spindly arms, which are the only wobbly things about the whole machine. If you wish, you can take the camera off and put your own camera on via an adaptor. You can also buy a sliding head assembly if you want to switch quickly from focusing to taking, although I have never found the need for it.

A good copying stand is like a dupe tranny service – once people know you have it, you will never be short of work for it. We have copied paintings, architectural drawings, artwork, photographs – even on one occasion separation negs using our light box on the easel. Add an Illumitran and there really is no limit to what you can do, and you can make a good profit doing it.

Mounting and lamination services

Another of the services which attract orders almost overnight is mounting and laminating. Mounting is sticking or gluing copy (photographs, artwork) to boards; laminating is attaching a protective plastic layer on top.

There are two basic techniques, hot and cold. Hot mounting, or "dry" mounting as it is still called, consists of gluing the print on to a mount using heat and pressure in a dry mounting press. Cold mounting means sticking the print to the mount with double-sided tape.

Because, in hot mounting, the adhesive melts once, it can melt again, and there are plenty of stories of exhibition displays unmounting themselves under the heat of spotlamps on exhibition stands. For this and other reasons, I feel that the dry mounting press is probably more at home in the social studio than in our commercial environment. Cold mounting techniques suit our requirements much better.

Cold mounting equipment consists of two rubber or neoprene rollers, adjustable for tension. Two passes are needed, the first to attach the adhesive film to the mount, and the second to add the print. It is a technique which requires a little practice, but once you have the knack it is extremely easy.

The completed mounted pic can then be hung on the wall using Velcro tabs. The mounting boards used commercially are usually foam-cored, which are very light and quite rigid. As there is no weight to the board there is no risk of the thing falling off, as can often happen with hardboard or plywood mounts. The mounting film, which is quite expensive, usually cures in 24 hours, and then nothing will induce the print to part company with its mount. Because foam-cored board is used, you can trim the completed mounted print with a sharp scalpel.

Occasionally, the client will want a protective film on top of the print. Unlike the mounting film, this film requires a fair amount of pressure to apply correctly. With foam-cored board it is easy to overdo it and reduce a 5mm board to 3mm or less in one pass! I had Ademco's rep show me how to do it, and I recommend you do the same. This protective film or lamination comes in all thicknesses and surfaces, from an attractive lustre to high gloss.

Be careful when the word gets around that you "do" lamination. Restaurateurs who serve "messy" food often have a protective film applied to both side of their menus to keep them clean. There are machines that do this kind of lamination quickly and cheaply, and you should refer enquiries for this to people that have them.

However, you may find clients who are willing to pay your price for this service. If you do it, make sure you leave a couple of millimetres as a border all round the menu for the laminating film to stick to itself. If you trim the film too close to the menu, bored diners waiting for their order will sit there and pull the menu to pieces. Naturally, it'll all be your fault. Better to stay away from it altogether.

A cold mounting machine about 24in wide will cost somewhere in the region of £750. With reasonable selling, it should pay for itself in six months or less. There are second-hand machines on the market, but be careful that they are true and that both rollers are parallel. One way to check this is to pop a business card under one side and adjust the tension so that you can just pull it out. Without altering the setting, try the same on the other side. If you can't pull it out or if it falls out, then the rollers need adjusting or the frame is out of true.

When you buy your cold mounting rollers, allow also for a large cutting mat. These extraordinary things are really essential, although one of the right size will set you back £60 or so. They are invaluable when trimming things that won't go into a normal trimmer, like oversize prints or Kappa board for example. Get a supply of Swann-Morton scalpels and blades, and a good steel straight edge about three feet long (the price of this item will bring tears to your eyes). That's all you need to mount prints up to 24x 36in, which will cover most eventualities. Mount everything on a good solid bench at the side of the studio.

If you go in for these extra services then you have a financial buffer for when times go slack in the studio – dupe tranny and mounting orders tend to come in a steady stream. They will often bring in studio business as well. Remember, customers who want prints mounting have to have the photographs taken somewhere.

Remember your mission

Nice though all this sounds, there are some dangers to advertising all these services. The odd client who comes in for a display print is fair game – as mentioned above, they could very well be a potential customer for your studio. Anything that increases your customer base is a good thing. What you do have to watch, however, is the agency that puts all the easy, profitable photography in one place, and all the tricky lab problems elsewhere.

You must remember – and from time to time remind your clients – that you are a photographic studio. The fact that you have processing facilities does not mean that you are a photofinishing laboratory with a studio stuck on the side.

For years, I had a client who kept giving us tricky lab work, things like transparency colour cast corrections, 8x10in dupe trannies and the like. On one occasion, we even stripped the emulsion off some Cibachrome prints so that they could be remounted on a flexible base. It appears they were to be used as displays in a cathedral, and were to be fixed around the main columns. We didn't get any photography though, and yet the pics we were dealing with were not particularly impressive or creative and were certainly within our competence.

After a year or so of talking around the subject, I asked directly why my studio was fine for the difficult lab work where the risk was high but the profit minimal, but not for the profitable standard pack shot work. I didn't get a straight answer, but I did get a very embarrassed client, who then proceeded to let the odd job come my way. But again, it was the difficult stuff – industrial interiors, special effects and the like. I decided we were not getting very far, and, perhaps wrongly, told the client that whilst we were happy to spend half the night correcting a poorly made dupe from somewhere else, it would sweeten the pill if we had some of the standard product work we knew he was giving to someone else around the corner. It didn't work, and we had to let the account go.

On another occasion we were asked to quote for a major trade catalogue by a local manufacturer. We lost the bid on price, and heard that the job had gone to a local social photographer. About ten days after the catalogue was shot, we were phoned by the company to quote on a "substantial" quantity of dupe transparencies. On inquiring further, it transpired that the photographer had shot the entire range without bracketing. There was only one transparency per product, and a wide variation in density. Our brief would be to take all the trannies and dupe them to identical densities, so that the repro house, in line with normal practice, could scan them together, page by page.

When we mentioned that we thought the photographer who did the shoot was probably in a better position to have this work done for them, we were told that he didn't have anything like our facilities. We asked to be excused the job.

If you are not careful you can end up becoming the saviour of people who are incompetent, poorly equipped, or who simply make wrong judgements. A pro lab is in business to do that – our little studio isn't, and we systematically refuse any work which we think is rectification of another photographer's mistakes. Let the client go back to where he placed the order and sort it out there. You get no kudos for making someone else look good.

Another area that perhaps comes under the heading of general policy is the access you allow clients to various parts of your studio, notably the darkroom.

Many people consider that possession of a Hasselblad immediately guarantees success in roll film photography. Equally, the same people consider that an old Rolleiflex or similar cannot possibly "take" good professional photographs. Most pro darkrooms contain a profusion of home made gadgets and many enlargers are old and dowdy De Veres – the average ad agency director can often get the wrong impression. Also, especially in black and white printing, the client should never see your struggle for perfection. Ban all clients from the darkroom; that is your private territory.

In a similar vein, I try not to let clients see contact sheets either, unless I know they are experienced in dealing with photographers. You can assume too much knowledge on your client's part sometimes.

I remember several years ago setting up a series of shots in an old forge where the client was making garden ornaments out of old horseshoes and the like. When I thought I had the Monolites balanced with the forge fire and the daylight streaming through the windows, I took a couple of Polaroids to check all was well before shooting the E6.

Shortly after I showed the Polaroids to the art director, I noticed there was a little huddled meeting in the corner, the client seeming quite upset about something. After the shoot was over, I asked the art director what the problem was. Well, he said, the client felt that I was quite expensive if all I was going to do was take Polaroid pictures. He had some of those which he had taken himself, which he didn't think were too bad, and they were free ...

THE PRODUCTION STAGE

Because most of a commercial photographer's work ends up in print, you would think that most of them would be reasonably knowledgeable about the reproduction and printing process. I thought so too.

Most people I have talked to in the business have a vague knowledge of what a "scanner" is. They have probably seen a "Cromalin" or two. However, they remain blissfully ignorant of what really happens to their transparencies and prints when they are taken away by the designer or art director.

I have always followed the principle that "knowledge is power" and the more I know about what is going on, the better I can serve my client. A simple understanding of what a graphic designer has to do, coupled with a knowledge of reproduction and printing processes, can often mean that photographer and designer can work much more effectively together. And it certainly helps to maintain their loyalty to you when the competition comes knocking on your client's door.

The design brief

When a client requires a brochure, or an advertisement or series of advertisements, it is normal for him to brief a graphic designer, who may be freelance or a member of staff at an advertising agency.

I define "the client" as the person at the end of the line who makes all the decisions and pays all the bills. It is easy to forget this, especially when a long chain of subcontractors is involved, each gaily marking up each other's work. At the end of the day someone has to pay all these charges, and this is the client. They are the boss, and for us all to stay in business they must consider the charges for our work reasonable and the work worthwhile. Don't ever forget it.

At the first briefing, the client will outline the requirements. The designer will then establish that the project is feasible and that he is capable of carrying out the work. In many cases the designer, in conjunction with other colleagues in the agency, will be expected to make a judgement as to whether the client's ideas are

158

the best way to reach the particular market. Because ad agencies and designers are often better informed as to how a particular market should be approached, often the agency role is that of marketing consultant. Indeed, many clients place their entire marketing strategy in the hands of their advertising agency, or "communications consultant" as many of these companies are beginning to be known.

Rough budgets and schedules are also discussed at the initial briefing. Usually the decision to proceed in principle and offer the commission to that particular designer or agency is made at this initial meeting. Their decision to accept the brief is similarly made at this time.

Visuals

The next thing that happens is for the designer to show the client his ideas, or his interpretation of the client's ideas, in the form of sketches or "visuals", sometimes called "roughs". How these are presented depends upon the level of design knowledge possessed by the client. Obviously a visual aimed at a sales director will be more complete and "professional" than one prepared for a former art director. I have seen them vary from beautifully (and expensively) prepared works of art to rough sketches "on the back of a fag packet". The purpose of them all is to stimulate discussion. They are first thoughts, and should in no way be regarded as final proposals cast in stone.

At this stage the designer will often ask the photographer to submit some first ideas in photographic form, sometimes just on Polaroids, to help fix in the client's mind the kind of finished result that can be expected. Incidentally, when you are asked for these "first ideas", be careful about your charges. At this point the designer is selling you as well as himself, and won't appreciate large bills that he is unable to pass on to the client at this stage.

Occasionally the designer will go ahead and commission photography for use in a visual, especially when a major advertising campaign is envisaged. If the client rejects the idea, then your invoice to the designer or agency represents a straight loss for them. Many feel this risk is justified on the basis that they can only really sell the idea with the photography. Those that do take this risk usually win. Sometimes though, they don't, and whilst you should never underwrite this risk totally, a sympathetic attitude towards the payment of your invoice will win friends.

When the client approves the visual the designer or agency fine tunes the costings, and it is at that stage that your quote for the photography becomes more or less firm. They will also finalise the timetable for the ads, and book the media space after having obtained from the client the final green light to proceed.

Commissioning

The designer now commissions all the creative work. He will brief
you and book the photography. If the copy is to be written by a freelance copywriter, this is also commissioned at this point. Any freelance artwork is also ordered, or produced in house. The type size
and faces are decided, the layout frozen, and the copy sent to the
typesetter.

Typesetting is a subject we'll look at in a moment, but for now,
the designer is ordering all the text to be supplied on a PMT for
cutting and pasting on the final artwork.

When all this is done, including the photography, the designer
prepares the final layout. This means deciding on the size the illustrations have to be, including artwork and photographs, and
pasting up all the text in its final position. Transparencies are sent
for separations, and the final film positives are made of the text.
The separations are married to the text and the whole thing goes to
the printer.

If all that sounds like double Dutch, don't worry, we are going
to look at each process in turn, starting with the typesetting.

Typesetting

Typesetters complain that their work is the most misunderstood
function in brochure or ad production, and yet is the most important. I would not presume to agree or disagree with that statement.
Certainly it is rare to hear of a young graduate aspiring to be a
typesetter, and yet there are plenty aspiring to be photographers or
commercial artists.

Typesetting consists of taking the copywriter's text, and the
designers typeface and size instructions, and producing a print of
the text on a piece of photographic paper to the designer's specification. Virtually all typesetting is now done by photosetting (also
known as filmsetting or photocomposition). There are two main
ways of doing this. The first is by using a photomechanical typesetter, which is a machine containing typefaces printed on negative
film. The other is to use a digital typesetter where the typeface is
produced by a CRT or laser from information stored in the
machine's memory.

In the mechanical device, light is shone through the film and
the image of the typeface (or "typeform") is printed on sensitised
paper, just like a contact printer or photographic enlarger. In the
digital version, a laser beam scans the paper, producing the typeface directly.

Until comparatively recently, the highest quality work was
always done on mechanical typesetters, as the quality of the type-

face produced was superior. Being an analogue system, the mechanical machine produces an exact replica of the typeface that was originally used to produce the film in the machine. Digital machines, on the other hand, create the typeface in much the same way as a dot matrix printer prints characters. The quality depends on the resolution of the machine, and type produced in this way has ragged edges if you examine it with a magnifying loupe. Having said that, modern machines are now very good indeed and improving all the time.

Depending on the machine, text is entered by sitting at a keyboard like a typewriter, or by digital input, provided from either the ubiquitous floppy disc or over the phone lines via a modem. At the end of the process, the finished product comes out either as a full page of text, or on a long strip of paper ready to be cut up and pasted on to the final layout.

Sizing

When the designer has the text from the typesetter, he then has to "size" the illustrations. He does this at this stage for two reasons. Firstly he has to make sure that the picture is suitable for the space he has designed for it. Secondly, a transparency or print cannot be sent for separations or screening until the final size is determined. Separation negatives and screened film are produced at the actual printed size, the designer specifying the degree of enlargement or reduction in percentage terms.

Sizing is done slightly differently according to whether the designer is working on a print or transparency. If he has a transparency he takes a tracing of the images on the total film area, either using a light box in a process camera or a simple photographic enlarger. This tracing, which is usually done to final size, is then "squared up" by drawing a true square frame around the whole image.

The designer then decides the crop of the transparency and draws new squared lines around the crop he has defined, shading off the parts of the image he has discarded. He then draws a diagonal line from opposite corners, usually from bottom left to top right. He marks off on the margin the actual size of the transparency, and draws in a rectangle representing the actual size of the original transparency. From this, he can calculate the percentage enlargement as follows:

$$\frac{\text{Size of final image}}{\text{Size of original}} \quad \text{x} \quad 100 = \%$$

Usually he will tape the transparency to the tracing, and write on the repro percentage – 152% for example. The transparency can then go to the repro house for scanning.

The procedure for sizing prints is very similar, except that a transparent overlay is usually taped over the print itself, and the scaling operation carried out on that instead.

What is important to note is that the designer needs to see all the image on the film or negative clearly. When printing, don't crop any of the image; let the designer do that. In the case of transparencies, don't supply trannies mounted in fancy black masks which crop off an eighth of an inch or so of image – the designer may need that eighth, and may not be aware that it exists. Present the trannies in clear sleeving, so that they don't have to be taken out of their protective covering for the selection and sizing.

At the end of all this, the designer has the text to size, and has the sizing of the illustrations defined. The repro house can now go ahead and produce the screened film for black and white, and the separations for colour.

Reproduction

Text is very easily printed. In letterpress, for example, you make a piece of metal with the character form raised in relief, put a layer of ink on it, and press it onto the paper. However, whatever you do, you cannot alter the intensity of colour on the paper. If you use black ink, you get a black image, red ink a red image. Unless you change the colour of the ink, you cannot get a grey or pink image from the black or red ink.

Yet a photograph consists of variable tones of colour; in black and white they vary from dense black through all the greys to white. Some means therefore has to be found of producing all the tones of grey using the black printers' ink used in monochrome printing.

This is done by printing photographs (or "tone") in a series of dots. A dense black layer will have large dots, and a light grey area will have small ones. The spacing of the dots is constant for any particular application, but varies depending on the type of printing envisaged. As the dots are produced by a "screen", the dot spacing is called the screen, and is measured in dots (or lines) per inch. If you look at any newspaper black and white illustration through a magnifying loupe, you will see the dot pattern, and as you move away you will see the dots blend into the tones of the original photograph. A photograph reproduced this way is called a halftone.

Screening, or producing a halftone image, is done by copying the original on to a piece of film through a dot screen of the required spacing. The resulting film negative is used by the printer to produce the printing plate.

The original print is placed on the copy board of a process camera, which is really an overgrown copying stand fitted with a camera capable of taking A3 or larger film. The screen is placed either in contact with the negative film or spaced just in front of it, depending on the type of screen used. The screen can consist either of a series of dots printed on a film or glass base at the required spacing, or two thin sheets of glass with intersecting parallel lines ruled on them, producing a pattern of dots.

The dot spacing depends on the type of printing envisaged, and the kind of paper to be used. A fine screen will allow much more detail to be reproduced, but if a coarse absorbent paper is used, such as newsprint, the detail will run together and produce a "blob" of ink. Fine art papers, on the other hand, will allow the ink to reproduce very fine detail, so a fine screen can be used. Newsprint will use a screen from 65 to 80 lines/inch, whereas fine, coated art paper can go as high as 200 lines/inch.

Screening is a skilled process, and the exposure given when producing the negative, as well as the choice and positioning of the screen, is critical. However, good screening seems to be a dying art, especially with the growth of desktop publishing.

The process is helped by a good mono print, with a full range of tones from white through to black. Hard, contrasty prints will be very difficult to screen, and muddy ones with no blacks and whites will end up even muddier. Highlights should have some tone in them; reserve "paper base" white for specular reflections. Be careful of shadows too – keep good tone in areas you want reproducing, dark tones will be lost with the blacks. Some magazines' quality of screening leaves a lot to be desired, but you can help by presenting a good print in the first place.

Colour tone is reproduced in exactly the same way, using coloured inks. However, first we have to separate the colours on the transparency into the three primary colours that will be used for printing – yellow, magenta and cyan. Just as a colour print is produced by exposing three layers of emulsion sensitive to the three primaries, colour printing is done by printing on the paper three (or more) times with yellow, magenta and cyan inks. To combine these to recreate our colour image, we need to produce three negatives of the transparency: one through a red filter to make the cyan "printer", one through a blue filter to make the yellow, and one through green for magenta ink. These negatives, or "separation negatives" are then used to provide the screened film, exactly like the black and white process above.

Until the advent of digital scanners, separation negatives were usually produced by copying the transparency on to panchromatic (black and white) emulsion through the three filters in turn. In fact, when producing the highest quality reproductions – of paintings for instance – this method is still used, using the original painting as the subject instead of a colour transparency of it. However, for most normal applications today, separation negatives are produced digitally from a transparency using a piece of equipment called a colour scanner, hence "scanning a tranny".

Before we look at how these things work, remember we have only talked about three colours – yellow, cyan and magenta. In practice, a fourth colour, black, is added to give the finished print additional substance. Also, because printing inks are never really pure, some colours cannot be produced by mixing our three colours alone. In very high quality work therefore, one or two extra colours can be added, making six-colour printing for instance. But normally we only encounter four colours, so we need four screened negatives for the printer – yellow, cyan, magenta and black.

Most repro houses use the Crosfield Magnascan scanner. This device scans the original – mounted on a rotating drum – with laser light through colour filters. It then directly produces the separation negatives for each colour, already screened to the operator's instructions. Sometimes, if the transparency is scratched, or high magnifications are required, the surface of the transparency is coated with oil before mounting on the drum. Most repro houses clean this oil off afterwards, but some don't.

The operator then mounts the drum on the machine, enters the percentage magnification (or reduction) into the computer's memory, tells the computer what screen size is required, and presses the button. The machine rotates the drum at high speed, scans the transparency, and exposes the individual film within the machine. This is then processed in rapid access chemistry, and within minutes you are presented with screened "seps" for proofing.

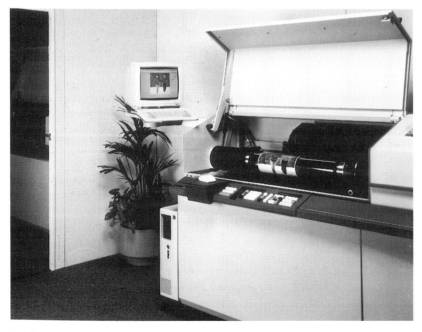

The Crosfield Magnascan scanner

Scanning prints is done in a similar fashion except that the light used for producing the "seps" is produced by reflection off the print rather than by transmission through a transparency. This does degrade the quality of the final image somewhat, and is one of the reasons why trannies are preferred.

Because the scanning process is expensive, when a page contains more than one illustration it is most economic to scan all the illustrations in one go.

It is possible with the digital scanner to "correct" all kinds of problems on a transparency. Colour casts can be removed if they are not excessive, contrast can be improved, and by selectively modifying contrast, even slightly out of focus trannies can be sharpened up a little. The ever-promised E7 process with the "sharpening bath" has become reality. However, most of these corrections can only be applied across the whole scan, and therefore if you have more than one tranny mounted, you should take some care in selecting them.

Most applications that are "gang scanned" are for trade brochures with six or eight illustrations per page, making sometimes an assembly of sixteen or so trannies for the double page. In order to make sure these scan well – if the trannies were not taken at the same time on the same set – I bracket a third of a stop on the flash. I can then easily assemble a set that match well.

I do this selection on a proper, professional light box, with frequently changed Philips Graphica 47 tubes. Don't buy a cheap light box – Hancocks, DW Viewpacks or KJP make suitable ones.

Many photographic magazines recommend underexposing tranny film "for better colour saturation". I think this is rubbish; I have found that the best final printed work comes from bright, correctly exposed film. Also, the best bracket seems to jump out at you on the light box, without the necessity for a great deal of poring over with a loupe. If you do have a problem selecting the right bracket, choose the brightest where detail is still present in the highlights before it starts to go grey. Going for a bracket that gives dark colours and veiled highlights may be great for camera club competitions, but it won't be welcomed by a client that wants the brightest, "happiest" representation of his product.

When you have selected the first tranny, borrow the designer's visual and assemble the others in position, selecting the brackets that look right. Once you have done this, and made sure there are no burnt-out highlights or "grey" whites, you should have a set of trannies that will scan together cheaply and reproduce well in print. And that's what we are all about.

The evidence that all is well and that the separations have been produced correctly is in a proofing process which results in a "print" called a Cromalin. This proof is normally produced by the repro house, and is an indication of the print quality that can be produced from the separation negatives made by the scanner. They are expensive, and are charged separately by the repro house, but it is normal for the designer to have these produced for every set of separations he has made.

Because the Cromalin is attractive, it is often used to show progress to the client and obtain approval to go ahead with the printing. Because a commercial photographer's work is so tied in with repro, I feel that a good Cromalin is the "sign off" point for the photographer. It is the final indication that you have done your work well, and I always ask to see them if the designer doesn't volunteer, which is rare.

Because the scanner is a digital device, there are all sorts of games designers can play if they are willing to pay the price. For instance, it is reasonably easy to distort images in one dimension or the other. If you add about a quarter of a million pounds worth of computer graphics equipment, you can also add one image to another, or modify the image you already have. You can lift an old manufacturer's logo and replace it with a new one. You can block out one background and replace it with another. You can change the colour of bits of the transparency at will. The technology is changing all the time, and the quality of these digital devices is improving all the time.

Desktop publishing

When "desktop" publishing programs first appeared, many people thought that they would sound the death-knell for the graphic designer. You can now sit at home, design magazine pages on a video monitor, digitally scan photographs and transparencies, run the whole thing off on your laser printer and send camera-ready artwork straight to the printer. Or so you think.

The fact is that a DTP system is just a tool – possession of a chisel doesn't make you a good cabinet maker, just as possession of a Leica doesn't make you a Cartier Bresson. It requires skill and graphic design training as much as the paste-up board and spray mount does. Also, the typefaces produced by a laser printer are not as good by a long chalk as those produced by a phototypesetting machine.

At the time of writing DTP systems are quite capable of producing magazines, but not really good enough for a quality advertisement or product brochure. However I am sure that this situation will soon change.

Printing

Where the finished product is an ad, the designer now puts the film work from screening or separations, plus a film positive of the layout, into the mail, with the hope that the various magazines' printers do justice to his work.

If a brochure is being prepared, then we are now at the final stage – platemaking and printing.

You will see from the above that each time an ad or illustration is prepared, a new set of separations has to be made. It is for this reason that designers can "run out" of trannies if you don't give them plenty to start with. I try to expose lots at the time of the shoot. Unfortunately this isn't always possible, and the client then has to use your duping facility.

Most printing work these days is done by a process called offset litho, which can be used for just about everything from the printing of company memos to large books and magazines. It uses the principle that grease and water don't like each other too much, and started as a printing process in Bavaria at the end of the eighteenth century.

One Alois Senelder of Solnhofen found that if a greasy image is formed on a piece of absorbent limestone, which is then dampened with water, then the greasy image will attract ink whilst the damp areas will repel it. Paper pressed against the stone will therefore show an inked image, whilst the damp areas remain clear. The name "lithography" derives from the Greek *lithos*. for stone, and indeed stones were used until the beginning of this century.

Early in the twentieth century, a new printing plate was devised which revolutionised litho printing. It consists of a thin aluminium plate, which is coated with a colloidal photographic medium. The plate is placed in contact with the screened film and exposed to high-powered light, which, after treatment, hardens the coating and makes it insoluble in water. The result is a plate containing an image of the screened film. If this plate is now dampened, greasy ink will be attracted to the image, and repelled from the damp non-image areas. This plate is flexible, which means it can be formed around a rotary cylinder and used in high-speed rotary printing presses.

In practice, the plate is first dampened by dampening rollers, then ink is applied via two smaller rollers. The image is not transferred directly to the paper, as the plate is fragile and abrasive paper would soon damage it. Instead, the inked image is transferred first to a rubber roller called the blanket cylinder. The rubber blanket cylinder then transfers the image to the paper, hence the term "offset" litho printing.

Multiple colour printing is done in exactly the same way, with each colour applied in turn. If you look at a colour reproduction in a magazine through a loupe, you will see each colour dot combined with the others in a "rosette" pattern. This pattern is produced by rotating each of the colour screens to an exact amount, and avoids the moiré patterning effect that occurs when two or more screens are superimposed at random.

When the plates are made, occasionally the printer is asked to produce a proof for approval before the run is made. This proof is usually done on a hand press, and checks things like colour balance (yes, you can still tweak it a little), registration between colours, and angles of screening. If it looks OK, the designer gives the thumbs up, and you see thousands of your photographs running off the press.

It still makes me a little excited, every time.

THOUGHTS FOR THE FUTURE

If you have followed most of the principles outlined in this book, you should by now be sitting on a small business founded on a firm, solid base, and looking towards the future. In this short section we will be looking at widening our horizons a little, perhaps hiring staff, expanding maybe. We'll take a quick look at the thorny question of regulation of photography in the UK, and at the role of professional institutions. Finally, we'll end with some more general thoughts.

Considering the options

Fairly quickly, you will get to the point where you you are regularly booking a couple of days a week for studio photography, with lab work in proportion. I find, working on my own, that two days a week is easily accommodated but that three days a week starts to become difficult to manage, especially when sets have to be built and disassembled. You have to consider whether to expand your turnover and production facilities to suit, or to maintain your level of bookings but charge more money for your services.

To a certain extent, your business profile and where you are located will affect this decision. If many of your clients are direct, and much of your business is in catalogue and brochure work, then to make more money you really need to increase the throughput. If, on the other hand, most of your work is in the advertising field, then you can increase your turnover by gently increasing your day rates, as advertising photography is less price sensitive than brochure work.

At the end of the day it is what you want to do that counts. You went into business for yourself because you wanted to "do your own thing" – so do it. If you are the kind of person that wants to expand the business into ever larger premises with increasing numbers of staff, building up a substantial company in the process, then good luck to you. If, on the other hand, you would prefer to "cherry pick" among available clients, and only work for those that appreciate your particular skills and are prepared to pay for it, then that is an equally acceptable policy for the future.

But whichever you choose, you will need a studio assistant.

Hiring an assistant

The first thing you should look at is the possibility of delegating those tasks which you currently do, but which do not necessarily require your level of skill or creativity. Loading dark slides for example, is a time-consuming task that just about anyone can do. I say just about anyone because I once had an assistant who couldn't, or more probably wouldn't, learn how to do it, ending up with sheets of film in the wrong way round, or forcing two sheets in instead of one. However most people can acquire this elementary skill. In the studio, you personally don't have to make all the preparations that have to be made, such as positioning the camera, or setting the lights in their approximate positions with their correct accessories, softboxes etc. So your first step towards an easier life is to take on an assistant.

Here you have two choices, you can hire someone with studio experience, or train a beginner. The former does appear to have some advantages, the chief one being that the new employee is "earning his (or her) corn" from day one. The disadvantages are that an experienced assistant will usually demand more money than a raw trainee, whilst the habits that may have been acquired elsewhere may not be the habits you particularly appreciate. Also, most assistants learn the business with one studio and then leave, either to set up their own business elsewhere or to take on a more senior position with another studio.

So, although you may be starting at square one, an inexperienced trainee is probably the best bet in your situation.

There are a number of government schemes for the hiring of young trainees, the best known being the YTS scheme, in which the government pays half the wages of the trainee, plus all the National Insurance contributions. This scheme has been criticised as a means for employers to hire cheap labour with government subsidies, but my experience has been that this is rarely the case, and I have seen more abuse of the YTS scheme by the trainees themselves than by employers.

Also, the agencies that administer these schemes are often way out of touch with the requirements of one or two person businesses. We once had a demand from a managing agency for us to release one of our YTS students for one week's leave to attend "lectures" on trade union legislation, industrial relations and assertiveness training. The notice given for this week's "leave" was three working days, in one of our busiest periods.

On the other hand there are many young people interested in commercial photography who genuinely do want to train in the profession. My advice would be to go ahead and hire someone outright.

Of course you do have to make as sure as you possibly can that your youngster is really interested in a career in photography.

Many just want to fill in time in what is generally considered a glamorous and trendy profession. Gone are the days when assistants would work for nothing to learn the business, but unless you detect something of that spirit in your candidate, look elsewhere.

A good assistant, after a few months, will definitely help you improve your throughput, especially if you add some responsibilities in the darkroom. But be careful not to let them enter the "creative" chain too soon, especially when your client is present. The client has hired you to do the job, not your assistant. Don't become one of those studios where the assistant does all the work, and you saunter in to press the button every now and again. They do exist – ask any West End advertising agency.

Finding your assistant can take time. Ads in the *British Journal of Photography* can often bring results, as can talking to the careers counsellor at schools and technical colleges. Advertising in the local press rarely works – I have found it tends to attract the wrong kind of candidate. Word of mouth can often put you face to face with likely aspirants.

When you have your candidate, you then have a couple of hour-long interviews at the most to judge their suitability. When I was in industry I attended several courses on effective interviewing, but I don't think they made me any better at this difficult task. I rely on my "gut feel" when hiring people, coupled with a little imagination of what life is going to be like with this person by my side all the time. You are taking a chance, and if your decisions generally are more right than they are wrong, then I suspect you are as good at choosing people as anyone is.

The secret, really, is to hire, then decide over the first few weeks or so whether it is going to work out. If you have serious doubts, then end it quickly and start again. An unsatisfactory relationship with someone who works for you can be a real catastrophe, and "trying to work it out" is just not worth the candle.

Assuming you have a good candidate, and have agreed on pay and conditions, you need to formalise the relationship with an employment contract. Simply, this is a piece of paper which confirms the terms of employment and is signed by both parties. You need to confirm the job title (trainee photographer or studio assistant), but leave the specific duties fairly open – "to assist the photographer on a day-to-day basis" is fine. Specify the weekly pay, and the notice required by either party to terminate the contract – a week or a month depending on how you feel. Build in a trial period; three months is usually long enough to evaluate someone's performance. State when the wages will be reviewed (usually annually).

Finally, include the policy on paid holidays. The norm is for the employee to earn holiday entitlement on the basis of, say, one and a half days per month during the first year, to be taken the following year. It is normal for the employee to take compulsory paid holiday during your annual shutdown period (if you have one), whether or not they have earned the entitlement.

Draw up the contract the day your assistant starts work, make sure you have both signatures on it, and keep your copy in a safe place.

You are also going to have to notify the Inland Revenue that you now have an employee subject to PAYE contributions. They will send you an enormous employers' kit, which is quite well done and answers most questions as to what deductions you make and how. You must also notify the DSS and make employer's and employee's National Insurance contributions.

You must also carry employer's insurance, and display your certificate in a prominent place.

Expansion

The next temptation is to look at larger premises, with a couple of studios maybe, and an additional photographer. But expansion along these lines is something that you should consider very carefully indeed.

A larger studio usually means a much larger studio, and you are going to have to increase your turnover substantially to cover the increased overheads, plus the actual relocation costs. As your market size remains the same, this increased turnover will have to come from a much greater penetration of your existing market. Are you sure your market will stand it, and are you sure you can achieve it? The death knell of many fine small businesses is often tolled when they expand too quickly for the available market.

Also, take a look at your motivation very carefully. A small commercial studio can turn over in excess of £100,000 p.a. with a partner (wife or husband) and a good assistant. Moving into larger premises brings its own new set of major problems. It is tempting to say that if you have a nice business going already, why knock it?

It all depends on what kind of person you are. For some, the small business they have just created and are beginning to enjoy is only the start of great and wonderful things. Those adventurous souls will have no need of this book from here on in, and I wish them good fortune.

The profession of photography

Most European countries have qualifications for professional photographers, and it is not normally possible to practise in those countries without having obtained them. In this country, however, we have not achieved harmonisation internally, never mind with the rest of Europe. From personal experience, I find that the professional photographer commands much more respect in Europe than in the UK. Whether this is because of the requirement to qualify in the profession, or whether our continental cousin just behaves more professionally, is a debate I would prefer not to enter. The fact remains that we have a lot of work to do to improve our status as a profession.

A number of people have long been in favour of bringing in legislation which would make it illegal for a photographer to practice professionally unless they have reached a minimum standard of professional competence (as evidenced by a formal qualification).

The reasoning behind this is easy to understand. Photography suffers as much as any profession, and more than most, from the "cowboy" operators who take clients' money and leave behind not only unsatisfactory work, but a poor reputation for the profession as a whole. Opponents of registration, however, argue that at the end of the day the true professional will always survive, and really it is up to the client to choose a photographer as carefully as he would choose any other similar service.

I don't really feel strongly about it either way. If pressed I would probably favour the free market approach, as I think we all have a bit too much government in our lives.

If the client needs to be satisfied that the photographer he is choosing is competent, the British Institute of Professional Photography (BIPP) publish a list of photographers who have satisfied their various levels of competence, and also place an ad in each volume of the local Yellow Pages. Photographers who wish to be considered by potential clients who may consult these lists should take the necessary steps to become qualified and therefore included.

Membership of a professional association like the BIPP should certainly be a priority for any commercial photographer. The recent 1988 Copyright Act was a result of extensive work and lobbying by a group of these organisations. These people are working in our interests all the time and it is only fair, in my opinion, that we should support them.

In closing...

During the writing of this book I have been looking even more closely than usual at the attitude of the people who have sought advice from me, either at the start-up phase of a new business, or about the running of their existing venture. I therefore think a few general comments in conclusion are definitely in order.

I have seen only two distinct types of situation; no in-betweens. There are those who I am sure will succeed, and those who I am sure will fail.

I have seen those with "fire in their bellies", with a driving enthusiasm to get their show on the road and a dismissive attitude to difficulties that can sometimes be a little frightening to an advisor.

On the other hand, there have been those "laid back" entrepreneurs who believe that it will all come out right in the end, and that there is no real need for all this planning and marketing and burning midnight oil.

In twenty years of managing businesses, my experience is that invariably the former win and the latter lose.

We also tend to find a divergence of opinion on quality. There are those who will tell you that if a client accepts a job then the quality is fine. They claim that the secret of success and good profitability is to provide the minimum quality that the client will accept.

I feel that such opinions are more at home in a cheap furniture store than in a creative business like photography. My belief is that if you constantly strive for perfection, then you will probably reach excellence. I prefer to be known for excellence than adequacy.

We as a nation seem to be more affected than others by the "let's not get too excited about this" attitude. We tend to sit back and look for the comfortable easy way, not to disturb the status quo too much, not to work too hard. Often the attitude seems to be that surely all this planning and forecasting is textbook nonsense, and that the "real" entrepreneur doesn't need it.

I met one aspirant to riches through self-employment who felt that a certain current magnate of a major retail chain would never have done cash planning when he started with his barrow in Covent Garden, and look at him now. We'll just start trading and see how it works out ...

Also, "Mañana" is as prevalent here as it is anywhere. In the last six months I have seen businesses wounded and opportunities missed because "we need a holiday", or "my wife can't leave work yet – we need the money", and so on. Sometimes I sit powerless on the sidelines and watch the opportunities go by, unchallenged, because someone just does not want to get off their backside and go and grab them. Tomorrow; maybe.

Happily, we are not all like this. One young tiger recently broke all records. Having reached the point of total frustration in employment, he knew he could do better on his own. With very little capital, in the space of less than a month he conceived his business, completed his budgets and cash planning, obtained his financing, leased and fitted out his studio, and started trading. His first month's turnover was nearly twice his forecast.

The armchair entrepreneurs at this point scream "luck". My reply is to quote Stephen Leacock, the Canadian economist:

"I am a great believer in luck, and the harder I work the more I have of it".

Appendix A
10 PRACTICAL EXAMPLES

In this section we are going to look at ten typical examples of the kind of work a small provincial photographic studio may be asked to perform.

The pictures have been chosen not to illustrate any particular creative skill, or even because I particularly like them. They are examples of how a client's brief can be satisfied, and every one of these was successful, being used several times in brochures or ads. In the case of the more experimental shots, each was also success-ful in having been used as the basis for a final ad or brochure shot.

Example 1: rubber stamps

Example 1: rubber stamps

This shot does break the rules in this selection, in that I actually quite like the pic!

The brief was totally open, except that the shot should be

landscape and crop to A3. The client (the manufacturer) came to me direct requesting the best shot I could produce for the cover of his sales brochure. He had felt an airy "high key" shot would be nice, but he'd leave it up to me – maybe a red flower somewhere? I have learned that what "would be nice" usually means "it is mandatory", so I set about producing a pleasing arrangement of the stamps incorporating a red carnation.

The products were set up on a sheet of 6mm glass which in turn was resting on a white Colorama roll on the studio table. The paper dropped to the floor behind the table, then ran up the studio wall about six feet behind.

The lighting on the background was chosen at 1 stop over the correct "highlight" reading to make sure there was little or no tone on the tranny. The camera was a Toyo 5x4G fitted with a Symmar S 360mm lens – it didn't look right with anything shorter. Film stock was Kodak EPN 100.

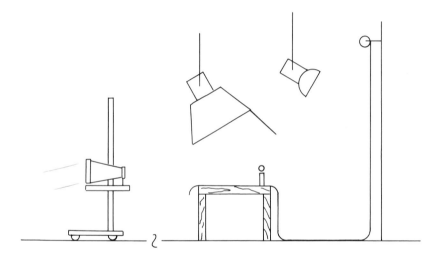

Studio set-up, rubber stamps

*Example 2:
salmonella*

Example 2: "salmonella"

The brief for this shot came after doing a "capabilities" brochure shoot for a local hi-tech company providing biological analysis services to the feed, food and pharmaceutical industries.

Most of the brochure was shot "straight", but a creative lead transparency was needed for a header for the microbiological assay section. My brief was to provide "something colourful".

I took several Petri dishes back to the studio with various nasties growing in agar – one dish was said to contain a virulent form of salmonella. In the past I had played with taking photographs through crossed polarisers, but only on a small scale. Using 20in square Lee polarisers, I tried various arrangements of dishes, with the result you see here.

The set-up consisted of a Bowens Monolite Silver mounted on a low level floor stand, fitted with a Squarelite and plastic diffuser. Taped to the top surface was a 20in panel of polarising film from Lee, with the Petri dishes arranged on top.

The camera, a Wista field, was mounted above the Monolite with a gelatine filter holder containing a 3in Lee polariser attached to the 210mm Symmar S lens. The filter holder was rotated until the polarisers were completely crossed, and the shot was taken on Fujichrome 50 RFP 5x4in sheet film.

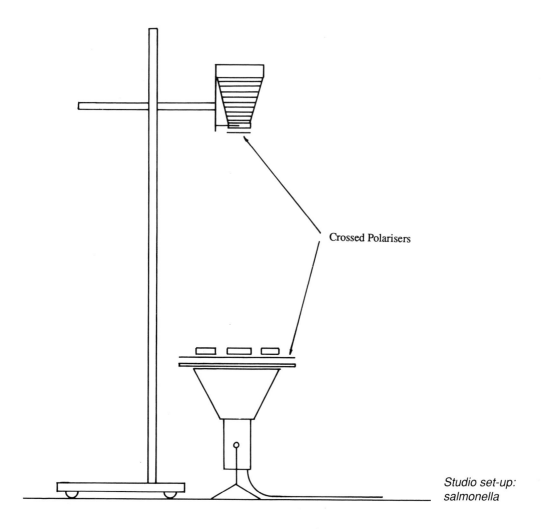

Crossed Polarisers

Studio set-up:
salmonella

*Example 3:
heating
elements*

Example 3: heating elements

This shot is a result of a couple of days spare studio time, knowing
that a commission was just around the corner.

The picture was required for the front cover of a trade catalogue, for a manufacturer of industrial and OEM heating elements.
The catalogue commission was in the hands of a design agency
which was looking for some inspiration as far as the cover was concerned.

179

When the products were delivered from the client, I began to appreciate the designer's problem. All the elements were coated with a matt black compound, and a pile of them on the table looked quite disgusting.

As the product range included halogen cooker elements, I decided to use a much enlarged shot of a lit halogen element as a background, with an assembly of elements photographed in front, using front projection techniques.

Firstly the cooker element had to be photographed, and a reddish filter had to be used to keep colour in the shot. About 30cc red with 10cc yellow was chosen in the end, with an exposure time of about 10 minutes on Kodak EPN film. Only a portion of the heating elements were included in the frame, and these were shot on the diagonal to create interest and a little tension. The elements were bolted to the studio table, which had previously been covered with a piece of brown melamine.

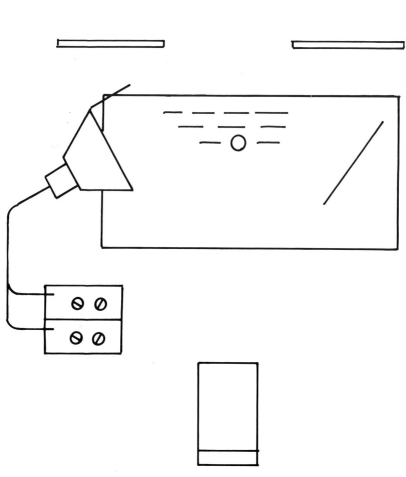

Studio set-up: heating elements

Before the front projection was set up, test shots were taken with Polaroid. These were disappointing as the elements absorbed all the light, leaving dirty black silhouettes. However, using a couple of Quad packs and Keylight reflectors changed the situation totally. These overexposed the elements by about 3.5 stops, giving them a silvery appearance but retaining their shape, hence acceptable from a product identification point of view. They were lit from one side by three Quad heads on full power, with a small silver reflector on the opposite side kicking back a little light into the shadow.

A screen was built just behind the table to keep stray light out of the front-pro screen. The halogen cooker element slide was put into the Hensel Super Compact 2 projector, which was fitted with a Bronica SQA camera with 105mm lens. Exposure was balanced using Polaroid, keeping the aperture small to keep the background as sharp as possible. The shot was taken on Kodak EPN stock.

The designer was delighted with the shot, and only very minor modifications were made for the final (commissioned) photograph.

Example 4:
the ten minute
ten-eight

Example 4: the ten minute ten-eight

This shot shows the virtue of a ready made product table, set up with its own soft box, ready to go. This floral study took literally ten minutes to set up and photograph using one light, a couple of side reflectors and an 8x10in camera fitted with a standard 360mm lens.

One of the problems of a "provincial" studio is that it is never seen to be as good as a proper "London" studio, and occasionally you will come across someone who takes great pleasure in ramming this down your throat. I had just finished a brochure shoot for one of my regular floral accessory clients, when we were visited by one of the many photographic "experts" you will be plagued with in this business, complete with his copy of the latest amateur magazine. "Of course", he said loftily, looking around the mess of cut flowers, discarded boxes and pools of water that usually remain after a floral session, "you really aren't equipped here to do the job properly on 8x10, you need much more lighting and facilities".

Without a word, I disappeared into the darkroom, loaded one 10x8in slide, popped the prepared arrangement on to the product table, and gave two exposures, one at the flashmeter reading, and one at a third of a stop more. The film was in the Jobo within five minutes of being shot and a dry tranny was on the light box within the hour.

Fits of pique apart, I showed the tranny to my client the next day, who promptly insisted on using 8x10 for the main shot for every ad shoot after that, whereas before he had never wanted to go to the expense of using it!

Incidentally, my 8x10in camera has paid for itself more quickly than just about any other piece of equipment, but clients do need to see an example before they will approve the considerably higher costs.

Lighting was a standard Bowens Mistylite fitted with a Quad 1500 head at full power. For the rest: f32 on EPN100 sheet film; E6 done in a Jobo CPA2 with Photo Technology three-bath chemistry. I put a very slight front tilt on the lens to maintain sharpness.

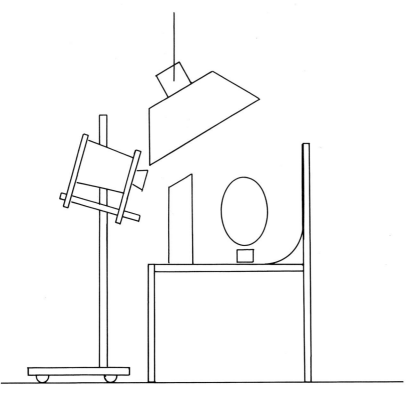

Studio set-up: the ten minute ten-eight

*Example 5:
microfilm unit*

Example 5: microfilm unit

Companies that advertise in county business magazines are often offered the front cover for free, or for very little, if they have a suitable transparency. In many cases all the design work is done by the magazine, so it represents a very economical way of getting your name in front of the punter.

I have included this tranny, which was commissioned for the front cover of *Cambridgeshire Business*, because it was a little tricky in that three different light colours were involved, each requiring separate attention.

The main lighting had to be set up first, and the designer wanted a "vignette" (light tapering off to dark at the top and back) so that the magazine title could be reversed out. The screen of the unit came out the most evil emerald green colour on Polaroid, and the standard tungsten light of the projector source was yellow. Obviously two exposures were going to be needed, one for the overall view with flash, and one for the screen, but with suitable filtration.

As there was no time to do a filtration test, I guessed at the filtration for the screen at about 40cc Magenta, but this would affect the light spilling out of the lamphouse of the unit. Magenta and yellow equals red, so I cut some cyan foil lighting filter material to fit inside the casing of the lamp house.

I bracketed filtration as well, giving two sets of exposures at 30 and 40cc magenta. 10 seconds or so handled the screen with the modelling lamps of the flash switched off, and the 30cc magenta left just a little green in the screen – this preferred by the client.

The main (unfiltered) exposure was f22 on 5x4in EPN with about 750 joules into a Bowens Litalite. The screen exposure was 10 seconds at f11 with the filtration. The lens was a 210mm Symmar S, and a little front tilt was applied to even up sharpness all over.

The resultant composite transparency worked quite well, and was later used for a brochure and advertising.

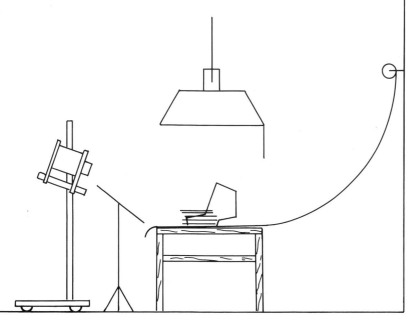

Studio set-up: microfilm unit

Example 6:
mannequins

Example 6: mannequins

I chose this shot because it shows the necessity of having a high ceiling, and that a transparency often has to cover much more area than the subject demands.

This was for a page in a sales brochure for protective racing clothing, where the designer wanted to superimpose the copy onto the same background as the illustration. Normally a catalogue like this would be shot on 6x7cm format, but the large area of empty space at the top would mean image sizes of less than 3cm, and definition would not be satisfactory. We therefore had the problem of shooting a set twelve feet high on 5x4in with a studio 28 feet long. This was the only time I have ever used a 150mm lens in the studio.

The more observant will notice that we used several mannequins and only one model. This was to economise on modelling fees, but offsetting this was time lost in dressing the mannequins – models usually dress themselves!

Lighting was standard. Two Bowens Monolite Silvers with Maxilite reflectors lit the top of the set, whilst the subjects were lit with two Quad heads into Litalite softboxes either side of the camera. A Toyo monorail was used, fitted with a Rodenstock Sironar "N" 150mm lens – still one of the finest lenses I've ever used.

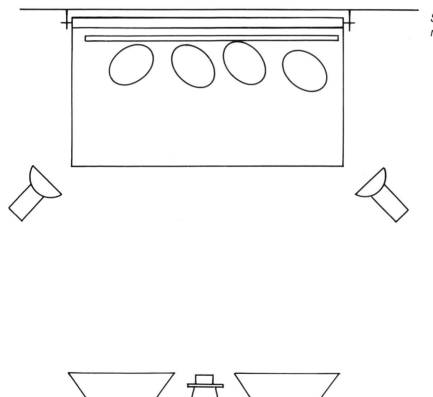

Studio set-up: mannequins

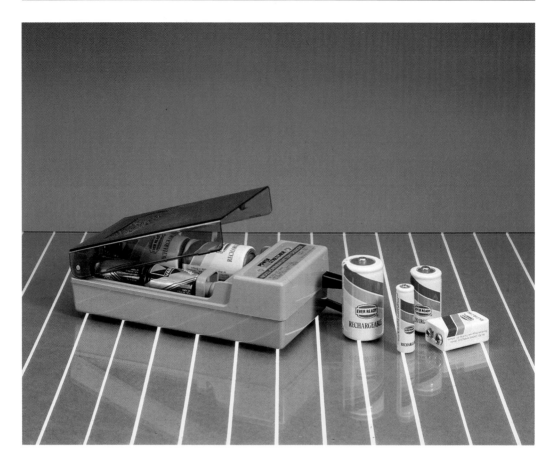

Example 7: battery charger

*Example 7:
battery charger*

Photography for packaging is an important part of the commercial studio's work. This shot has been included because it shows the importance of correct positioning of the product in the transparency. It also illustrates some of the set techniques described earlier.

In any packaging photograph it is absolutely essential to have a copy of the fold diagram before you even start to consider setting up the shot. In this example, the product and the batteries take up the top and right hand end of the box, plain tone being used on the back. I actually used a tracing of the fold pattern to 5x4in scale before finally shooting, so that the folds would occur in the right places.

The set was lit from both above and below. The background was a Colorama Rainbow sheet, orange to black, hung vertically behind the table, about one foot away. This was lit with "spill" light from the top light, a Bowens Quad fitted to a Litalite softbox. The "sandwich" on the table was a sheet of 6mm float glass, a sheet of diffusing mylar, a yellow foil, strips of brown art card taped 4mm apart, and finally another sheet of float glass on top to give some reflections of the product. The diffuser was taken off the bottom Litalite, which was mounted right up against the lower sheet of glass.

From the camera point of view, the standard Toyo with the 210mm lens was used, with the back tilted to exaggerate the perspective a little. The front was then tilted to give almost the "Scheimpflug" conditions of depth of field. Lighting was balanced using Polaroids, as flashmeters aren't much use in these conditions. Several sheets of film were exposed at each bracket.

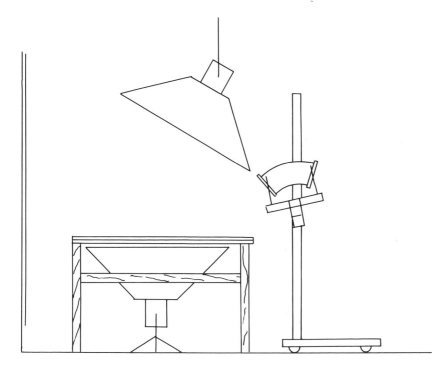

Studio set-up: battery charger

Example 8: glassware with "condensation"

Every now and again you will be asked to "do something like this" – a client will see an ad in a magazine that he likes, and wants something similar. I don't feel there is anything wrong in this providing the result is not out and out plagiarism. This shot of

Example 8: glassware with "condensation"

glassware was inspired by some beautiful work in a French consumer magazine.

The photography was used for both advertising and packaging, which meant that plenty of "air" was needed around the products. The set-up was classic – the glassware was shot as a silhouette, with a piece of ground glass between the lit white Colorama and the products.

The condensation "runs" were painted on the reverse with Canada Balsam, and bits of black paper were stuck on the white background in strategic places to darken the "wet" areas. Be careful with Canada Balsam, it doesn't set, so a "condensation run" continues to run all afternoon. We worked quite quickly after we noticed this!

Sinar P2 with 240mm Symmar.

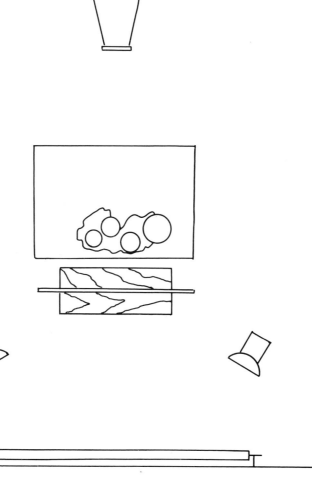

Studio set-up: glassware with "condensation"

Example 9: fire and ice

From a commercial point of view, this is the most successful photograph I have ever taken. It is still being used at the time of writing,

some five years after the shoot.

The brief was to "hit 'em hard – be totally unsubtle", and show that this top of the line motorcycle glove could cope with anything the elements could throw at it.

Having established that this was going to be a fantasy shot, totally "over the top", the designer and I sat down to some lateral thinking. Could we have a hand holding a ball of fire with icicles hanging from the other side, and maybe a thunderstorm in the background? Why not, said I, front pro is a wonderful tool.

The first problem was to get a nice, round, fiery ball. The ball had to be about 6 inches in diameter to fit neatly into the glove, so we set about finding one of suitable size that we could set fire to. We also started looking at fuels that would provide the right kind of flame. Gas burned too blue; oil took too much lighting; petrol was just plain dangerous. We also found that we needed an absorbent ball, to retain the burning fuel long enough to take the pic.

Eventually we gave up trying to find something ready made, and approached a local potter to throw a hollow ball on his wheel, but not to fire or glaze it since we needed absorbency. He made exactly what we wanted, and we took this limp, fragile thing away to practise pyrotechnics in our back garden, much to the disgust of the neighbours. At about midnight, with all the neighbours' curtains drawn, we found that if the ball was hot, and if we then poured about two tablespoonsful of lighter fluid on it and threw a match at it, we were rewarded with a shapely flame of high luminosity.

After rewarding ourselves with G&Ts, we agreed to put the flame on EPN the following afternoon.

This passed without particular incident, using an RB with a 180mm lens. We used two tins of lighter fluid and four rolls of film, and almost set fire to the black Colorama backdrop, but when the film came out of the drier we had every shape imaginable, including one that was a perfect treble clef. We mounted this in a 645 mount for the Hensel, and I popped out to take some storm cloud pics (heavily Cokined) over the Cambridgeshire fens.

The following day we set up to shoot the combination. The glove, suitably decorated with perspex icicles (lovingly made by the art director's assistant) was positioned on a Studio Accessories stand about four feet off the ground and about six feet in front of the front-pro screen.

Format was decided at 6x7cm as I was sure we would eat film, and also the RB67 would be a lot quicker than the monorail. Film was to be EPN. The power settings for the two front pro exposures (sky and ball of fire) were found using Polaroids. Luckily they were both one third power at f16, which meant I wouldn't have to remember to change power as I switched the trannies in the Hensel.

Then we lit the glove, using two Quadmatics fitted with squarelights, one 45 degrees above and in front of the glove, with barn doors keeping stray light off the front pro screen. The other sat under the glove pointing upwards, with a deep blue gel for the icicles.

The first exposure was made for the sky with the Hensel only and the Quads switched off. Then the tranny in the projector was changed for the ball of fire, the Quads switched on, and the fire tranny centered in the glove with the modelling lamp. The second exposure put the glove and the fire on the film. I bracketed one stop either way with each light source, and two rolls of film were all that was needed.

The original 6x7cm transparency was then duped up to 5x4in for the colour separations.

There are a lot of faults in this shot. You can see the Black and Decker Workmate behind the flame; there are other faults if you look carefully. On the other hand, it has been used in brochures, catalogues, point of sale material, countless ads, and has even gone on to a record cover.

It has certainly killed loads of Russians...

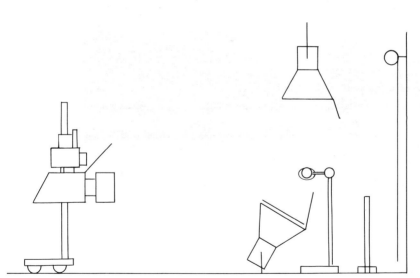

Studio set-up: fire and ice

Example 10:
"Jodi"

Example 10: "Jodi"

Again this is a shot that has already been referred to in the text. Although the major ad campaign for this client was run in colour, the original concept was for black and white. The Ektachrome was only shot as an afterthought.

This was really quite a simple shot to take, the only difficulty was in having a soft enough quality of light for the model coupled with a sharp cut-off at the edge of the table, as the designer specifically did not want the table lit. His instructions were that the table should be visible, but not lit.

The lighting was originally set up using two softboxes, one

above the other, but there was so much light flying around the set I removed the bottom one, replacing it with a white polystyrene reflector. Light was kept off the table by means of black screens.

The shot was taken on a Bronica SQA with a 105mm lens, on Kodak Plus X film. The colour shots were taken on Ektachrome EPN roll film, and duped up to 5x4in for the ads.

This shot shows what can be achieved when an art director, model, photographer and stylist work well together.

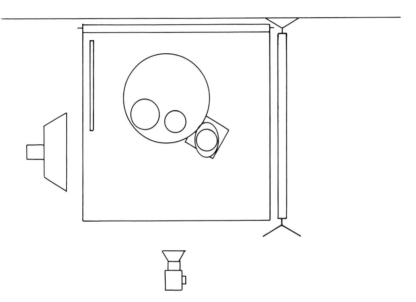

Studio set-up: "Jodi"

Appendix B
A MONORAIL PRIMER

The average monorail camera can be an intimidating beast, especially some of the newer ones. But like most complex things, it is based on the simplest of principles. Once you have a reasonable grasp of them, using a monorail need hold no terrors for you. Jobs in the studio which are difficult to handle, if not impossible, on a standard roll film reflex, will become almost routine on your trusty "five-four".

If you have bought one of the simpler models, a Cambo SC2 or Toyo C, for example, you will find it a little easier to master at first than one of the more advanced "yaw free" models. You can always progress later, one of the advantages of five-four being that when you change cameras you keep the lenses.

The basic monorail camera consists of two frames or "standards" which slide along an accurately machined base or rail. One standard carries the lens, and the other carries the back, in which is mounted the focusing screen and holder for the film cassette or "dark slide". The two standards are joined together by the bellows, which is interchangeable in all but the most elementary cameras.

Both standards are equipped with mechanisms for swinging or tilting the back and lens up or down, and from side to side, and also for shifting up, down and sideways at right angles to the monorail. It is these mechanisms which allow us to solve particular problems of depth of field and perspective, and are known as "movements".

Let's look first at the movements which shift the lens or back up, down and sideways. These are known as the "decentring" movements, because they move the lens or back off the optical centre.

Let's leave five-four for the moment and look at a problem we often have in 35mm photography. People who, like myself, are lucky enough to live in East Anglia, are constantly occupied photographing the most beautiful small village churches, many like miniature cathedrals. If you stand in a position which gives the most natural perspective, to fill the frame with church you need to fit a 50mm or 35mm lens, and tilt the back of the camera upwards "to get it all in".

The result looks horrible, with the sides of the building leaning in. So, we remove the 35mm lens and fit a 24mm. Now the building is square, but the image is much smaller on the film. You will also

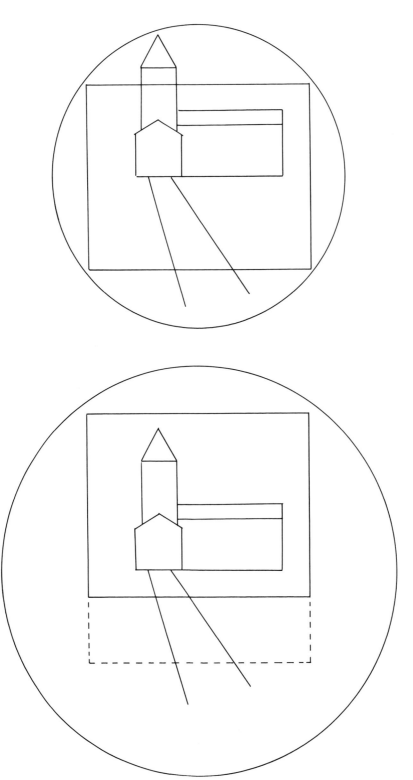

Top: normal focal length, normal coverage. Bottom: normal focal length, wide coverage

have noticed that for the sides of the building to be square, the back of the camera has to be vertical, and that the ground level cuts the pic exactly in half, giving you loads of foreground. If you are shooting on negative material, then you can always crop it off, but then you are only enlarging a portion of the negative. A loss of quality is inevitable.

In a 35mm camera, unless you fit a "PC" (perspective control) lens, the area of film illuminated is just large enough to cover the 24x36mm film frame, and consists of a circle about 45mm in diameter. Imagine, however, a lens that has the same focal length, but has a much larger circle of illumination, or "coverage". Such a lens produces the same image size as your 35mm lens, but has a much wider field of view. If the total circle of illumination were 60mm diameter, for instance, then there would still be an image formed outside the 24x36mm frame you see through the viewfinder.

So if you had a means of moving either the lens or the film up or down, then you could select a part of the larger image formed by the lens, and have a full frame pic of the church without distorting the sides. Compare the two lenses shown opposite.

The first illustration shows that the coverage of the standard 35mm lens is not enough to include the top of the church without tilting the camera. The second shows another lens in use that has the same focal length, but a wider field of view. From the illustration you can see that if you could raise the lens, or lower the film, then you would be able to obtain a full frame pic of the church, without any distortion of the verticals.

Put into practice, the two illustrations on the next page show the same subject photographed with 35mm lenses, the first with a standard 35mm lens, and the second with a 35mm PC lens. The difference is not just in the fact that the PC lens allows vertical movement, the lens itself must have a wider angle of coverage to allow the use of such movement.

Back to our monorail. Large format lenses, like the PC lens, have much larger circles of illumination than is required to just "cover" the standard sheet of film. As a result you can use extensive rise, fall and cross movements, both on the front and the back – you can "crop in the camera".

In the studio, it is rare to use a rising front; the most commonly used shift movement is the drop front. In many pack shots, the client often wishes the writing on the top of the pack to be visible, forcing you to look down on the product somewhat. Without any movements, the pack sides diverge towards the top, and the shape of the pack is distorted. If you keep the back of the camera vertical, and either drop the front standard or raise the rear standard until the pack is central in the frame, then you will have vertical verticals and be able to see the top of the pack.

This "correction", if applied freely, can distort the pack in

another way. With the shift movements out to nearly maximum, you are at the edges of the field of a wide angle lens, and the familiar "wide-angle" distortion becomes apparent, with elongated shapes and elliptical circles. The compromise I find acceptable is to fully correct initially, then back off the shift a little, tilting the camera slightly off the vertical to have slightly diverging verticals, but a visually more acceptable picture.

You will use this position frequently in product photography. The design of the top of a coffee pot is as important to the designer as the side elevation, and he will want this detail in the picture. Similarly, kitchen pots and pans need to show the non-stick interior. You will come across endless applications.

Just as the vertical rise and fall is useful, so is the side-to-side movement. Most textbooks these days show how a mirror can be photographed without showing a reflection of the camera and photographer by using side shift, but there are more practical uses in the studio. In conjunction with a drop front, a side shift can show the side as well as the top of a product if the movements aren't used to excess. Chrome coffee pots, for example, can often give a beautiful reflection of the camera, which can sometimes be minimised by moving the camera a little to one side and shifting the front. Be careful though; remember that you are in effect selecting

Left: In order to "get it all in", the camera has to be tilted upwards, distorting the perspective. 35mm Nikkor lens.
Right: Here, a "shift lens" has been used to select an undistorted portion from the larger available image. 35mm PC Nikkor lens

bits off the edges of a wide angle lens, with its own associated distortion. Sometimes what looks acceptable on your ground-glass screen looks terrible on a tranny – if in doubt, take a 5x4in Polaroid and look at it in the front office.

The shift movements exploit an already formed image by selecting particular bits of it for the film. The swing movements actually alter the image on the ground-glass screen, either by affecting the perspective, or the depth of field. Generally, we use the front swings to alter depth of field, and the rear swings to alter perspective. Let's take the front movement first.

In a camera with no movements, the front and rear limits of depth of field are parallel with the film, because the axis of the lens is parallel to the film. If the back of the camera is not parallel to the lens mount, then the plane of sharp focus will not be parallel to the film, and one side of the pic can be sharp whilst the other is not. This effect is exploited in the swing movements of a monorail camera. Let's look at a typical example.

The illustrations below show a monorail camera set up to photograph a long carpet. In the top sketch, no movements are applied, and the camera is set up to have all of the carpet from A to B visible on the ground-glass.

Point A on the carpet is brought to a focus at point a; similarly the far point B is sharp at point b. The dotted line ab shows the plane of focus with the lens in that particular position, and it can be seen that if you moved the lens, or the back, backwards or

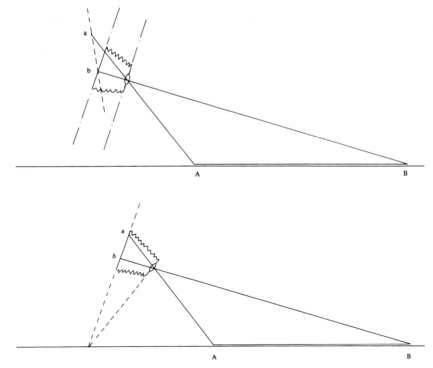

Swing front illustrations

forwards, you could get either point A sharp, or point B, but not both at the same time.

From the illustration, you can see that if you were to just swing the back into the ab plane, then everything would be in focus from A to B, and indeed this is one way to achieve overall sharpness. Swinging the back, however, will additionally alter the perspective, so that the shape of the carpet will be different on the film than it would be if your eye were at the back of the camera. The correct way to handle the problem is to swing the lens forward as shown in the lower sketch; then you have the whole carpet in focus, with correct perspective.

There is one particular set of conditions which is very useful to the 5x4 photographer. On the lower sketch on the previous page, extend the line AB to the left, under the camera, to A'. Then, extend the line through the back ab to cross the line AA' at C. Then, swing the lens panel so that the line through the lens mount LM crosses both these lines at C also. Under these conditions, anything on the line A'AB to infinity will be in focus.

This is the "Scheimpflug" principle, named after the Austrian sage who first discovered it. Properly defined, it states that if the planes of the film, lens mount and subject intersect in a single line, then depth of field in the subject plane will be infinite.

What this means is that when your art director is laying out a group of products to photograph, you need have no worry about the distance from the front to the back of the set. Providing you can draw a line through the set – a mean "plane of focus" – then you can swing the front to establish the Scheimpflug conditions, and be sure that all products in the set are sharp. A typical example is shown on the next page.

In this example, the "near" and "far" limits of depth of field are above and below the "plane of focus" line. Because the eye is normally used to things going out of focus at the back, you can let the focus slip a little at the base of the set, and you won't have a problem. This is one of the occasions where your competitor with no movements on his roll film reflex will fail, whereas you can give the client a good sharp shot.

Now, let's look at back swing.

If you position yourself to one side of a building and point the camera "square on" to the front, you usually have a fairly uninteresting record of a parallel front and sides, with no "depth" to the shot. Normally you would move further to one side and take a three-quarters view, but in this instance say there is a ten foot brick wall in your way. You can help things a little by swinging the back, and introducing some perspective into the front by making one side of the building taller than the other. If you leave the front alone, then you will have to shoot at a small stop to give adequate depth of field. But if you swing the front, to introduce a

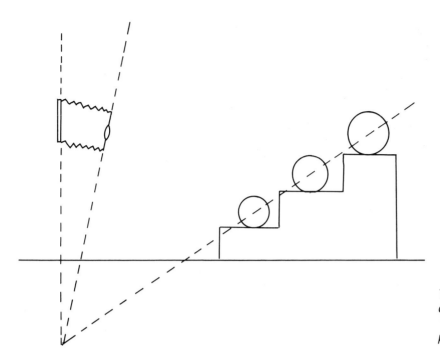

*Typical use
of swing
for product
photography*

little Scheimpflug effect, then you can have the front sharp all over as well.

In the studio, the back can alter the shape of products viewed from unusual angles. Moved one way it can exaggerate perspective. Board games, for example, can benefit from this treatment, especially if a little front swing sharpens the board up all over. Swinging the back the other way will often soften a hard perspective because you are too close to a product.

The rule is, get the shape right with the back, and sharpen up all over with the front. Like the shift movements, you can use both vertical and horizontal swings, separately, or in combination.

This is basically all you need to know to get started with your monorail. If you have a simple camera, then you will probably have noticed that when you swing a lens or back, you have to re-focus to get the image back into focus. Fancy monorails swing the panel around where the manufacturer thinks the optical axis of the lens is, and re-focusing movements of this kind are less severe. Personally, I believe the simpler a camera is the better to start off with, and the standard Toyo C or Cambo SC2 take some beating in my book.

Before we leave monorails, note that most dealers will sell you a 150mm lens with your camera. I have found this focal length to be near useless in the studio. A 210mm or 180mm is a much better bet for still life work, whilst outside, for architecture, a 120mm or 90mm is much more use. Unless you plan on moonlighting and doing scenic work for calendars and suchlike, save your money and get a 210mm and 90mm combination.

Also bear in mind that most roll film back adapters of the sliding type are difficult to use with the 150mm. The bellows end up so compressed that any movement is severely restricted.

Buy loads of dark slides – most dealers have heaps of them around second-hand for a fiver or so each. Twenty is the minimum; you can be comfortable with thirty. Clients don't appreciate paying £40 – £50 per hour for you to disappear every five minutes to load a couple of dark slides, although you never know, you might just find an assistant that can do it for you ...

Appendix C
A BASIC THEORY REFRESHER

In Chapter 1 we discussed the need for a sound foundation in photographic theory. The problem with modern automatic cameras is that if you use them a lot, you tend to rely on the automation and forget the theory you learned a long time ago when you first took up photography. Generally, if you don't use something for years, it tends to become a little rusty. However, a quick clean is usually all that is necessary to get things going again.

This is the "quick clean" on your photo theory.

Basic optics

A camera consists of a light-tight box containing photographic film at one end, and a lens at the other. Between the lens and the film there is some means of interrupting the flow of light through the box, called a shutter. This can consist of interleaving blades of thin metal mounted in the lens, and is thus called a "between lens" or "leaf" shutter, or can consist of fabric or metal blinds mounted immediately in front of the film, called a "focal plane" shutter because it is situated almost in the "focal plane" of the film.

The lens is mounted in such a way so that the distance from the lens to the film can be varied, or the lens "focused". This section on theory is primarily concerned with the focusing of the lens, and the effect of focusing on the sharpness of the image on the film.

When discussing optical theory, we do have to make some assumptions to make the mathematics manageable. One of these assumptions is that a lens is "thin", and has therefore no thickness. There are corrections to the formulae that can be applied for the true "thick" lens, but they need not concern us.

A thin lens has two principle properties, the focal length and the aperture. If you hold a thin lens up to the sun and focus a sharp image on a piece of white paper, then, if you can measure the distance between the lens and the paper before it catches fire, then that distance is the "focal length" of the lens. Rays of light from infinity are brought to focus at the "focal point" of the lens, which is situated at a distance equal to the focal length from the lens.

Because our thin lens is symmetrical, it has two focal points, one in front of and one behind the lens, called the front focal point and the rear focal point respectively. We'll look at aperture in a moment.

If we now need to produce a sharp image of a subject situated between the front focal point of a lens and infinity, then the image formed by the lens will be found behind the rear focal point. If the film is situated in a camera at the rear focal point, then to bring the sharp image of our subject onto the film, the film has either to be moved back, or the lens moved forward. Look at the diagram below.

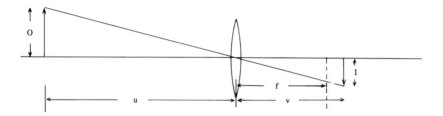

What we have here is a representation of an object of height "O" at a distance of "u" in front of a thin lens of focal length "f", producing an image of height "I" at a distance of "v" behind the thin lens.

By similar triangles:

O/I = u/v

But, because v is approximately equal to f, O/I is approximately equal to u/f.

O/I is called the "Reduction", and u is called the "Range", and we know that f is the focal length. Our formula therefore in words means that:

Range is approximately equal to reduction times focal length; or, reduction is approximately equal to range divided by focal length.

Let's look at a practical application. Among other things, this formula tells us whether our studio is large enough for a particular application.

A client has just phoned wanting us to photograph an object 3 metres high on 5x4in sheet film. We have a 150mm lens on our camera, and the studio is 6 metres long. Our client wants a landscape format picture. Can we do it?

Taking into account background rolls and the length of the camera, let us assume the maximum distance we have between the lens and object, the "range", is 4.5 metres. A sheet of 5x4in film is actually 10cm by 12.4cm, and you lose a few mm all round in processing. For safety's sake, allow an image height on the film of 8cm. "Reduction" is therefore 300/8, or 37.5. Our camera therefore needs to be placed 37.5 focal lengths away from the object, or 37.5 times 150mm. This works out at 5.63 metres. We can just do it.

This little formula is easy to keep in your head. Calculate the reduction on to the film (object size divided by image size), multiply the result by the focal length of your lens, and you know whether you can do the job or not. The formula is an approximation, but it is certainly accurate enough for our purposes. Let's move on.

If you look at the next illustration, you will see that an object of height "O" is situated at a distance of "p" in front of the front focal point, and the image of height "I" resulting is situated at a distance "q" behind the rear focal point. The focal length of the lens is f.

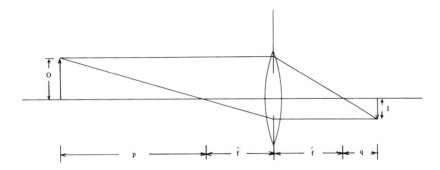

If the object were at infinity, then the image would coincide with the rear focal point, and q would be zero. Spend some time understanding this sketch; most optical theory is derived from it (physics students are excused).

From similar triangles:

O/I = f/q
and
O/I = p/f

Therefore:

f/q = p/f
or:
$p \times q = f^2$

These formulae are useful to calculate the amount a lens has to be moved forward to bring an image in focus on the film. Because the formulae measure from front and rear focal points they are accurate for all distances. Now, we can go on from this:

If an object is "n" focal lengths in front of the front focal point, then:

p = n x f.

So, from the above:

n x f x q = f^2

Or:

q = f/n

Or: if the object is "n" focal lengths in front of the front focal point, then the image is 1/n focal lengths behind the rear focal point.

This is a very important formula to have around. Most roll film and all 35mm cameras are equipped with focusing scales so that we can see at a glance whether we can focus a close object or not. Monorail cameras on the other hand have no such facilities. If we need to find out whether our lens/bellows combination will allow us to focus on an object close up, we have to use this formula. Just "trying it out" in front of a client is not very professional. Let's look at an example:

Suppose we have a monorail camera with a 150mm lens and a bellows capable of 300mm of extension. How close can we get to a subject to photograph it for maximum magnification?

We can do it in our head. With the bellows out to the 300mm maximum, the image will be 150mm behind the rear focal point. 1/n therefore equals one, therefore n=1. The object will therefore be one focal length in front of the front focal point. The front focal point is one focal length in front of the lens, so the object will be two focal lengths in front of the lens, or 300mm.

These two formulae are surprisingly useful, and while you don't need to know how to work them out, you should have them off pat in your mind. Many times, when you are visiting a client to discuss a job, you will be asked if a particular studio task is feasible. These formulae enable you to decide whether your studio and equipment can handle extra large or extra small product shots, and give you the confidence to talk with authority in front of your client. They are called the "range" and "extension" formulae respectively. Think in terms of numbers of focal lengths and you won't go far wrong.

Depth of field

It is well known that when you focus a camera on a particular subject, objects in front of your subject become progessively more and more unsharp as the distance away from it increases, and similarly, objects behind the subject progressively become more unsharp the further away they are. There is a zone in front of and behind your subject in which the sharpness is acceptable, and this zone is called the "depth of field".

The first thing we need to define is the acceptable limit of sharpness. This is purely arbitrary, and depends upon the degree of enlargement that the negative or transparency will have to undergo later. When a point goes out of focus, it changes into a blurred circle. When we define the size of that blur circle, we can calculate depth of field.

Most people use a figure of 1/1000 radians, and this is acceptable for day-to-day use. For more critical applications, a figure of 1/2000 radians is used. Using the methods described above, students of maths can prove that, for a lens of effective aperture A, distance "u" away from the focused image, depth of field on the "near" side is equal to:

$$u^2/(1000 \times A + u)$$

and depth on the "far" side is given by:

$$u^2/(1000 \times A - u)$$

This doesn't make much sense until you put some figures in the calculation. "A" is measured in the same units as the other dimensions, so you have first to know the relationship between f stops and effective aperture.

I remember asking candidates years ago at a job interview what "f stops" meant. It is surprising how many people who were supposed "experts" in photography didn't know. Here's the answer: the f stop is the focal length of the lens divided by the effective aperture, the actual diameter of the iris opening. The effective aperture A, therefore, is the focal length divided by the f stop. In good old feet and inches, a 6 inch lens at f8 has an effective aperture of three-quarters of an inch.

Going back to our formulae therefore, if we have our camera with a 150mm lens set at f8, (A therefore equal to 18.75mm) and focused on a subject at 3 metres, the "far" depth of field is:

$$df = 9/((1000 \times 0.01875) - 3) = 0.57 \text{ metres}$$

And the "near" depth of field is:

$$dn = 9/((1000 \times 0.01875) + 3) = 0.41 \text{ metres}$$

Looking at these figures, we now know that if the camera were focused exactly on 3 metres, everything would be sharp (within our limits) from 2.59 metres to 3.57 metres, and depth of field behind the subject is greater than that in front.

We can also see that depth of field decreases very rapidly as the camera/subject distance is reduced – close-ups have very little depth of field. We can also see that depth of field has nothing to do with camera size; it is the focal length of the lens that determines depth of field for any given aperture. It is the image size which counts: a 135mm lens on a 35mm SLR will have exactly the same depth of field as a 135mm Symmar on a 5x4in monorail, at the same aperture and subject distance.

Hyperfocal distance

I have included these two formulae for interest's sake; no-one is suggesting you go around with a calculator every time you need to establish depth of field. But starting with them you can arrive at some very useful rules of thumb, especially if you do a lot of company PR work or convention photography.

The first of these concerns the "hyperfocal distance". In the formulae above, if you make the object distance equal to 1,000 times the effective aperture, then depth of field extends from half this distance to infinity.

1,000 times the effective aperture is called the hyperfocal distance, and if you work it out for two or three apertures on your favourite location lenses, then, whether you can see to focus or not (or have time to focus), you can be sure of having enough depth of field.

If we look at a practical example, the effective aperture of a 35mm lens at f11 is about 3.5mm. 1,000 times this is 3.5 metres. If you set your lens to 3.5 metres, then everything will be in focus from 1.75 metres to infinity. If you are more particular and use 1/2000 radians, then you simply double the figures, set your lens to 7 metres and enjoy sharp pics from 3.5 metres to infinity.

These two basic formulae give us more. We can work out two very useful guides for banqueting photographers here. The first enables us to find where we should focus the camera given near and far limits, and the second gives us the f stop we should use. Looking at the first, if we call the near limit of depth of field "x" and the far "y", then:

x = u – dn, and y = u + df

Mess around for a while, and you end up with this:

u = 2xy/(x+y)

Or, the focusing distance is twice the product of near and far limits divided by the sum.

Practically, if the first person round a large table is 2 metres away from you, and the farthest guest is 4 metres away from you, you should set your lens to:
2 x 2 x 4 / 6 metres, or about 2.5 metres. In dimly lit dining rooms, sometimes this is the only way of focusing, unless you have a Leica....

The next is a little more involved, but not much.

First, find the hyperfocal distance. If you bothered to go through the maths for the formula above, you have found at one point that 1000 x A, or "h", is equal to:

$$h = ux/(u-x)$$

Or, hyperfocal distance is the product of focusing distance and near limit divided by the difference. So, in our case:

$$h = 2.5 \times 2 / (0.5), \text{ or } 10 \text{ metres}$$

h also equals 1000 x A, so A (effective aperture) is 1/100 metres, or one centimetre.

We are using an 85mm lens, and as:

$$A = \text{focal length/f stop}$$

$$f \text{ stop} = \text{focal length/A} = 8.5/1, \text{ or about } 8$$

We set our lens to f8.

These formulae are not really that difficult to use, and I have a little card with them written down in my camera bag. Let me restate them before we change the subject:

1. Focus the lens on twice the product of near and far limits of field divided by the sum.

2. Find the hyperfocal distance from the product divided by the difference of the focusing distance and the *near* limit.

3. Effective aperture A is h/1000 or h/2000 (your choice).

4. f stop is the focal length of your lens divided by effective aperture A.

I know all this seems quite a lot to take in, and is it really necessary?

That has to be up to you, but if you do spend the time to get familiar with the formulae you are in a much better situation than your competitor who relies on chance. Situations where you need to know what is going on include dim industrial interiors, the banqueting examples already mentioned, and group shots in dim lighting conditions. Theoretical knowledge of this type separates the men from the boys, and gives you enormous confidence in difficult situations.

Perspective

Before we leave optical theory, let's look at perspective. Often you hear, "let's change the lens and get a different perspective". This remark is very misleading, because perspective has nothing to do with the lens that you use. A scene is in "correct" perspective when the image that you see through the ground-glass of your camera is identical to the one that you see with the unaided eye.

If you set up a camera with a 50mm lens (on 35mm), then the perspective of the picture will be more or less correct. If you now change to a 24mm, then the angle of view immediately becomes wider. If, however, you were to select a portion of the view equivalent to the 50mm view and enlarge it to fill the frame, then the perspective would be identical to that produced by the 50mm lens. If you now walk forward so that the image in the viewfinder becomes the same size as the 50mm shot, then the perspective is distorted, the so-called "wide angle distortion". To alter the perspective we have had to move camera position.

You can prove the same thing with a telephoto lens.

Go back to the original position and fit a 90mm telephoto lens. You will now see a small section of the 50mm image. Reduce the size of that image so that objects are the same size as the 50mm shot, and the perspective remains the same. Move back so that you have the same field of view in the finder, and you have compressed telephoto perspective distortion.

Perspective is correct when the scene looks natural, when everything is in correct proportion, and is only changed when camera position is changed.

Exposure

The human eye is a near perfect camera. Not only does it autofocus with extraordinary speed, it has automatic aperture control and can cope with different levels of light that are far outside the range of any film/lens combination.

Illumination, or light falling on a subject, is measured in "foot candles", one foot candle being the illumination resulting from the light of one standard candle one foot away. If that light falls on a perfectly white surface, then the "luminance" is equal to one foot lambert.

Having some idea of that level of luminance, the light levels that a camera and film have to put up with vary from a sunlit snow scene at about 10,000 foot lamberts to dark shadows in a church interior at less than one hundredth of a foot lambert. This represents a ratio of a million to one. Standard transparency film can tolerate about five stops, or 32:1, so we see that accurate exposure measurement is something we should all know about.

The amount of light reaching the film in a camera is controlled by the shutter and the lens aperture. The shutter settings are obvious – 1/60 of a second admits twice as much light as 1/125, but the aperture values are less clear. We seem to have got stuck with a system of numbers which many have tried, unsuccessfully, to change.

Around the lens you have numbers from f2.0 to f22, and these, as we saw earlier, represent the focal length of the lens divided by the effective aperture. Each setting represents a doubling of the light entering the camera, as you go up the scale. Thus, f11 lets twice as much light in as f16, f5.6 lets four times as much in as f11. Lovers of maths will see that each number is the previous multiplied or divided by the square root of two, depending on whether you go up or down. This is how we change it; we now need to measure it.

There are two main ways to measure light. We can measure the intensity of light falling on a subject, the incident method, or we can measure the reflection of light from the subject, unsurprisingly called the reflected light method.

The first method, if used without corrections, will place the exposure evenly between the brightest and darkest areas of the subject, and, over the tolerance range of the film of about five stops will give the most information on the transparency. The extreme highlights will be a little overexposed, and the darkest shadows underexposed.

The measurement is taken using a normal exposure meter fitted with an incident light "integrator" or dome, and pointed at the camera from the subject position. If the lighting is from the side, I tend to move the cone slightly to one side to position it facing about a third of the way between the camera and the light, but this you find out in practice. (Don't do this if you are using a Weston with invercone – you don't need to.)

For normal subjects this is all you have to do, and you will be surprised at the accuracy of your exposures.

You can make modifications to your exposures if you have very dark or very light subjects. I photograph a lot of dark leather clothing, and I find that an extra stop on the incident light reading puts detail into the dark leather if the client doesn't like fill flash. Similarly, very light subjects such as white leather benefit from about half a stop underexposure.

Remember, however, that these modifications to the incident light reading will also affect the background.

If your client wants all the detail in black leather and the background right, then you have to introduce extra light, either with a reflector or fill flash. In the case of the light subject, you need to get it in the shade.

The second technique, which I use rarely, is the reflected light method, which measures the average of the light reflected from the subject. I find it unreliable, because most of the things I photograph have bright colours in them, or are biased towards the dark and dingy. If you use the meter in your camera, usually centre-weighted average, then the chances are you will be wrong. On the other hand, out shooting landscapes for stock, the average method tends to be not far off. However, I still prefer to use the incident light technique, especially if for any reason bracketing is impractical.

One meter which does use reflected techniques accurately is the spot meter. This measures a very small angle of reflected light, usually only 1 degree. With this meter you can select an area of the subject and expose specifically for it. If you habitually shoot white things, a spot meter is a good investment.

Most are equipped with three calibration marks, one which is set for shadow areas and gives the right exposure to give detail in shadows, one which is the standard 18% grey, and a third which is set for highlights and keeps the exposure under control when registering detail in whites and things. The shadow/highlight limits are usually 5 stops apart, keeping everything right in the film department. I have more problems with highlights than shadows, so I always take a spot highlight reading when confronted with a white car, or a white motorcycle suit, or a sunlit snow scene.

When I go out taking photographs on the motor racing circuit, a common problem that occurs is that of a white car against a background of dark trees. An uncorrected incident light reading will usually overexpose the car, as will an average centre-weighted reflected measurement. The only method I know is to use a spot meter or knock half a stop or so off an incident reading. The new matrix metering systems don't seem to cope too well with this situation either. And you can't bracket exposures on a car travelling at 180 m.p.h.!

Before we leave exposure meters, a word about the "Zone" system. Many darkroom workers extract the maximum from their film and papers by calculating exactly the exposure a film requires to reproduce a particular tone accurately on the paper, given specific processing.

The system works by dividing up a scene into a series of grey tones, each one stop apart, from a very dark shadow (Zone 1) to white (Zone 9). The standard 18% grey comes out at Zone 5.

These Zones are 8 stops apart, outside the range of colour transparency film.

Our type of work is not critical enough to use the system; all we have to know is that if we expose a scene at Zone 5 (most exposure meter indexes) then there is no wanted detail in the shadows below Zone 2.5, and no wanted detail in the highlights above Zone 7.5. If there are, they won't "come out".

I refer readers interested in this system to Minor White's excellent treatise on the subject, published by Morgan and Morgan, "The New Zone System Manual".

Finally we need to look at the effect of magnification on exposure.

When we photograph a subject at infinity, then the f-stop numbers on the lens are accurate. If your exposure meter indicates that you should shoot a landscape at 1/250 at f8 using a 50mm lens, then f8 represents the correct effective aperture to expose the film correctly. However, if you move the camera round and shoot an insect using your 50mm lens on extension tubes at 1:1, then your photo will be substantially underexposed at f8. Why?

If the range is very short, then the distance between the lens and the film is considerably greater that the focal length. In our insect photo, it is twice the focal length. You can work it out from the formulae we've already looked at, or you can take my word for it and use the following formula:

$$E\ new = E\ meter \times (1 + M)^2$$

M being the magnification. For our insect shot, the new exposure is the hand meter reading multiplied by 1+1 squared, or four times. You therefore need to open up the lens two stops to f4, or decrease your shutter speed to 1/60. Cameras with TTL metering compensate automatically, but I find I get better results with a separate meter and the little formula above.

The inverse square law

In the studio, we have to deal with a law called the "inverse square law", which says that if you double the distance between a lamp and a subject, you reduce the light falling on it by a quarter. Properly put, the light falling on a subject is proportional to the square of the distance.

So, if you need a stop of f32 on a product table for depth of field, and you only can get f22 on your flashmeter, you only have to move the light 1.4 times closer (the square root of two, because you need to double the light) and you are there. Similarly, if you want a greater difference between a key light and the fill, you only have to move the fill 1.4 times further away to halve the light.

You need to know this effect, but not worry about it unduly – it is useful when you have run out of adjustment on your flash but still need to alter the flash intensity up or down.

Conclusion

This is really all you need to know about basic photo theory. There is lots more of course, and if the subject interests you, go ahead and read up on it. However, the above will equip you well enough to operate efficiently in a normal professional environment. Perhaps more importantly, it will enable you to continue to operate when things go wrong, when equipment breaks down on you.

Remember George in QC – you have been hired to come up with the goods, every time. There are no excuses.

GLOSSARY

People often commend my wife on her knowledge of things photographic. When she gets to know them better, she confides that actually she knows nothing, but knows all the right words.

Whilst I think she is underselling herself, knowledge of the correct terminology does avoid misunderstandings and always impresses. This list is not designed to be exhaustive, but is my choice of the terms you are most likely to come across.

A/W
abb. artwork (qv).

Air
A large amount of white space in a layout, or a large amount of space around the subject in a transparency. "Plenty of air" around a shot means make the subject small on the transparency, usually because the designer wishes to insert text or "copy" into the pic.

Airbrush
A miniature spray gun used for illustration and photo retouching.

Angle of view
The maximum angle that a lens can "see" and produce an image within certain specification limits. Normally it is defined as the angle subtended by the diagonal of the circle of coverage at the lens position.

Aperture
The "hole" in the middle of the lens, controlled by the iris diaphragm.

Apochromat
A high quality lens specifically corrected for all three primary colours.

Art paper
Heavily coated paper with a hard smooth surface.

Artwork

Any illustrations, photographs, diagrams etc prepared for reproduction.

ASA

American Standards Association. A system of speed ratings for film now replaced by the ISO system.

Aspect ratio

Ratio of width to height, usually applied to figures or letters.

Back focus

The distance between a lens, usually measured from the mounting panel, to the film, when the lens is focused on infinity. It is approximately equal to the focal length for large format lenses.

Back projection

Usually used to create special backgrounds in the studio. A background transparency is projected on to the rear of a special translucent screen, and photographed from the front.

Back up/back to back

Printing on both sides of the paper.

Backlighting

Positioning the main light behind the subject. Produces "depth" to the picture, but sometimes requires fill light from the front to relieve shadows.

Bag bellows

A leather bellows capable of a large amount of displacement when large movements are used with wide angle lenses on mono-rail cameras. Expensive and not always necessary.

Barn doors

Movable panels used on studio flash to mask and control the beam of light.

Barrel distortion

Distortion produced by a lens which gives convex edges to the image produced. Common with cheap (and some not so cheap) wide angle lenses.

Bas relief

In design, a shallow three-dimensional design in which the subject stands in relief from the background. In photography, a composite print technique producing a relief illusion.

Baseboard camera
Another name for view camera (qv).

Bellows
Leather (usually) concertina type sleeve between lens and back on monorail camera.

Bleed
Strictly, that part of an image that extends beyond the trim marks on a page, but normally applied to an illustration that goes right to the edge of the paper.

Blister pack/card
A form of encapsulated packaging for small products, usually illustrated with photographs.

Blocking out
Painting or airbrushing out sections of artwork before reproduction. Usually used to remove distracting backgrounds.

Blow-up
Enlargement.

Bounce lighting
Reflecting the light from a flash head from an umbrella or surrounding walls to give a larger source of light and hence softer shadows.

Bracketing
Shooting several frames at varying exposures to ensure at least one correct value. Normal interval for colour transparency material is half a stop.

Bromide
A normal black and white photographic print. Used to be used to describe the output from a phototypesetting machine, now more usually described as a PMT (qv).

Bullet
Accent points used in copy to emphasise particular parts of text, items of particular interest.

C Type
A standard neg/pos print as opposed to a direct reversal print made from a transparency.

Camera movements

The adjustments found on large format cameras (usually) to alter the position of both back and lens panel.

Camera-ready

A term used to describe artwork or copy which is ready for reproduction.

Chroma

A printers term to describe the strength or purity of a colour.

Cibachrome

A direct reversal process to provide prints from transparencies giving a particularly brilliant print, marketed by Ilford Ltd. The name of the process has recently been changed to "Ilfochrome".

Colour positives

Screened colour separations (qv) used to produce the actual printing plates used in multi-colour printing.

Colour separations

Film (negative or positive) of the original colour illustration photographed through colour filters corresponding to the colours used in final printing.

Colour temperature

The colour of a light source, defined in degrees Kelvin. The higher the temperature, the bluer the light. Daylight (blue sky plus clouds) is around 5,500 degrees, as is electronic flash. Household bulbs give yellower light at about 2,900 degrees. Filters are available to fit over the light source or lens to modify colour temperature.

Colour transparency

Normally understood to be a camera exposed positive colour original on direct reversal colour film, format from 35mm to 10x8in and beyond. Designers sometimes confuse transparencies with "slides". Slides are normally understood to be 35mm transparencies for projection only. Therefore, all slides are transparencies, but not all transparencies are slides.

Colour value

The "grey value" of a colour when reproduced as black and white.

Contact print

A photographic print made by direct contact with the original negative or strip of negatives.

Contact screen

A halftone screen consisting of a dot pattern used to produce a screened negative from a tone original. The screen is placed in contact with the film.

Continuous tone (or Tone)

A photograph or illustration where the subject contains continuous shades of grey or colour between light and dark.

Contre jour

See Backlighting.

Cool colours

Colours which depict cold temperatures, particularly blues and greens.

Copy

Subject matter set in text.

Copy date

The final date for submission of copy and/or artwork to a magazine for an advert. Often much abused.

Copywriter

A member of the creative team in an ad agency, responsible for producing the text for an ad or brochure.

Covering power

The circle of image produced by a lens within defined quality criteria.

Cromalin

A rapid proofing process, patented by DuPont, to evaluate separations before final printing.

Crop marks

Marks on the four corners of a page indicating the limits to trim to.

Cut out

A process where the background dots are removed in an illustration to provide only the subject image. When a designer indicates that an illustration is to be "cut out" you don't need to worry about the background.

Dark slide
A light-tight film holder for sheet film.

Deadline
The final date for delivery of a particular job.

Densitometer
Instrument for measuring the density of particular colours, used for control in colour processing laboratories.

Depth of field
The distance between the nearest and furthest acceptably sharp points.

Depth of focus
The amount by which the film can move before the image becomes unsharp.

Diaphragm
A series of interleaving thin plates controlling the aperture of a lens.

Dot etching
Chemical manipulation of the size of dots on a printing plate. One of the ways a printer can correct poor colour balance.

Double extension
A bellows extension equal to twice the focal length of the lens in use, allowing macrophotography up to 1:1 reproduction ratio.

Dry mounting
Mounting prints by means of heat sensitive glues, normally shellac.

DTP
Desk Top Publishing. The use of small computers to design and "paste up" magazine pages and ads.

DTP scanner
A device connected to a computer to digitally produce halftone film from tone illustrations.

Element
Any part of an advertisement.

Emulsion
A colloidal coating of silver halides on acetate or paper/PVC

bases to provide photographic films and papers.

Exposure
Combination of aperture and time to expose a photographic film.

Exposure meter
Instrument for measuring light intensity or luminance, and equipped to convert the measurement into a combination of aperture and shutter speed.

Extension
Distance from the lens to the film.

Fill-in flash
A means of illuminating dark shadows to reduce contrast without destroying the original lighting effect. Often overdone.

Filmwork
General term for all the completed film negatives and positives used for the production of the printing plates used in litho printing.

Flare
A reduction in contrast due to internal reflections in the lens and camera body. Often confused by designers with reflections from shiny products; don't argue with them.

Flip
Reverse a transparency left to right. Often done when a reversed image looks better in a particular page design. Can't be used when there is text (for obvious reasons).

Focal length
Lens/film distance for a simple lens set at infinity.

Focal plane
The plane in which the image is formed.

Foreshorten
Distortion in perspective caused by too close a camera position, and "corrected" by the use of a wide angle camera lens. Sometimes a "foreshortened" perspective will be asked for by an art director, and can also be provided with the swing back on a monorail camera.

Four-colour printing
The standard method of colour printing, by using four printing

plates produced from four colour separations, usually in cyan, magenta, yellow and black.

Fresnel lens
Condenser lens normally used in conjunction with a ground-glass screen to improve image brightness.

Front projection
Technique of projecting a background image on to a highly reflective prismatic screen to create special studio effects.

Gang up
Printing one sheet of paper with several different jobs, to economise on colour separations and press time. Often used for trade catalogues and economy A4 brochures. Although a cost saving technique, it makes colour adjustment for one page or individual illustration impossible as any adjustment affects the whole. If the technique is to be used, the photographer should provide matched transparencies.

Glossy
Normally a 10x8in glossy black and white print.

Gutter bleed
An illustration allowed to spread across the centre margins of a double or centre page spread.

Halation
A spread of light around the highlights of a photographic image, caused mainly by the light source being included in the scene.

Halftone
The process used to convert a continuous tone illustration into a series of dots of various sizes.

High-key
Photographs lit to provide only light tones. Popular with baby food ad shots and female portraiture.

Hyperfocal distance
When a camera is focused on the hyperfocal distance, depth of field extends from half the distance between the camera and the hyperfocal distance, and infinity.

ISO
International Standards Organisation; the current system of

film speed definition.

In pro
In proportion. A designer will request a series of shots to be "in pro" when he needs to show the relative sizes of a range of products. Start with the largest product, then don't move the camera or subject position for the series.

Infinity
A point far away from which light rays are supposed to be parallel, in practice, the horizon or 1000 metres away.

Internegative
A negative made from a transparency or flat copy as an intermediate to producing a high quality print. Practically the best way of getting a print from a transparency.

Inverted telephoto
A wide angle lens made as a wrong way round telephoto to allow sufficient back focus to clear the mirror of a reflex camera.

Joule
Watt/seconds, used as a measure of the power of studio electronic flash.

Laminate
To coat a print with a transparent plastic film for protection.

Landscape format
Horizontal format.

Latent image
The image "stored" on the film after exposure but before development. A delicate child.

Layout
A sketch (usually) of the finished page or advert, showing the relative sizes and positions of illustrations and text. Used normally as the discussion document between the designer and photographer when directing photography.

Line copy
Copy consisting of black lines or blocks on a white background only, with no halftones or greys.

Linen tester
A folding magnifier much used by designers to look at halftone

dot patterns and sizes, and occasionally at transparencies.

Lith film

Extreme contrast film, usually orthochromatic, for producing line images.

Luminance

Intensity of light reflected from a subject and determines reflected light exposure measurement.

Macrophotography

Close-up photography producing images varying from life-size up to about ten times magnification.

Magnification

Size of the image relative to the size of the subject.

Mask

A faint black and white negative combined with an original transparency to reduce contrast in transparency duping. Not normally used today as low contrast duping stock is readily available.

Mechanical

American term for camera-ready artwork.

Mechanical tints

Different dot patterns giving different shades of grey for laying down on to artwork before repro.

Offset litho

Lithography in which the ink image is transferred from the printing plate to the paper via a second roller called the "blanket". By this means the paper doesn't touch the plate itself, and thus the delicate plate is protected from paper abrasion.

Orthochromatic

Emulsion sensitive to blue and green but insensitive to red.

Panchromatic

Emulsion sensitive to all colours.

Pantone

A commercial system of colour matching for inks and papers.

Perspective

The relative appearance of three dimensional shapes in two dimensions. Controlled only by viewpoint.

Photomicrography
Photography through a microscope.

Pincushion distortion
Distortion produced by a lens giving concave edges to the produced image.

PMT
Photo Mechanical Transfer. A photographic print made in a process camera, for use in producing camera ready artwork.

Polarisation
Polarised light is light vibrating in one plane only, produced by the use of a polarising filter, fitted either over the light source or the lens.

Portrait format
Upright format.

Posterisation
The separation of two or more tones from a continuous tone original, producing a set of negatives, one for each tone. A composite print is then made from a combination of these negatives.

Process camera
A large camera fitted with a copy board and lights for producing photographic prints from flat artwork. The prints (PMTs) are made using a rapid diffusion process, and are used in the preparation of artwork.

Process lens
A lens specifically computed for flat copy work in a process camera.

Proofing press
A small hand operated printing press used when the client wishes an additional proof to the Cromalin.

Proxar lens
A close up lens. The Proxar is a lens produced by Zeiss for use with the Hasselblad camera.

R types
Direct reversal prints from transparencies.

Reciprocity failure
The breakdown of the rule that equates light intensity (aperture)

with time (shutter speeds). Manufacturers give data with film application notes.

Reduction
See Magnification.

Resolving power
The ability of a lens to reproduce fine detail.

Reverse out
A process used to produce text as white on a solid or tone background.

Scrim
A term used to describe a large diffusing panel, normally made from mylar film stretched over a wooden frame and illuminated by two or more flash heads. Useful for producing soft light and also for reflective subjects.

Separation negatives
Negatives of original illustrations taken through colour filters.

Snoot
A conical tube fitted over a flash head to give a narrow, small diameter beam of light.

Softar filter
A filter, produced by Zeiss, to soften detail, especially useful in female portraiture.

Solarisation
Tone reversal on film or paper produced by extreme overexposure or by secondary exposure during processing.

Spot meter
Exposure meter designed to measure reflected light over a very small angle. Used to evaluate small areas of the scene, especially useful for stage and sports photography.

Squaring up
Sizing an illustration to give percentage increase or decrease on the original size for graphic design and for instruction to the repro house. Also a "squared up shot" is a pic taken directly from the front of a subject and not from a diagonal or oblique position.

Tint
An area of halftone grey or colour produced by a pattern of dots

of a particular density. The amount of white paper showing through determines the density of the colour on printing. Tints are defined in "percentages" of colour.

Tone
    See Continuous tone.

Tone separation
    See Posterisation.

Trim marks
    See Crop Marks

Uprating
    Deliberately underexposing film for "push" processing.

View camera
    Large format stand camera, usually used for exterior views and landscapes, normally made from wood.

Warm colours
    Colours depicting warmth, browns, reds, orange, etc.

USEFUL ADDRESSES

This list of addresses is not just copied out of the latest directory. It is a list of people that we have contacted in the last few years who have shown themselves genuinely helpful to the professional photographer and sympathetic when problems have arisen. For this reason, the list is not over-long.

Naturally we cannot guarantee that companies which have been co-operative in the past will always be so in the future – staff change and so do policies. At least this is a starting point.

Ademco Seal
Chesterhall Lane, Basildon, Essex SS14 3BG.
Tel: (0268) 287650.
Mounting and lamination materials and equipment.

Agfa UK Ltd
27 Great West Road, Brentford, Middlesex TW9 9AX.
Tel: 081-560 2131.
Importers of Agfa film, paper and chemistry.

Association of Model Agents
The Clock House, St Catherines Mews, Milner Street, London SW3 2PX.
Tel: 071-584 6466.

Association of Photographers
9/10 Domingo Street, London EC1 0ZA.
Tel: 071-608 1441.

Bowens Ltd
Promandis House, Bradbourne Drive, Tilbrook, Milton Keynes, Bucks MK7 8AJ.
Tel: (0908) 366344.
Manufacturer of Bowens electronic flash.

British Association of Picture Libraries and Agencies
13, Woodberry Crescent, London N10 1PJ.
Tel: 081-883 2531.

British Institute of Professional Photography
Amwell End, Ware, Herts SG12 9HN.
Tel: 0920 464011.

Bureau of Freelance Photographers
Focus House, 497 Green Lanes, London N13 4BP.
Tel: 081-882 3315/6.

Canon UK Ltd
Brent Trading Centre, North Circular Road, London NW10 0JF.
Tel: 081-459 1266.
Importers of Canon photographic equipment. Membership of
Canon CPS gives extra facilities to professional users of Canon
equipment.

Commission for the New Towns (CNT)
For opportunities throughout the country.
Tel: 071-828 7722

De Vere Ltd
Vulcan Way, New Addington, Croydon, Surrey CR0 9UG.
Tel: (0689) 842222.
Manufacturers of De Vere darkroom equipment and importers of
Cambo cameras, Deville sinks, Maron slide duping equipment,
Rodenstock lenses and Wing Lynch rotary processors.

Dun & Bradstreet Ltd
Kimberley House, 11 Woodhouse Square, Leeds LS3 1ND.
Tel: (0532) 459265.
Debt collection and receivable management services.

DW Viewpacks Ltd
Unit 7/8, Peveral Drive, Granby, Milton Keynes, Bucks MK1 1NL.
Tel: (0908) 642323.
Transparency viewing, filing and storage systems. Light boxes.

George Elliott and Sons Ltd
London Road, Westerham, Kent TN16 1DR.
Tel: (0959) 62198.
Importers of Exacta 66 cameras, Liesegang projectors, Meteor
Siegen processors, Schneider lenses, and Toyo large format
cameras and accessories.

Hasselblad UK Ltd
York House, Empire Way, Wembley Middlesex HA9 0Q.
Tel: 081-903 3435.
Importers of Hasselblad cameras and Metz flash equipment.

Ilford Photo Ltd
14-22 Tottenham Street, London W1P 0AH.
Tel: 071-636 7890.
Manufacturer of film, paper and chemistry, including Ilfochrome (Cibachrome).

Interlink Express Parcels Ltd
Brunswick Court, Brunswick Square, Bristol BS2 8PE.
Tel: (0272) 426900.
Overnight parcel service with offices in most large towns. Can also give same day service from some of its depots.

Introphoto Professional
Priors Way, Maidenhead, Berks SL6 2HR.
Tel: (0628) 74411.
Importers of Arca Swiss large format cameras, Bronica cameras, Jobo processors, Kinderman projectors, LPL enlargers, Shepherd meters and Tokina lenses.

Jessops of Leicester Ltd
Proline Dept, 98 Scudamore Road, Leicester LE3 1TZ.
Tel: (0533) 320232.
Photographic dealer. Studio equipment including Powerflash, darkroom equipment and materials. Branches of Jessops can be found in most large towns for day-to-day needs.

Johnsons Photopia
Hempstalls Lane, Newcastle, Staffs ST5 0SW.
Tel: (0782) 717100.
Importers of Cokin filters, Fotima bags, Gepe slide accessories, Mamiya cameras, Tamron lenses, Teleplus convertors and Zeiss Ikon projectors.

KJP Ltd
Promandis House, Bradbourne Drive, Tilbrook, Milton Keynes MK7 8AJ.
Tel: (0908) 366344.
Dealer and importer. Studio equipment includes Bowens studio flash, Horseman cameras, Manfrotto tripods, Sekonic meters, System Hi-power flash battery systems, Wein flash triggers, Master light boxes, Peak magnifiers, Colourshade backgrounds, darkroom and processing equipment. Trade counter for materials. Large hire department. Branches in London, Aberdeen, Belfast, Birmingham, Bristol, Manchester and Nottingham.

Kodak Ltd
Kodak House, Station Road, Hemel Hempstead, Herts HP2 7EH.

Tel: (0442) 61241.

Manufacturers and importers of film, paper and chemicals, and projectors. Kodak has several telephone numbers throughout the country linked directly to the Hemel Hempstead number, so it is often possible to talk to their customer service and technical departments for the cost of a local call.

Mid Counties Photographic Supplies
617 Jubilee Road, Letchworth, Herts SG6 1NE.
Tel: (0462) 679388.
Photographic dealer, film, paper, chemicals, mounts, albums and accessories.

Nikon UK Ltd
Nikon House, 380 Richmond Road, Kingston on Thames, Surrey KT2 5PR.
Tel: 081-541 4440.
Importer of Nikon camera equipment. Nikon has a VIP service for professional photographers giving priority for service and repairs.

Royal Photographic Society
The Octagon, Milsom Street, Bath BA1 1DN.
Tel: (0225) 462841

Small Firms Service (Department of Employment)
Tel: Freefone Enterprise 0800 222999.
Government information on starting and running your own business.

Studio Accessories Ltd
443-449 Waterloo Road, Blackpool, Lancs FY4 4BW.
(0253) 694340.
Studio backgrounds and props.

Studio Professional Sales
56 Marchmont Street, London WC1N 1AB.
071-278 1004.
Importer of Hensel flash and front projection equipment.

Robert White,
199 Bournemouth Road, Parkstone, Poole, Dorset BH14 9HU.
Tel: (0202) 723046.
Photographic retailer specialising in the supply of equipment to the professional and advanced amateur. Good second-hand selection. One of the last "real" photo shops.

INDEX